# CIVIL WAR KANSAS

# Civil War Kansas

*Reaping the Whirlwind*

The Authorized Edition
with a New Preface

## Albert Castel

01 4242

UNIVERSITY PRESS OF KANSAS

Originally published in 1958 by Cornell University Press as
*A Frontier State at War: Kansas, 1861-1865.*
New preface and textual corrections
© 1997 by the University Press of Kansas.

Published by the University Press of Kansas (Lawrence, Kansas 66049),
which was organized by the Kansas Board of Regents and is
operated and funded by Emporia State University, Fort Hays State
University, Kansas State University, Pittsburg State University,
the University of Kansas, and Wichita State University

Library of Congress Cataloging-in-Publication Data

Castel, Albert E.
[Frontier state at war]
Civil War Kansas : reaping the whirlwind / Albert Castel. —
Authorized ed.
p.    cm. — (Modern war studies)
Originally published: A frontier state at war. Ithaca, N.Y.:
Cornell University Press, 1958. With new pref. and textual corrections.
Includes bibliographical references and index.
ISBN 0-7006-0872-9 (alk. paper)
1. Kansas—History—Civil War, 1861-1865.  2. Frontier and pioneer
life—Kansas.  I. Title.  II. Series.
E508.C3   1997
973.7′09781—dc21                                        97-21546

British Library Cataloguing in Publication Data is available.

Printed in the United States of America

10 9 8 7 6 5 4 3 2

The paper used in this publication meets the minimum requirements of
the American National Standard for Permanence of Paper for
Printed Library Materials Z39.48-1984.

*To the memory of my parents,*
*Albert E. and Dorothy W. Castel (1903–1971)*

*They made it all possible*

# Contents

*(photographs follow page 20)*

# Preface to the Authorized Edition

THIS was my first book. Like the vast majority of maiden efforts by historians of the species *academicus,* it derived from my doctoral dissertation. What follows is an account of how it came into being and what I tried to achieve in it.

I did most of the research for what became *A Frontier State at War: Kansas, 1861–1865,* and what has now been retitled *Civil War Kansas: Reaping the Whirlwind* at the Kansas State Historical Society in Topeka during the autumn of 1954. Every morning, Monday through Saturday, I left my room at the YMCA, ate breakfast at a nearby restaurant, and then walked the short distance to the Historical Society where I waited for the front door to open at 8 A.M. Once inside, I worked without pause, not ceasing for lunch, until the society closed at 5 P.M., whereupon I returned to my room, took a short nap, and then hustled over to the Senate Cafeteria for supper. Usually I spent evenings sorting notes before going to bed where I would fall asleep while listening to a portable radio.

Such was my routine for close to six weeks, with the only break coming on Sundays, when I took long walks, once even hiking twenty-some miles to Lawrence (returning by bus). Because photocopying machines had not yet come into being, I had to write hundreds of notes and transcribe long passages from sources with pen or pencil. A modern photocopier probably would have enabled me to complete my research in no more than two weeks and spared me much eyestrain. Sometimes, after a day of reading the small print of old newspapers on microfilm, I literally was half-blind while groping my way back to the YMCA.

I returned, by train, to my parents' house in Wichita with enough notes to fill a Brooks Brothers suit box. During late November I organized these and other notes acquired elsewhere by chapters and by topics within the chapters. On the day after Thanksgiving I began writing my dissertation, a task I continued in January in room 1203 in the tower of the International House at the University of Chicago. All went well until I reached the most dramatic event of the tale I was telling—the Lawrence Massacre. I got Quantrill's raiders on a hill overlooking Lawrence, but it took me a week to find satisfactory words for getting them off that hill and into Lawrence to perform their bloody deeds! (As if in compensation, I wrote the first draft of a subsequent chapter in one morning.)

In May 1955 I completed the dissertation and successfully defended it the following month, after having its format approved by the redoubtable Master of the Footnote, Kate L. Turabian, and arranging to have it final-typed in triplicate. Early in September, with my parents present, I received a Ph.D. in History and Political Science at Rockefeller Chapel. All I needed now was a job.

A month later I had one—in the United States Army, where I added to my newly acquired title of "doctor" that of "private." In effect I volunteered for the draft. I desired a vacation from things academic and in the army I obtained it and benefited from it.

In December, having graduated from basic training at Camp Chaffee, Arkansas, and on a two-week leave, I took my dissertation to the director of the University of Oklahoma Press. He expressed interest in publishing it but said that its 549 pages needed to be greatly reduced in number. During the spring and summer of 1956, while at the Military Intelligence School at Fort Holabird outside of Baltimore, I did this, working for the most part at the post library but sometimes in the barracks with my footlocker serving as a desk. Upon completing the task, I submitted the much-shortened manuscript to the University of Oklahoma Press. Presently, the press notified me that it would publish it, provided I finance one-half the cost of publication. My parents would have furnished the money; but I disliked the prospect of paying to be published and therefore wrote my dissertation director, Professor William T. Hutchinson, seeking his advice. He suggested that I enter the work in the American Historical Association's Albert J. Beveridge Award competition. Although I believed that my chance of success was close to nonexistent, I decided to do so on the principle of nothing ventured, nothing gained.

By then I had become a "special agent" in the Counter Intelligence Corps, assigned to Region VIII, 113th C.I.C. Detachment, in Kansas City, Missouri. Wanting a neater manuscript than the one I had prepared for the Oklahoma press, I employed Wilma Strong, wife of a fellow agent, to retype it. She performed a rapid and excellent job, and early in 1957 I submitted my would-be book to the Beveridge Award committee. Then, quite truly, I virtually forgot about it. My main concern was securing a college teaching position before I finished my two-year army hitch in October, by which time it would be too late to obtain academic employment.

Late in the spring of 1957 I obtained a one-year appointment as a history instructor at the University of California at Los Angeles and in August received an early discharge from the army. During the autumn I was so busy preparing lectures and writing some articles that I gave little thought to the Beveridge Award— and that little thought was pessimistic. Then early in December I received a letter from John Hope Franklin, chairman of the Beveridge Committee. To my delighted surprise it stated that the committee "has voted to confer the Honorable Mention for 1957 on your manuscript, 'A Frontier State at War: Kansas, 1861–1865.'"

Unlike the award itself, the honorable mention did not bring with it $1,000, but it did result in publication, and that was the main thing. That evening, in company with an American Airlines hostess from Canada named Patricia, I celebrated with Lobster Newberg and Champagne at a restaurant in Santa Monica. While sipping the bubbly, I remembered the YMCA and the Senate Cafeteria in Topeka. The change in my circumstances was most gratifying.

Less than a year later my manuscript became a book with its publication by the Cornell University Press on behalf of the American Historical Association. Reviews generally were favorable, and I was especially pleased when told that Dr. James C. Malin of the University of Kansas and the doyen of Kansas history spoke highly of my work. The only irksome criticism came from a member of the staff of the Kansas State Historical Society, who in a review complained about what he considered to be the excessively grim picture of frontier Kansas that I painted in the first chapter. Why should he think that I would traduce my native state when in its infancy? And how could he have failed to notice that my description took the form of a collage of quotations from contemporary observers, many of them Kansans, something clearly indicated in the footnotes? But, as Edgar Allan Poe demonstrates in his classic tale, "The Purloined Letter," not seeing the obvious is a common human failing, one that I readily admit to sharing.

Nearly forty years later I encountered a far more baffling assertion about my book. It came from an able young historian at one of Kansas's state universities. According to him, had I written the book in recent times instead of back in the 1950s, it would have been much different, particularly in respect to the amount of attention given to women, blacks, and Indians. Possibly he was right; historians are influenced by the present when depicting the past. On the other hand, possibly he was wrong; after all, people can react negatively as well as positively to the intellectual fashions of the day and often do. In any case, as I told the young historian, I would gladly have dealt more with women, blacks, and Indians had the sources available to me in 1954 justified doing so given the purpose of my book. As set forth in the preface to the original edition, this purpose was to remedy a "long-standing deficiency in Kansas historical literature by describing the political, military, social, and economic events and developments of the state's first four years" and to "contribute to a better understanding of the Civil War in the Trans-Mississippi West." Consequently, as I also noted in that preface, the "primary focus throughout the book is on Kansas, and if I have emphasized political and military matters, it is because this period of Kansas history was essentially political and military in character."

Since the mid-1950s a number of new sources, books, and articles pertaining to Civil War Kansas have appeared. Some of them, had they been available when I did my research, would have been useful, in particular Stephen Z. Starr's *Jennison's Jayhawkers: A Civil War Cavalry Regiment and Its Commanders* (Baton Rouge: Louisiana State University Press, 1973) and Thomas M. Goodrich's *Bloody Dawn: The Story of the Lawrence Massacre* (Kent, Ohio: Kent State University Press, 1991). None of them, however, challenges the basic account and key interpretations presented in my book but on the contrary tend to reinforce them. Likewise, although several general histories of the Civil War west of the Mississippi now exist, I see no need to remove from this new edition the statement that appears on page 97: "The story of the Civil War in the West has yet to be well and fully told, but when so recounted should prove fascinating."

Hence I welcome the opportunity to offer again my old book, with a new title, some factual errors corrected, and some new photos added, to the history-reading public. In doing so, I am confident, as well as hopeful, that those who peruse it will find it informative, interesting, and sometimes even exciting. The

Civil War is the most dramatic event in American history, and in no Northern state was it so dramatic as in Kansas, where the wind that had been sown by struggle between pro- and anti-slavery forces in the 1850s was reaped in the form of a whirlwind.

ALBERT CASTEL

*Hillsdale, Michigan*
*March 1997*

# *Acknowledgments*

FIRST and foremost I wish to thank Fred Woodward, director of the University Press of Kansas, for giving my old book a new lease on life by, somewhat to my surprise but much to my gratification, deciding to republish it and also for giving me the opportunity to remedy a number of errors, replace the original preface with one that would now be more appropriate, and to add what, for unaccountable but unforgivable reasons, I failed to provide forty years ago—a dedication to those to whom the book should have been dedicated.

Most of the illustrations appeared in the original edition of the book, but a large proportion are different. To further complicate matters, after the passage of forty years I no longer possessed copies of most of the original prints. Hence I needed many new prints and fast. Four people enabled me to obtain them that way: Thomas Goodrich of Topeka, Kansas; Nancy Sherbert, curator of photographs at the Kansas State Historical Society; and Larry and Priscilla Massie of the Allegan Forest, Michigan. I here record my gratitude to all of them, especially to Larry and Priscilla, who again made possible what otherwise would have been impossible.

Finally, I wish to credit Stephen Z. Starr's *Jennison's Jayhawkers: A Civil War Cavalry Regiment and Its Commanders* (Baton Rouge: Louisiana State University Press, 1973), pp. 366–368 and 382–385, for enabling me to write a fuller and more accurate account (p. 229) of the termination of Charles Jennison's military career and of his post–Civil War life.

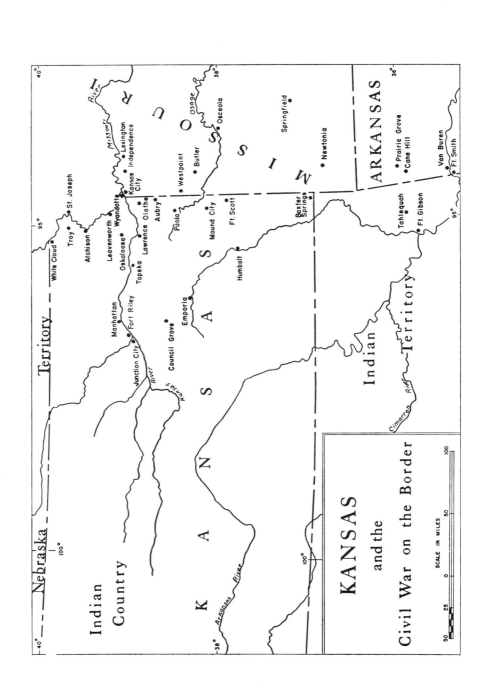

KANSAS
and the
Civil War on the Border

SCALE IN MILES

50 25 0 50 100

# I

# *The New State*

"THE LONG AGONY" was over: Kansas, as of January 29, 1861, was a state—it had "moved to America." In Leavenworth, Lawrence, Topeka, and other towns Kansans celebrated the "glorious news" of the coming of statehood in a "fury of excitement." Cannons boomed, cheering crowds gathered on the street corners, a judge and a militia general stood on their heads, and the saloons were scenes of inebriated revelry. A few despondent officeholders in the now defunct territorial government at Lawrence were the only exceptions to the general jubilation. "Damn it," exclaimed one of them, "Kansas ought not to have been admitted for ten years!" [1]

The way of Kansas to the stars had been difficult—or at least so the state motto, *Ad astra per aspera*, was to declare, and so Kansans believed. For over six years, ever since Kansas was opened up as a territory by Stephen A. Douglas' Kansas-Nebraska Bill

---

[1] Leavenworth *Daily Times*, January 30, 1861; Elwood *Free Press*, February 2, 1861; *Lawrence Republican*, January 31, 1861; *Topeka Tribune*, February 2, 1861; Emporia *News*, February 2, 1861; Oskaloosa *Independent*, February 6, 1861. The Kansas Statehood Bill passed Congress on January 28, 1861, and was signed by President Buchanan the following day. Owing to an oversight it was not ratified by the Kansas legislature until January 23, 1862.

of 1854, its prairies had been the stage for an almost incessant series of political conventions, elections, raids, massacres, pitched battles, and atrocities, all part of a fierce conflict between the Free State and proslavery forces that had come to Kansas to settle and to battle. By 1857 the Free State Party won their almost inevitable victory, and in 1859 they wrote a constitution and élected a state government. But for nearly two more years, at least as the majority of Kansans saw it, the pro-Southern government in Washington continued to deny Kansas statehood and kept it under the control of "proslavery" territorial governors in order to punish it for rejecting slavery. Thus most Kansans hailed the advent of statehood as meaning "deliverance from vassalage" and as marking the successful termination of the struggle to make Kansas a Free State. On February 2 the territorial legislature, in session at Lawrence, adjourned *sine die*. A week later Dr. Charles Robinson, famed leader of the old Free State Party, took the oath as the first Governor of the Commonwealth of Kansas. The history of the new state was under way.

What sort of people were they, these Kansans, now full-fledged citizens of the Union? Fire-eating Senator Louis T. Wigfall of Texas, for one, had no doubts on this score. "The inhabitants of that so-called state," he declared, "are outlaws and land pirates. . . . I shall not consent that Texas shall associate herself with such a state." [2] Many others, both North and South, shared this opinion of Kansans, although perhaps in less extreme and biased manner. The circumstances accompanying the settlement of Kansas during the 1850's had given its population a reputation for violence and lawlessness and had created the still-persistent myth that they were stern New England puritans who had gone to Kansas as crusaders to preserve it from slavery. The truth of the matter was that the "troubles" in Kansas had been greatly exaggerated, mainly by young Eastern newspaper correspondents engaged in the manufacture of Republican political propaganda

[2] Quoted in Leverett W. Spring, *Kansas: The Prelude to the War for the Union* (Boston, 1890), p. 264.

and of their own careers. And as for Kansans being of New England origin, census figures were available for anyone to see that most of them came, not from that section, but from Ohio, Missouri, Indiana, Illinois, Kentucky, Pennsylvania, New York, and Iowa, in that order. Obviously, if the reigning spirit of Kansas was puritan, it was a puritanism which came by way of the Great Lakes, not direct from Massachusetts Bay.

Nor did the settlers of Kansas go there simply to wage a holy war against slavery. "We came to Kansas," said one of them afterwards, "to better our conditions, incidentally expecting to make it a free State." [3] But even this confession of motivation probably holds true only for the more idealistic upper stratum of the immigrants. The bulk of the thousands who poured into Kansas between 1854 and 1860 were driven by sheer land hunger and little or nothing else. Yet in actuality there was little or no difference between coming to Kansas in quest of free land and coming to make it a land of the free. The average settler, whether Northern or Southern, regarded slavery as an economic curse to the small white farmer and believed that only by making Kansas a Free State could he protect and improve his socioeconomic status.

Another facet of the reputation of Kansans, closely linked to that of their supposed puritan New England origin, was that they were a Bible-toting, hymn-singing lot, deeply steeped in the somber hues of evangelistic Calvinism. This too, however, seems to be largely a myth, deriving mainly from political propagandists who constantly contrasted the pious Free State Kansans to the whisky-swilling, tobacco-spitting "Border Ruffians" of Missouri. "One remarkable feature of the social conditions here," wrote young John Ingalls from the "miserable" little town of Sumner, Kansas, to his father back home in Massachusetts, "is a total dis-

[3] William H. Carruth, "The New England Emigrant Aid Company as an Investment Society," *Kansas Historical Collections*, VI (1897–1900), 93. In subsequent references the *Kansas Historical Collections* will be cited as *KHC*.

regard of the Sabbath; perhaps because there are no churches. No change of dress or manner indicates the advent of holy time, and the most of the citizens employ the day in hunting prairie chickens or ducks and geese." A newspaper reporter commented on the absence of religious observance among the men of Topeka by writing, "Suggest to a friend the propriety of attending church; he stares at you for a moment with a look of ineffable surprise, then indulges in a boisterous guffaw, subsiding, at length, into low gutturals, amidst which such syllables as 'pshaw,' 'damn,' and the like, are plainly discernible." If any group were bona fide puritans, it would have been the Congregationalists. Yet they numbered only about 800 and centered mainly about Lawrence. The largest denomination was the Methodist Church with 3,932 members, followed by the Baptists with 1,231 adherents and the Presbyterians with 600. There were only a very few Episcopalians, Catholics, and Jews. The total number of church buildings was 97.[4]

Possibly the indifference to religion merely reflected the youthfulness of the settlers. Almost 90 per cent of them were under forty years of age, and over 40 per cent were between twenty and forty. Anyone over forty usually had "Old" prefixed to his name when referred to by others. Such prominent political leaders as Marcus J. Parrott, Thomas Ewing, Jr., and Martin Conway were in 1861 aged respectively thirty-one, thirty-two, and thirty-four. The majority of the state legislators were in their twenties and early thirties, and it was an ordinary occurrence for them to pelt speakers with paper-wads during sessions. Much in the early history of Kansas which some historians might be disposed to attribute to an abstract influence of the "frontier" can be explained better by the more concrete fact that the men who made that history were very young.

[4] William E. Connelley, ed., "Some Ingalls Letters," *KHC*, XIV (1915–1918), 103; Leavenworth *Daily Times*, March 26, 1861; Andrew Stark, ed., *Kansas Annual Register for the Year 1864* (Leavenworth, 1864), pp. 84–95.

Like all people everywhere in all times, Kansans of the early 1860's were a mixture of the good and the bad and of the stupid and the intelligent. When John Ingalls, very much aware of his own personal superiority and New England breeding, described the members of the Kansas bar as an "ignorant, detestable set of addle-headed numbskulls and blackguards" and when newspaper correspondent Albert Richardson opined that the delegates to a Kansas convention possessed a high degree of "intelligence and culture" and were better speakers than the run of Congressmen, both men were probably right. Yet, as the pages of this history may serve eventually to demonstrate, Amos Lawrence, financier of the famous New England Emigrant Aid Society, had some justification for writing in 1858 that "the world is made up of all sorts of men, but Kansas seems to have more than its share of the weaker brethren and rogues." [5]

In the Kansas of 1861 "the pulse of civilization had just begun to beat—very feebly." There was hardly more than one person in the state for each of its 82,158 square miles of prairie soil. Settlement was confined almost entirely to the eastern third of the state and was distributed roughly in the form of a "T" on its side: north and south along the Missouri River and down the Missouri border, east to west up the Kansas River. The western frontier was marked by Marysville, Salina, Council Grove, and Emporia, the last a "forlorn hamlet" where the inhabitants occasionally killed stray buffalo in the streets. Beyond was "droughty country," considered by most contemporaries as unsuitable for agriculture and fit only for the Indians whose hunting parties roamed it. To the south the rim of settlement was the "Neutral Lands," corresponding to present-day Crawford and Cherokee counties. Nominally this area belonged to the Cherokees by a treaty of 1855, but by 1861 fifteen hundred white "squatters" had pene-

[5] Connelley, ed., "Some Ingalls Letters," *KHC*, XIV (1915–1918), 115; Albert D. Richardson, *Beyond the Mississippi* (Hartford, Conn., 1867), pp. 43–44; Charles Robinson, *The Kansas Conflict* (Lawrence, 1898), p. 388.

trated into it. In the language of the day, "Western Kansas" meant the region beyond Topeka, and the dividing line between North and South Kansas was the Kaw.

The majority of the people lived in lonely, wretched little log cabins or dugouts, "black holes of evil smell," where humans, dogs, pigs, and chickens "all huddled pell-mell on the floor around the cooking . . . one and all looking for a chance of a snap at it." Frame houses were rare because of the scarcity of sawmills and the lack of suitable native timber. Many buildings were constructed of cottonwood, the prevalent tree, but these had a startling tendency to "twist about like a corkscrew" as the wood warped under the hot Kansas sun. Richardson, during his travels through the state, was "pained by the absence of fruit and shade trees" and by the "slovenly log houses, with jet-black bare soil all around them, and stiff frame dwellings with naked walls and glittering paint." The houses of Kansas, he concluded, were uglier than those of any other state.[6]

The daily life of the Kansas pioneer was the dreary, grinding one customary to the frontier. Long hours of hard work, exposure to intense heat or bitter cold, little time or facilities for recreation—such was the monotonous substance of his days. Perhaps the worst hardship he experienced, however, was illness. Journals and letters of the time often speak of little else. The most common form of sickness was malaria or the "ague." Its prevalence in the state gained it the nickname "Kansas fever." Some, who were accounted lucky, caught the "Kansas itch." Although covering the body with blotches and scabs, it seemed to result in immunity to the "ague" and other afflictions.

The lot of the women, testified one of them, was not extraordinarily hard. They were so few that the males placed a high value on them and so relieved them of the "worst drudgery." The letters of Sarah Everett, a farm woman who lived

[6] Adela Elizabeth Orpen, *Memories of the Old Emigrant Days in Kansas, 1862–1865* (Edinburgh and London, 1926), pp. 2, 40; Richardson, *Beyond the Mississippi*, pp. 53, 560.

near Lawrence, made it clear, however, that they shared fully in the privations and labor of the frontier. This particular woman died at the age of thirty-four from overwork and childbearing. Women from the East especially found it difficult to adjust to pioneer conditions. Mrs. Adela Orpen, who spent her childhood in the Kansas of the sixties, related that one spring she discovered her governess, a New Yorker, crying—"crying because there was nothing beautiful to look at: everything was hopelessly ugly, and even the floor was always dirty, and it was useless to wash it, for it would be dirty again before night." Yet, by way of contrast, it is interesting to note that a highly refined woman from Boston was, after several days in Kansas, going about in the same manner as most Kansas farm women—attired in short skirt and trousers and barefooted.[7]

Not least of the hardships experienced by Kansans in the early 1860's were the extreme dearth and poorness of transportation and communication facilities. There were in the state only a few miles of railroad tracks, laid in 1860 at Elwood. Except for the Missouri, the rivers, best described as "amphibious—half water and half mud," were unnavigable. Leavenworth was the only point in direct telegraphic contact with the East. News had to be relayed from there to the interior by messengers or via the recently established "pony express." Lawrence, in January, 1861, while the territorial legislature was in session there and the statehood bill pending in Washington, was cut off from outside news for more than two weeks because of heavy snows. In some of the more remote and sparsely populated sections the settlers were over sixty miles from a post office. Once a week "a stagecoach ran, or rather crawled," from Kansas City to Mound City. Agriculture and stock raising could never be really profitable in Kansas unless and until communications with the

---

[7] Orpen, *Emigrant Days*, pp. 45, 51–52, 65–73, 105, 114, 132, 193–194, 218; "Letters of John and Sarah Everett, 1854–1864," *Kansas Historical Quarterly*, VIII (August, 1939), 288, 303–307. In subsequent references the *Kansas Historical Quarterly* will be cited as *KHQ*.

East were improved. Thus Kansans looked to the coming of railroads with an eagerness that was little short of desperate.

The Indians still effectively possessed much, if not most, of the new state. They were of two types: semicivilized tribes like the Sac and Fox, Delawares, and Pottawatomies and more or less savage nomads like the Osages, Pawnees, Comanches, Cheyennes, and Arapahoes. The semicivilized tribes resided in fixed communities on permanent reservations located in the eastern and central sections of Kansas. The nomads held an ill-defined sway over the southern and western plains. Except to the outer fringe of settlers the Indians were not a serious menace, and up to 1861 Indian troubles had not obstructed the development of Kansas. In fact, the Indians were in far greater danger from the whites than the whites were from the Indians. White whisky and diseases decimated their numbers and destroyed their morals; white squatters encroached upon their lands and massacred their game; and large land speculators and ambitious railroad promoters, supported by the Government, plotted to deprive them of all their territory.

There were in Kansas in 1861 only ten towns with over 500 inhabitants. The principal ones were Leavenworth, Atchison, and Lawrence. Leavenworth, with a population of approximately 5,000, was the largest. It boasted three daily newspapers, several fine hotels, a public gymnasium and a college, and many substantial houses and buildings. And if it did not boast of, neither did it bother to conceal, a large number of saloons and brothels, with appropriate accompanying personnel. The economic base of Leavenworth was its wholesale trade with the inland districts and the local business provided by the nearby garrison at Fort Leavenworth. Its levee was lined with huge warehouses in which were received the goods and products brought by steamboat up the Missouri from St. Louis. It was also the main stopover for travelers entering and leaving Kansas, since it was only a few miles by boat from Weston, Missouri, western terminus of a branch line of the Hannibal and St. Joseph Railroad. Leavenworth's ambition was to become the leading city west of St. Louis.

Atchison, twenty-five miles up the Missouri, was Leavenworth's chief rival in control of the river and inland trade and in the political and economic domination of northern Kansas. It had a population in 1861 of only about 2,500, but it was supremely confident of the future, despite the fact that its streets were ungraded, crooked, and covered with stumps and underbrush and that it was referred to even by one of its own leading citizens as a "hog-pen." This confidence stemmed from Atchison's advantageous geographical position on the westernmost bend of the Missouri, which made it an ideal point of departure for commerce coming both by river and by rail from the East. In quest of their goal of commercial pre-eminence, the businessmen of Atchison stood as a unit, with such former "Border Ruffians" as B. F. Stringfellow working in close harmony with such leaders of the Free State and Republican parties as Samuel C. Pomeroy.

Thirty-five miles from Leavenworth and about forty miles from the Missouri line was Lawrence, a town already possessing great fame and much history. Founded in 1854 by the first parties sent out by the New England Emigrant Aid Company and named after the financial angel of that company, Amos Lawrence of Massachusetts, it had been the "Free State Fortress," the storm center of the struggle of 1855 and 1856. As such, its present appearance must have been disconcerting to anyone whose imagination had been fired by the story of its past. It consisted simply of a few hundred structures, scattered over uneven, hilly land on the south bank of the Kaw, with Mt. Oread rising abruptly to the southwest, the ruins of a fort built on it in 1855 still visible. To Eastern eyes Lawrence presented a "mean, slender appearance," and it had scarcely 2,000 residents. Yet these citizens were the key to its prestige and importance. At one time or another practically all the prominent Free State leaders had resided in Lawrence, and many continued to do so—Charles Robinson, James H. Lane, Martin Conway, Samuel Walker, Solon Thacher, to name the more outstanding. Others had moved on to become leading citizens in other towns —Samuel N. Wood at Council Grove, D. R. Anthony and Thomas Ewing, Jr., at Leavenworth, Pomeroy at Atchison, G. W. Brown at Paola. Politically, the quality of its population gave Lawrence a role in Kansas affairs greatly disproportionate to its size. Economically, it competed with Leavenworth for trade in the Kaw Valley and to the south and west.

Other towns of note, none having more than several hundred residents, were Wyandotte, then as ever overshadowed by Kansas City across the river; Topeka, in 1861 the provisional, but ambitious to become the permanent, capital of the state; Manhattan, boasting "some very creditable buildings" and a hotel "free from bedbugs"; Mound City, with a few dozen houses and buildings strewn about at random; and Fort Scott, the largest town in southern Kansas and, like Mound City, a vortex of much of the violence in that region during territorial days. Add to this list Troy, Elwood, White Cloud, and Hiawatha in the "Northern Tier," Olathe, Oskaloosa, Baldwin City, Osage, Burlingame, Paola, Osawatomie, Council Grove, and Junction City in the central row of counties, and Garnett, Humboldt, LeRoy, and Emporia in southern Kansas, and practically all the places of any importance are named. Other settlements had even less right to the title of "town," and the claims of some of the above were extremely tenuous. Yet, however "cheap, shabby, and rude" these Kansas towns were, they all cherished high hopes of future growth and prosperity, and all were to greater or lesser degree centers of political power and activity. Moreover, their economic rivalries and aspirations, especially those of Atchison, Lawrence, and Leavenworth, provided much of the substance of Kansas politics in the sixties, and had profound bearing upon the history of the state.

Nearly all the towns had one or more newspapers—whether

they supported them or not is another matter. In general these journals were as unpretentious as they were insignificant, but in several instances they were of decidedly high caliber. Constantly proclaiming itself the "leading" newspaper of Kansas, not without justice, was the *Daily Conservative* of Leavenworth. The first edition of this paper appeared on the day Congress passed the statehood bill, and it was the first to report the news. It was owned by Daniel R. Anthony, brother of Susan B., "a hot-headed, impracticable, energetic, smart, money-making ambitious abolitionist," and edited by another abolitionist, D. W. ("Web") Wilder, possessor of the Franklin Medal from Boston Latin School, recipient of the Bowdoin Gold Medal at Harvard, and a member of the Boston bar. Early in January, Wilder had been chased out of St. Joseph, Missouri, for his "incendiary" writings there, and he now proposed to practice the same kind of incendiarism in the more favorable atmosphere of Leavenworth and Kansas. Under Wilder's direction the badly misnamed *Conservative* became the most radical, most-hated, most-read, and most-news-containing paper in the state.[8]

Competing with the *Conservative* for readers and influence was the Leavenworth *Daily Times*. This journal had been founded in 1857, and prior to the advent of its local rival was probably the pre-eminent newspaper in Kansas. Its owner was J. Kemp Bartlett, its editor Edward F. Schneider, an able wielder of the pen, but not the equal of "Web" Wilder. Both the *Conservative* and the *Times* were Republican, and the third major Leavenworth daily, the *Kansas Herald*, was Democratic. At one time the *Herald* had been of considerable importance, but by 1861 it was moribund, if not almost extinct, sustained

[8] Leavenworth *Daily Times*, January 7, 1861; Leavenworth *Daily Conservative*, July 3, 1863; Richard B. Taylor, "Kansas Newspaper History," *KHC*, II (1879–1880), 182; Daniel W. Wilder, *The Annals of Kansas* (Topeka, 1886), p. 309; Noble L. Prentis, *Kansas Miscellanies* (Topeka, 1889), p. 86.

principally by government printing. In addition to the *Conservative*, *Times*, and *Herald*, a German-language paper, the *Zeitung*, also was published in Leavenworth.

Up at Atchison twenty-four-year-old John Martin's *Freedom's Champion*, originally the proslavery *Squatter's Sovereign*, was the best and dominant journal. Lawrence had two newspapers, both weeklies: the *Kansas State Journal*, edited by H. E. Lowman and Josiah Trask, and the *Republican*, under the management of John Speer, a Kansas editor since 1854. Topeka likewise possessed two weeklies: Edmund and William Ross's *Kansas State Record* and the *Tribune*, whose editor at the beginning of 1861 was J. F. Cumings, but in February was succeeded by John P. Greer. Several other noteworthy newspapers were the Emporia *News* of Jacob Stotler, H. D. Hunt's Elwood *Free Press*, and the Oskaloosa *Independent* of J. W. Roberts, who employed female compositors.

The outstanding editor in Kansas was Solomon Miller, proprietor of the *White Cloud Kansas Chief*. Miller had come to Kansas from Ohio in 1857, his "printing office" on his back. He was independent, outspoken, "cranky," and witty. The columns of his weekly contained the most penetrating observations on domestic politics and politicians of any paper in the state.

The newspapers, and the men who owned and edited them, were influential factors in Kansas politics. Anthony was several times mayor of Leavenworth, Martin was elected Governor in 1884, and John Ingalls (who was an editor of the Atchison *Champion*), Edmund G. Ross, and Preston B. Plumb (who was associated with the Emporia *News*) subsequently became U.S. Senators. Miller, Stotler, and S. N. Wood of the *Council Grove Press* were all prominent members of the state legislature; Wilder and Speer received top Federal posts in Kansas as rewards for their political activities. All these newspapers, of which there were about twenty-seven in 1861, were of course fervent boosters of the interests, real or fancied, of the communities where they were published.

A more poverty-stricken state than Kansas probably never entered the Union. Senator John Green of Missouri was not totally unwarranted in contending prior to its admission that Kansas was doomed to be "weak, puerile, sickly, in debt, and at no time capable of sustaining herself." [9] Thirty thousand would-be settlers had abandoned the state and returned East, 30,000 others lived in destitution so great that although they wanted to leave they were unable to do so. Currency was scarce and what there was of it almost worthless, having been issued by "wildcat" banks in Illinois, Wisconsin, and Missouri—there were no banks of issue in Kansas. Personal indebtedness was widespread and heavy, and the state government had inherited from territorial days $100,000 in liabilities but not a cent of revenue. Many men were going about attired in blue jeans or even converted gunny sacks.[10]

This "miserably depressed and wretched" state of affairs was largely the consequence of the mania for land speculation which characterized the early settlement of Kansas. A high proportion of the immigrants during the fifties were more interested in acquiring land than in farming it. Acting either for themselves or as agents for big speculators, they observed the pre-emption laws only to the barest, most literal minimum possible by resorting to such practices as laying four logs on the ground and calling them an "enclosure" or by erecting a veritable dollhouse and entitling it a "home." Thousands of newcomers hopped aboard the real estate merry-go-round. Land warrants were used in lieu of currency; huge paper fortunes accumulated; men in rags deemed themselves prairie nabobs. Speculation in town lots

[9] Quoted in Spring, *Kansas*, p. 265.
[10] *Ibid.*, p. 271; Alfred Theodore Andreas, *History of the State of Kansas* (Chicago, 1883), p. 178; Connelley, ed., "Some Ingalls Letters," *KHC*, XIV (1915-1918), 122; *Journal of the Kansas House of Representatives, 1861*, p. 37 (this publication will hereinafter be cited as the *House Journal* with appropriate dates); Paul Wallace Gates, *Fifty Million Acres: Conflicts over Kansas Land Policy, 1854-1890* (Ithaca, N.Y., 1954), pp. 70-71.

became so intense that "wags proposed an act of Congress reserving some land for farming purposes." It was a time of "unexampled prosperity." Then came the Panic of 1857. Creditors called for their debts and insisted that they be paid in hard cash. Immigration, the main source of currency, slowed to a trickle, with as many people going back as came. President Buchanan vetoed the Homestead Act and refused, despite the frenzied pleas of Kansans, to postpone the sale of public lands. This last was a crushing blow to the Kansas pre-emptors, for large numbers of them had proceeded on the assumption that this sale would not take place on the date scheduled. Consequently they found it extremely difficult to meet the government price, and many lost their claims outright; others either went heavily into debt at usurious interest rates or sold livestock, farm machinery, and portions of their claims.[11]

Following close upon the collapse of the land boom was a severe and prolonged drought, the "granddaddy of all Kansas droughts." It began in the autumn of 1859, after building up since 1854. Through 1860 and well into 1861 barely a drop of rain fell, and the winter of 1859–1860 passed without snowfall. During the summer of 1860 the rivers ceased to flow, the ground became like iron, the air was "the very breath of hell." In September grasshoppers inundated the fields. The result was an almost universal failure of corn and other crops. This crop failure, attended and intensified by the economic depression, brought much suffering to the already sorely afflicted state. The New York *Tribune* remarked that "in fact, had the tillers of Kansas kept their seed out of the ground and their hands in their pockets throughout 1860, they would probably have been in quite as good a position, on the average, as they now are." [12]

[11] Gates, *Fifty Million Acres*, pp. 52, 70–71, 98–105; Connelley, ed., "Some Ingalls Letters," *KHC*, XIV (1915–1918), 116, 119; Richardson, *Beyond the Mississippi*, pp. 57–60; Richard Cordley, *A History of Lawrence, Kansas, from the First Settlement to the Close of the Rebellion* (Lawrence, 1895), pp. 143, 161–162.

[12] Cordley, *A History of Lawrence*, pp. 170–171; James C. Malin, "Dust

From the very beginning Kansas had been the constant recipient of relief and aid, both organized and private, from the East. Thaddeus Hyatt of New York therefore followed customary procedure when in the fall of 1860 he organized the Kansas Relief Committee. With headquarters at Atchison and under the local direction of Samuel Pomeroy, this committee by March 15, 1861, distributed to the hundreds of applicants 7,173,614 pounds of provisions and "large quantities" of clothing, medicine, and seeds. Another organization, the New England Kansas Relief Committee, supplemented and in a measure competed with Hyatt and Pomeroy's efforts. In all, estimated a contemporary, well over a million dollars in aid went into Kansas before the end of the winter of 1860–1861, not counting what could only be guessed at—"the vast sums of money, clothing, and other articles received by private gifts." [13] Wrote Sarah Everett to an Eastern relative: "Every dweller in Kansas owes a lasting debt of gratitude to 'the East' for what she has done for the suffering here."

Some rogues, of course, benefited from the largesse of the East, and some honest people did not receive their due. There was much bitterness against freeloaders and those "that might have helped themselves" but "neglected their plain duty." Not a few Kansans felt that such as these "ought to suffer some!" Moreover, supposed corruption in the distribution of the relief funds and "abuse" of aid supplies "reflected on Kansas for a decade" outside the state and caused much grumbling inside it. In addition, exaggerated and false accounts of the drought and

---

Storms: Part One, 1850–1860," *KHQ*, XIV (May, 1946), 133; Thaddeus Hyatt to C. C. Hutchinson, undated, Thaddeus and Theodore Hyatt Papers, Kansas State Historical Society (henceforth the Kansas State Historical Society will be referred to as KSHS); New York *Tribune*, February 5, 1861.

13 "Report of the Kansas Relief Committee to and Including March 15, 1861" (n.p., n.d.), pamphlet in Kansas Relief Pamphlets Collection, KSHS; Leavenworth *Daily Conservative*, March 15, 1861; Wallace E. Miller, *The Peopling of Kansas* (Columbus, Ohio, 1906), p. 88.

suffering in Kansas, published in Eastern newspapers, served to discourage immigration by spreading the myth that only a small portion of the state, along the Missouri border, was suitable for agriculture and settlement.[14] Finally, the combination of drought and economic depression had a demoralizing and disheartening effect upon the people of Kansas, a fact which should be kept in mind as their history during the next four years unfolds.

Such, then, was Kansas when, upon the eve of the Civil War, it entered the Union.

[14] "Everett Letters," *KHQ*, VIII (November, 1939), 369–370; Samuel J. Crawford, *Kansas in the Sixties* (Chicago, 1911), pp. 7–9; James C. Malin, "Dust Storms: Part Two," *KHQ*, XIV (August, 1946), 265. Contemporary Kansas newspapers contain many angry references to statements in the Eastern press about the unsuitability of Kansas for agricultural settlement. Such statements caused Kansans, anxious for immigration, to go to the opposite extreme of asserting that nothing was wrong with the climate of Kansas.

# II

# *The Political Gallery*

I asked Mr. Colton if Kansas politicians were generally honest and reliable. Mr. Colton looked up and smiled, whereupon I looked down and blushed.[1]

KANSAS in 1861 was already the political preserve of the Republican Party. In the 1859 elections for state officers under the Wyandotte Constitution the Republicans had elected their ticket by a large majority and gained overwhelming control of the legislature. The Democratic Party, except at Atchison, Leavenworth, Wyandotte, and a few other localities, was only a negligible force in the state. Although many of its leaders and adherents had been stanch Free Staters, it was in disrepute with most Kansans as the "Pro-Slavery Party." Furthermore, the unpopular and disastrous land policy of Buchanan had caused thousands of debt-ridden and land-hungry settlers, including erstwhile Democrats, to give their allegiance to the Republican Party, with its promise of free homesteads.[2] The Republicans,

[1] C. M. Chase to the Sycamore, Ill., *True Republican and Sentinel*, August 15, 1863, C. M. Chase Letters, KSHS. Colton was a local Kansas politician met by Chase while traveling in Kansas.

[2] Leavenworth *Daily Conservative*, March 21, 1861; *White Cloud Kansas Chief*, January 16, 1861; Edmund N. Morrill, "The Early Settlers of Kansas: Their Trials, Privations, Hardships, and Sufferings," *KHC*, V (1891–1896), 150.

on the other hand, had inherited the prestige as well as most of the leaders and following of the Free State Party and were favored by the fact that the bulk of the immigration into Kansas "was in sympathy northern Republican." [3] The Wyandotte Constitutional Convention was completely dominated by the Republicans, who used it to strengthen their hold by so apportioning the state senatorial and representative districts that it would be practically impossible for the Democrats to capture the legislature or elect a United States Senator. Republican control of political affairs was further clinched by the termination of the territorial government and the inauguration of Lincoln, which deprived the Democrats of their sole advantage and main substance—Federal patronage.

As would be expected under these circumstances, the real and vital struggle for political power in Kansas was within the ranks of the Republican Party itself. At the beginning of 1861 the main combatants were the factions headed by Charles Robinson and James Henry Lane. These two men were the most prominent of all Kansans and were so important in the early history of the state that their careers and characters require detailed discussion.

Robinson possessed international renown for his outstanding part in the Kansas conflict of the fifties. Born in 1818 in Massachusetts, he had been a physician in New England and a prospector in California, where he was the ringleader of a squatters' riot in Sacramento, was shot and imprisoned, and afterwards served in the legislature. In 1854 he became the Kansas agent of the New England Emigrant Aid Company and conducted the initial settlement of Lawrence. Following the "Bogus Election" of 1855, in which the Missourians "invaded" Kansas and stuffed the ballot boxes to gain control of the first territorial legislature, Robinson sent for the famous Sharps rifles and helped organize the "Topeka Movement" to make Kansas a "Free State." He became the "Free State Governor" and directed the

[3] Miller, *Peopling of Kansas,* p. 74.

strategy of the Kansas antislavery forces during the violen
dramatic days of the Wakarusa War and of 1856. Declared a
outlaw by the Federal authorities in Kansas, he was arrested an𝔲
imprisoned for a brief period at Lecompton, the proslavery and
territorial capital. Called by his admirers "the George Washington of Kansas," he was the natural choice as the state's first
Governor following the formation of the Wyandotte Constitution.

In appearance Robinson was "tall, sinewy and bald," with
cold blue eyes which some regarded as "keen," others as "rather
calculating and furtive." All testified to his "pre-possessing presence," and one observer described him as being "more than or-
dinarily handsome." Despite his background of squatters' riots
and Sharps rifles his manner was quiet and dignified, and he
held a tight rein on his emotions. A clear, forceful, and ready
writer, he was but an ordinary speaker. His character was aus-
tere, his intellect high. He was ambitious, hard-working, and
strong-willed. He had tremendous self-pride—a source to him
of much strength, but also of much weakness.

Robinson's rival, "Jim" Lane, is the most colorful and fascinating personality in the history of Kansas. He looked, as one
writer expressed it, "like nobody else." He was tall, extremely
skinny and bony, yet very strong. His face was sallow and
hollow-cheeked, with the "sad, dim eyes of a harlot," wild,
matted black hair, and thin saturnine lips curling in a "Mephis-
tophelean leer." He moved about nervously, tirelessly, always
on the alert, "like one at bay and apprehensive of detection." His
customary costume consisted of overalls, a calfskin vest, and a
black bearskin overcoat, which he is said to have worn even in
summer. Vulgar, tempestuous, of fluctuating courage, and utterly unscrupulous, he was a cynic who posed as a zealot, a
demagogue who claimed to be a statesman. His private life was
that of a satyr, and he was utterly irreligious except at election
time. Then, with much fanfare and a great showing of repent-
ance, he would join the politically influential Methodist Church,

only to lapse into his old ways once the votes were tallied. Reproached once too often by a Methodist preacher for backsliding, he exploded: "The Methodist Church may go to hell!"

Lane had been born on June 22, 1814, in Lawrenceburg, Indiana. His mother wanted him to be a preacher, but his father was a politician, and he chose to follow the paternal example rather than the maternal wish. During the Mexican War he was colonel of an Indiana volunteer regiment and participated creditably in several battles. With his military record as a springboard he became Lieutenant Governor of Indiana, then a member of the House of Representatives in Washington. His vote in favor of the Kansas-Nebraska Bill wrecked his political career in Indiana, and he came to Kansas early in 1855 to repair it. He was at this time a Democrat, and his first public act in Kansas was to call a convention for the purpose of organizing a Douglas Democratic Party. The failure of this move, coupled with the refusal of the proslavery territorial legislature to grant him a divorce, caused him to espouse the Free State Party. He quickly rose to prominence, presiding at the Topeka Convention of August, 1855, and becoming major general of the Free State militia. His participation in the troubles of 1856 and 1857 was accompanied by much flamboyant publicity, but was largely barren of practical results. He became, however, the popular hero of thousands of Kansans who thought that his "campaigns" and "battles" rescued Kansas from the "Border Ruffians."

The main basis of Lane's power and popularity was his oratory. No one in Kansas could compete with him on the stump. Speaking in a voice that would range from deep, canine gutturals to high-pitched, feline mewings, he would pace up and down waving his lanky arms and doffing surplus clothing; then he would stop to point a long, bony finger at his enrapt auditors and shriek "Great God!" in a manner said to be weirdly electrifying. Apparently he had one of those voices which have the power to sway others simply by its sound or timbre.

Despite, or perhaps because of, his grotesque appearance and

James H. Lane
*(Kansas State Historical Society)*

Charles Robinson
*(Kansas State Historical Society)*

Samuel C. Pomeroy
*(Kansas State Historical Society)*

Thomas Carney
*(Kansas State Historical Society)*

Charles R. Jennison
*(Kansas State Historical Society)*

D. R. Anthony
*(Kansas State Historical Society)*

Marshall Cleveland
*(Kansas State Historical Society)*

William C. Quantrill
*(From William E. Connelley,* Quantrill
and the Border Wars *[Cedar Rapids,
Iowa: Torch Press, 1910])*

"Quantrill's Raid." Painting by Lauretta L. Fox Fisk. *(Kansas State Historical Society)*

"Lawrence After the Raid." By an unknown artist, *Harper's Weekly*, September 19, 1863.

James G. Blunt
*(Kansas State Historical Society)*

Samuel Ryan Curtis
*(Iowa State Historical Society)*

Thomas Ewing, Jr.
*(Kansas State Historical Society)*

John M. Schofield
*(U.S. Army Signal Corps)*

"Order No. 11." Painting by George Caleb Bingham. (*Missouri State Historical Society*)

General Sterling Price
*(Chicago Historical Society)*

"Close Up, Double Quick." Painting by Samuel J. Reader, who served in the Kansas militia against Price in October 1864. *(Kansas State Historical Society)*

"Battle of Big Blue, October 22, 1864." Painting by Samuel J. Reader. *(Kansas State Historical Society)*

mannerisms, he exercised tremendous personal magnetism. Even enemies confessed to his "wonderful tact" and intriguing personality. Already in his own lifetime he was a folk figure, regarded by Kansans as "one of our things." His sallies and catch phrases were repeated throughout the state, and countless anecdotes were told about him. Men who were fully aware of his faults overlooked them and gave him their support and even their respect. He was, in all, a master politician. In the opinion of John Ingalls, who knew him well both as friend and enemy, he could have been "a great leader" had he possessed "a rudimentary perception of the value of personal character as an element of success in public affairs." [4] Very likely, too, he was mentally unbalanced and a paranoid.

From the start Lane and Robinson were at odds. Robinson regarded Lane with suspicion and contempt; Lane loathed Robinson as the main obstacle to his achieving political control in the state. Although their rivalry was essentially a struggle for personal power, it involved also a political conflict between the factions of the Free State Party that they respectively headed or represented. Originally more "conservative" than Robinson —he opposed sending for the Sharps rifles—Lane in the course of events became the leader of the "radicals." This element, of whom John Brown was the most spectacular representative, advocated a program of terrorism against so-called proslavery settlers and armed defiance of the territorial government. Their objective was less to make Kansas a Free State than to promote the fortunes of the Republican Party nationally and to bring about a situation in Kansas which would lead to civil war and the abolition of slavery. In pursuance of this goal they actually endeavored to foster and perpetuate the strife in Kansas. Robinson

[4] John J. Ingalls, "Kansas, 1841–1891," in William E. Connelley, ed., *A Collection of the Writings of John James Ingalls* (Kansas City, Mo., 1921), p. 454. For a remarkable contemporary article on Lane, written by Nicholas Verres Smith, a Kansas journalist, see Leavenworth *Daily Conservative*, July 3, 1863; see also article on Lane by Ingalls, *ibid.*, May 10, 1861.

and the conservatives, on the other hand, had no such far-reaching aspirations as the radicals, but were primarily concerned with wresting the local machinery of government away from the proslavery party. This group, which controlled the Free State Party throughout most of the territorial period, based its strategy on the fact that most of the settlers entering Kansas were Northern free-soilers. They correctly believed that all the Free Staters need do was bide their time and avoid bloodshed and conflict with the Federal authorities and that eventually they would have a clear majority of the voters and could take over the territorial government peaceably and legally. By the summer of 1857 this strategy paid off as the Free State Party elected a majority of the territorial legislature. The Kansas conflict then for all practical purposes came to an end, notwithstanding the fact that John Brown and James Montgomery continued to keep southern Kansas disturbed and Lane talked wildly of wholesale assassination of proslavery leaders.[5]

In 1858 Lane's popularity suffered a temporary eclipse as the result of his killing Gaius Jenkins, a prominent Lawrence Free Stater, in a land quarrel. Lane greatly regretted the homicide—murder some called it—and for the rest of his life suffered horribly from night visions of Jenkins, "the 98 buck shot wounds in bold relief." [6] During this period he went about "care-worn,

[5] The best accounts of the career of Lane and of territorial politics yet written are by Leverett W. Spring in his *Kansas* and in his article "The Career of a Kansas Politician," *American Historical Review*, IV (October, 1898), 80–104. Many illuminating additional facts and insights are provided by James C. Malin in his *John Brown and the Legend of Fifty-Six* (Philadelphia, 1942) and in his series of articles, "Notes on the Writing of General Histories of Kansas," beginning in the *KHQ*, IX (Autumn, 1954).

[6] *Kansas State Journal* (Lawrence), March 26, 1863; James Christian to Charles Robinson, May 3, 1892, Charles Robinson Scrapbooks, vol. IV, University of Kansas; G. W. Brown to Charles Robinson, December 18, 1893, William E. Connelley Collection, Public Library, Kansas City, Kansas.

haggard, reduced almost to a skeleton, the picture of despair." He engaged in law practice and corner-lot speculation, but was so poor that he once walked forty miles to obtain a twenty-dollar fee. Yet never did he lose sight of the fixed goal of his ambition, the United States Senate. He had been a senatorial candidate from the first day he set foot in Kansas. Every session of the legislature, every convention, every meeting, he asked for an "endorsement," and usually obtained it, either through eloquence or persistence. In 1860, with statehood in the offing, he redoubled his efforts, traveling constantly and tirelessly, "with dilapidated garb and equipage, across the trackless prairies," speaking wherever there was a gathering, denouncing his enemies, defending his own character and record, and promising anything that would conceivably win supporters.[7]

In 1860 the Lane-Robinson fight broke out with greater intensity, if possible, than ever before following Robinson's appearance before a congressional committee investigating John Brown's raid on Harper's Ferry. Robinson in his testimony sought to clear the Kansas Free State Party of any complicity in the raid by stating that Brown, John Kagi, Josiah Hinton, John Redpath, William Phillips, and others of the Kansas radical faction were never true members of that party and that the troubles in southern Kansas were caused by Lane's military expedition through that region in 1857. A venomous newspaper quarrel, involving not only Kansas but Eastern journals, took place. Lane and his friends harped on a "bond swindle" allegedly perpetrated by Robinson and accused him of blackguarding the Free State movement. Robinson and his supporters elaborated on Robinson's testimony before the committee and presented lurid data on Lane's sex life and the Gaius Jenkins affair. By the end of

---

[7] John Speer, *Life of Gen. James H. Lane* (Garden City, Kansas, 1896), p. 221; Wendell H. Stephenson, *The Political Career of General James H. Lane* (Topeka, 1930), pp. 96–99; Ingalls, "Kansas," in Connelley, ed., *Writings of Ingalls*, p. 445.

1860 Lane's hatred of Robinson verged on insanity, and Robinson deemed Lane a menace to society whose ambitions must be frustrated at almost any cost.[8]

Lane and Robinson, although the central figures, were by no means the only important actors on the Kansas political stage in early 1861. Others worthy of note included Marcus J. Parrott of Leavenworth, territorial delegate to Congress; Frederick P. Stanton of Lawrence, former Secretary and Acting Governor of the territory; and Samuel Pomeroy of Atchison. All these men were Republicans and, like Lane, were senatorial aspirants. Stanton was a friend of Robinson and was Robinson's candidate to defeat Lane as the Senator from southern Kansas, there being a tacit understanding in Kansas political circles that one of the state's two Senators would be from north of the Kansas River, the other from south of that geopolitical boundary. Parrott and Pomeroy were the principal competitors for the northern senatorship, although Thomas Ewing, Jr., of Leavenworth, Chief Justice of the State Supreme Court, was also very much interested.

Pomeroy was a short, pudgy man of forty-five, with a bland smile and sanctimonious air that led Kansans to call him "Pom the Pious." Like Robinson he had come to Kansas in 1854 as an agent of the New England Emigrant Aid Company, but his role in the territorial conflict was not nearly so distinguished. He was, however, popular with the influential abolitionist element, and he had the powerful backing of the railroad and commercial interests of Atchison, which he headed. In addition, his services as agent of the Kansas Relief Committee had secured for him the gratitude of numerous indigent Kansans, many of whom wore pants made out of grain sacks with "S. C. Pomeroy, Atchison, K.T." stenciled on them. He was personally wealthy and had

[8] Various newspaper clippings of the period in Robinson Scrapbooks, vol. II, University of Kansas; James Christian to Robinson, January 21, 1889, *Kansas City Times*, January 27, 1889, clipping in Newspaper Articles by and about Charles Robinson (Scrapbooks), vol. II, University of Kansas.

received large sums of money from Thaddeus Hyatt to aid him in his campaign for the Senate. As a consequence he had the best-filled political war chest of any of the candidates, and his rivals feared that he would simply buy his way into the Senate chamber.[9]

Parrott was a South Carolinian, only thirty-two, a highly cultured gentleman and a graceful, polished orator able to speak eloquently on any given subject and always doing so. His services as territorial delegate gave him a sort of original claim on the senatorship, and he was deemed by most political observers to have the lead on Pomeroy. Despite this, and although he was identified with the conservative branch of the Republican Party, he had entered into an alliance with Lane, promising Lane the backing of his legislative adherents in return for that of Lane's. This partnership, of course, brought him into conflict with Robinson, who during January and February worked hard to halt Lane's push for the Senate. In order to counteract Parrott's candidacy and so reduce Lane's chances, Robinson backed Thomas Ewing, Jr.[10]

A "very prince in appearance," possessing "the most sturdy, massive and comprehensive mind of any man" in Kansas, Ewing was the son of the distinguished Ohio statesman whose name he bore and the brother-in-law of William T. Sherman. He had come to Kansas in 1856 seeking an open field for his driving ambition and had gained great distinction during the territorial struggle. By profession a lawyer—he and Sherman at one time were partners in a law firm at Leavenworth—he was also active in business affairs and one of the principals of the Leavenworth, Pawnee and Western Railroad Company. Self-confessed to be

[9] Pomeroy to Hyatt, March 14, 1861, Hyatt Papers; Theodore to Thaddeus Hyatt, July 15, 1861, Theodore Hyatt Letter Book, Hyatt Papers; Thomas Ewing, Jr., to Hugh Ewing, January 17, 1861, Thomas Ewing, Jr., Papers, KSHS.

[10] Leavenworth *Daily Times*, February 20, 22, 1861; Speer, *Life of Lane*, p. 227; Robinson to Mrs. Robinson, January 11, February 5, 1861, Charles Robinson Papers, KSHS.

"inordinately ambitious" and feeling that he had "few equals in mental vigor," the chief justiceship was not at all to his liking, being the result of an agreement forced on him by the Republican Central Committee, by which he was to receive that post in return for not opposing Parrott for Senator.[11] Therefore it required no urging from Robinson for him to disregard the agreement and to seek, though somewhat covertly, the senatorship in opposition to Parrott. The Ewing-Robinson combination was facilitated by the fact that both men were antiradical and that they shared mutual railroad and land interests which would be greatly aided if Ewing became Senator. In addition, neither had any use for Pomeroy—Robinson because of an old grudge against his former colleague in the Emigrant Aid Company, Ewing because Pomeroy headed railroad interests antagonistic to his own.

The key to victory in the senatorial struggle was Federal patronage. Like their fellow Republicans throughout the nation in early 1861, those of Kansas were ravenous for office. Not only had they been on a starvation diet patronagewise during the long years of Democratic rule, but the drought and depression had made securing a government job almost an economic necessity for many of them. Moreover, practically "every third man" in the state was "either a military character or politician, and most of these office seekers." Consequently, the person who could hold out the greatest patronage inducements would be almost sure to win the senatorial contest. And whoever won that contest would largely control Federal patronage for the state and so tend to dominate it politically.[12] Thus patronage was both the weapon and the prize of the senatorial election of 1861.

Robinson, as Governor, had extremely little patronage to administer directly, nor could he hope to exercise much influ-

[11] Ewing to Mrs. Ewing, February 16, 1863, Thomas Ewing, Jr., Papers, Library of Congress; O. E. Learned, "Organization of the Republican Party," *KHC*, VI (1897–1900), 315.

[12] *Lawrence Republican*, May 9, 1861; Leavenworth *Daily Conservative*, March 22, 1861; Robinson, *Kansas Conflict*, p. 436.

ence on such matters in Washington. Therefore he endeavored to obtain the post of Commissioner of Indian Affairs, being quite willing to forgo the rather empty honor of serving as the first state Governor of Kansas. The Indian Commissioner was very "influential in matters of great interest to frontiersmen," for he had at his disposal a large number of agencies, clerkships, and lucrative contracts. Ewing did not overstate the case when he wrote his father that if Robinson became Commissioner he, Ewing, would gain the senatorship with little difficulty and that the appointment "would go far to secure Lane's defeat." [13] In order to have sufficient time in which to secure the commissionership and bring its power to bear upon the senatorial contest, Robinson did not convene the legislature until March 26, although that date was nearly two months after the attainment of statehood. Meanwhile, he and Ewing pulled what Washington wires were available to them, and early in March, at the time of Lincoln's inauguration, Robinson went to Washington in person to look after the matter. But he and Ewing were doomed to disappointment. Robinson may have saved Kansas from slavery, but William P. Dole of Indiana had played a key role in Lincoln's nomination, and it was he who got the coveted post. This was a severe blow to the plans of Robinson, and it practically wrecked any chance Ewing and Stanton had for the senatorship, for neither man had much popular support.[14]

Kansas political circles took Robinson's failure to mean that he was not in favor with the Administration, but that Lane was.[15] Lane reinforced this impression by inducing Martin Conway,

[13] Ewing to Hugh Ewing, January 17, 1861, to his Father, January 20, 1861, Ewing Papers, KSHS.

[14] Ewing to Robinson, February 12, 1861, to Caleb Smith, January 21, 1861, to John Sherman, January 22, 1861, to J. J. Coombs, January 22, 1861, to Thomas Corwin, January 22, 1861, *ibid.;* Robinson to Mrs. Robinson, January 11, 1861, Robinson Papers, KSHS; *Lawrence Republican*, March 19, 1861.

[15] M. J. Parrott to Alfred Gray, March 12, 1861, Alfred Gray Papers, KSHS.

Kansas' sole Representative to Congress, elected in 1859, to consent to an arrangement under which all Kansas patronage appointments would be postponed until the legislature elected the
Senators. This arrangement was faithfully carried out by Conway, who in return was promised the support of Lane for
re-election. Lincoln, informed of the Conway-Lane agreement,
gave it his approval—which approval, along with the agreement,
was duly taken into account by Kansas politicians in making their
calculations.[16]

In his campaign for the Senate, Lane received his most enthusiastic support from among the large numbers of Kansans
who hailed from his native state of Indiana, from that influential
element known as the "Fifty-Sixers," and from the radical
abolitionists and roughly dressed, hard-drinking, gun-toting
"b'hoys" so numerous in the state. He also had behind him the
keenest practical politicians in Kansas, among whom Chester
Thomas and John Speer were probably outstanding. Thomas, or
"Uncle Chester" as he was usually called, was a professional
politico from Pennsylvania, who on coming to Kansas had deserted the Democrats for the Republicans because "there's more
of 'em." He was unabashedly corrupt, skilled in managing men,
and highly skilled in the techniques of low-level politics. Speer
was, as previously mentioned, editor and owner of the *Lawrence
Republican*, which he had purchased with money furnished by
Lane. He was intensely devoted to Lane and spent his entire life
working and writing in his behalf. Lane sought to obtain additional support by advocating stay and minimum-interest laws
designed to appeal to the thousands of Kansas debtors and by
outlining magnificent but highly visionary canal and railroad
systems which would be built following his election. Above all,
however, he promised influential members of the legislature and

[16] Conway to S. N. Wood, February 24, 1861, Samuel Newitt Wood
Papers, KSHS; Leavenworth *Daily Conservative*, March 21, 22, 1861; Con-
nelley, ed., "Some Ingalls Letters," *KHC*, XIV (1915–1918), 122; Speer,
*Life of Lane*, p. 221.

local political chieftains that he would see to it that they got choice Federal patronage jobs if and when he went to Washington.[17]

The prevailing opinion among political observers when the legislature assembled was that Lane was sure to win and that the real contest would be between Pomeroy and Parrott, with Parrott standing the best chance. In any event, John Ingalls was certainly not the only person who anticipated "a lively time" in Topeka.[18]

Topeka in the spring of 1861 was a straggling "town" of 800 surrounded by a "howling wilderness." Its appearance gave "a stranger the impression that the people now there, are not expecting to stay, but merely holding on till they can sell out at a big figure, and leave." Lawrence and Leavenworth, Topeka's rivals for the state capital, scornfully maintained that the town would always be too far west from the center of population to be a suitable place for the seat of government. Its businessmen and politicians supported Pomeroy because of common railroad interests with Atchison, but were divided between Lane and Stanton.[19] The state government had only the most makeshift accommodations. The Governor's and other executive offices

[17] Letter by "Kaw" in Leavenworth *Daily Conservative*, July 3, 1863; Emporia *News*, April 13, 1861; *Fort Scott Democrat*, March 16, 1861; Speer, *Life of Lane*, pp. 224–225, 232–233; Lane to Delahay, December 18, 1860, Mark W. Delahay Papers, KSHS; James C. Horton, "Reminiscences of Hon. James C. Horton," *KHC*, VIII (1903–1904), 204; R. S. Stevens to S. N. Wood, August 6, 1860, Wood Papers.

[18] M. J. Parrott to Alfred Gray, March 12, 1861, Gray Papers; Connelley, ed., "Some Ingalls Letters," *KHC*, XIV (1915–1918), 122; David E. Ballard, "The First State Legislature," *KHC*, X (1907–1908), 234; Isaac T. Goodnow, "The First Kansas Senator," Topeka *Capital*, January 29, 1893, Kansas Election Clippings, Scrapbook, I, 195–196, KSHS (hereinafter cited as Goodnow, "First Kansas Senator," Topeka *Capital*, January 29, 1893).

[19] Leavenworth *Daily Conservative*, March 26, November 6, 1861; *Council Grove Press*, June 8, 1863; Leavenworth *Daily Times*, March 15, 1861; *Kansas State Journal* (Lawrence), October 24, 1861; *Kansas State Record* (Topeka), March 26, 1861; *Topeka Tribune*, March 26, 1861.

were located in a few rented rooms in the corner of a building
on whose third floor the Senate met. The House of Representatives first assembled in an "old shack" which it had to abandon
because of a leaking roof in favor of the Congregational church.
The legislative chambers were "inconvenient" and "dirty," and
the members were compelled to remain standing "or perch upon
miserable substitutes of desks," while spectators could either
"sit on the floor or stand on their heads as best suited their tired
limbs." The desks were "small tables, covered with the meanest
cotton velvet," scattered haphazardly about the floor, and "each
expected to accommodate the elbows of two members." William
Updegraff, Speaker of the House, wielded a gavel described by
a St. Louis correspondent as "a clumsy machine, consisting of
the top of a bed-post with a chair round stuck in it—a handy
weapon of offense and defense." At night the legislators, "hungry
and sleepy," crowded into "incompetent hotels" or the "wet gar-
rets of distant buildings." Throughout the entire session a fierce
wind blew coldly and constantly down the wide, unobstructed
streets, and the drought gave way early in April to rains so heavy
that the Leavenworth *Conservative* sarcastically urged Pomeroy's
relief committee to send East for umbrellas.[20]

Most of the state officers and legislators, along with the mob
of lobbyists, journalists, and interested onlookers who accompanied them, gathered in Topeka several days before the legislature convened. The senatorial candidates were also soon on
hand to look after their respective interests. Pomeroy displayed
excellent foresight by having constructed beforehand a $2,000
"Senatorial Residence" for himself and his followers, which because of the free liquor and food lavishly dispensed there was
dubbed "Fort Sumptuous." Lane, on the other hand, arrived in
Topeka with only a few dollars in his pocket and "as ragged as

[20] Franklin G. Adams, "The Capitals of Kansas," *KHC*, VIII (1903–
1904), 347–48; Ballard, "First State Legislature," *ibid.*, X (1907–1908),
235; *Kansas State Record* (Topeka), April 4, 1861; Leavenworth *Daily
Conservative*, April 5, May 9, 1861.

Diogenes." He opened up his headquarters in a hotel, from which some of his political foes tried to evict him by telling the landlord that Lane was bound to lose and so would never be able to pay the rent. Lane remained, however, although prepared, if necessary, to "move into a store box on Kansas avenue, and get ahead of the hounds." [21] On March 26 the first state legislature of Kansas met in joint session, listened to Robinson deliver his message, then proceeded to the preliminary formalities of organization before taking up the business uppermost in all minds. In the meantime politicking in all its various forms ran rife in the bars, boardinghouses, and streets and even among the woodlands and underbrush of Topeka.[22]

The first move occurred on April 1. State Senator E. R. Bancroft, a Robinson-Stanton man, presented a resolution calling for the Senate to vote immediately and as a body for a United States Senator from "south of the Kansas River." The strategy behind the resolution was obvious: instead of having, as customary, a joint session of both houses to elect the Senators, each house would vote separately. In this manner Lane would be defeated, since the Senate, which had been elected in 1859, was filled with a majority of Robinson-Stanton adherents. Bancroft's resolution passed, and the balloting that followed resulted in a 16 to 9 vote in favor of Stanton over Lane. The anti-Lane men, Robinson prominent among them, filled the Senate chamber and jubilantly celebrated the "downing" of Lane.[23]

The rejoicing of the Robinson faction, however, was premature. That evening Pomeroy sent word to Lane that he would

---

[21] Leavenworth *Daily Conservative*, March 27, 1861; Speer, *Life of Lane*, p. 227; Sidney Clarke, "Lane of Kansas," Kansas City *Journal*, September 14, 1879, clipping in Kansas Reminiscences by Kansas Authors, Scrapbook, KSHS.

[22] Leavenworth *Daily Conservative*, March 28–April 4, 1861.

[23] *Journal of the Kansas Senate, 1861* (hereinafter cited as *Senate Journal*), pp. 33–34; Troy *Kansas Chief*, February 7, 1889, clipping in Robinson Scrapbooks, vol. III; P. P. Elder, "Our First Senators," Topeka *Capital*, February 5, 1893, Kansas Legislature Clippings, vols. I–II, KSHS.

like to make a deal. Pomeroy was in as much need of help as Lane. The votes on which he had been counting prior to the convening of the legislature had failed to materialize. Lane, who was "terribly disheartened" by the action of the Senate and alarmed because a large number of Parrott's followers had voted for Stanton, was delighted by Pomeroy's proposal. He at once hastened over to "Fort Sumptuous" and had a long talk with Pomeroy, after which the two slept together, bedfellows in fact as well as in politics.[24]

The next day the united Lane and Pomeroy forces rallied enough support in the Senate to nullify the resolution and election of the preceding day. Another day of frenzied political maneuvering ensued, during which Parrott, realizing that he had been dumped by Lane, formed an alliance with Ewing, who withdrew from contention in his favor.[25] Finally, on the afternoon of April 4, with both houses assembled in joint session, the long-awaited balloting began. Since both Senators were to be elected simultaneously, each legislator cast two votes when the clerk called his name. This made it possible for the members to play coy, to engage in trading and jockeying right on the floor and in the midst of the balloting. As a result a scene of frenetic confusion and disorder occurred which a witness likened to a stampede. Fifty-eight of the niney-eight members present changed their votes from one to six times each, and 297 different votes were cast in all. At times as many as eight men, all shouting, were on their feet trying to alter their votes. The clerks were unable to keep an accurate tally and either proceeded by guesswork or, as some charged, simply kept the count to suit themselves.[26]

When it was all over, Lane and Pomeroy were the victors by

[24] Goodnow, "First Kansas Senator," Topeka *Capital*, January 29, 1893; The Diary of Isaac T. Goodnow, April 1, 1861, MS, KSHS; Speer, *Life of Lane*, pp. 228–230; Elder, "Our First Senators," Topeka *Capital*, February 5, 1893, Kansas Legislature Clippings, vols. I–II, KSHS.

[25] Leavenworth *Daily Conservative*, April 4, 1861; Leavenworth *Daily Times*, March 29, April 4, 1861.

[26] Leavenworth *Daily Conservative*, April 7, 11, 1861.

slim majorities.[27] No one expressed any doubt concerning the validity of Lane's election, to which even many of his enemies had been resigned as inevitable. Pomeroy's success, however, was an unpleasant surprise in several quarters. Parrott men were especially bitter. They accused Pomeroy of bribery and asserted that their candidate had been "counted out" by the clerks after having been actually elected. The reaction of the badly routed Robinson faction to the election was expressed by Robinson's friend, G. W. Brown, who lowered the flag above the *Kansas State Journal* building in Lawrence to half-mast.[28]

During the balloting Lane sat on a sofa in the lobby of the "capitol," anxiously awaiting the outcome. When the good news was announced, tears of joy flowed from his "easy lachrymals," and he pulled out a pistol and avowed that if he had lost he would have blown his brains out on the spot. He remained in Topeka only long enough to receive the congratulations of his friends and to assure them that he would forget neither them nor his promises. On April 8, accompanied by Pomeroy, he left for Washington, having first secured a loan on his life insurance policy and an advance on his senatorial salary in order to purchase some respectable clothes and pay the steamboat and railroad fares. "Now," he said as he departed, "we will see what a *live* man can do!" [29]

Lane and Pomeroy had been preceded to Washington by a

---

[27] *House Journal, 1861,* p. 76.

[28] Speer, *Life of Lane,* pp. 230–231; Crawford, *Kansas in the Sixties,* pp. 19–20; Goodnow, "First Kansas Senator," Topeka *Capital,* January 29, 1893; Leavenworth *Daily Conservative,* April 7, 1861; *White Cloud Kansas Chief,* April 18, 1861; *Lawrence Republican,* April 11, 1861. The bribery charges against Pomeroy were probably well founded. John Ingalls, Secretary of the Senate in 1861, stated in 1862 that "it was through his 'manoeuvering' that Parrott was defeated" (*White Cloud Kansas Chief,* October 23, 1862).

[29] Jacob Stringfellow (Nicholas Verres Smith), "Jim Lane," *Lippincott's Magazine,* VI (March, 1870), 274; *White Cloud Kansas Chief,* July 5, 1866; Leavenworth *Daily Conservative,* April 9, 1861; Speer, *Life of Lane,* p. 233; S. C. Pomeroy, "The Times of War and Reconstruction," Kansas Biographical Scrapbook, "P," VI, 144, KSHS.

swarm of office-seeking Kansas politicians. A correspondent of the Leavenworth *Conservative* reported that in the corridors of the Interior Department "every other column has a Kansas applicant leaning against it" and that the request for Indian agencies "exceeds anything ever known." Because Kansas did not have a senatorial delegation and because the Lane-Conway-Lincoln agreement suspended all Kansas appointments until there was one, Kansas office seekers had so far been largely frustrated in their efforts. Therefore they hailed the arrival of Lane and Pomeroy as signifying the end of the patronage drought. Additional numbers of Kansans accompanied or followed the Senators, including so many members of the legislature that for awhile it had a hard time obtaining quorums.[30]

Lane and Pomeroy arrived in a Washington filled with tumult and excitement over the Confederate bombardment of Fort Sumter. When a rumor circulated that the Virginians planned to strike across the Potomac, Lane promptly marshaled his. fellow Kansans into the "Frontier Guards" and offered their aid to Lincoln in protecting the nearly defenseless capital. Lincoln gladly accepted the offer, and the Frontier Guards bivouacked in the White House itself for several days, then guarded a Potomac bridge. From this point they made a scouting foray into Virginia and captured a "secession flag," which Lane displayed proudly from his hotel window. After serving about two weeks they were mustered out in a ceremony at the White House in which Lincoln personally thanked them.[31]

Lane received considerable publicity from the Frontier Guards and became something of a national hero. The most significant aspect of the affair, though, was its bearing on his relations with the President. To begin with, Lane for several years had been

---

[30] Leavenworth *Daily Conservative*, March 22, April 15, 1862.

[31] Speer, *Life of Lane*, p. 241; "The Frontier Guard at the White House," *KHC*, X (1907–1908), 419; Oskaloosa *Independent*, May 8, 1861; Pomeroy, "War and Reconstruction," Kansas Biographical Scrapbook, "P," VI, 149, KSHS.

assiduously cultivating Lincoln's friendship. In this he was greatly aided by his close alliance with Mark W. Delahay of Leavenworth. Although of little consequence himself, this individual had the good fortune of being the cousin and close friend of Lincoln. When Lincoln visited Kansas in 1859, Lane was on hand with Delahay to welcome and dine him. Later, during the 1860 campaign, Lane went to Illinois and Indiana to, as a friend of Robinson's expressed it, "howl" for Lincoln and "so secure, if possible, the confidence of that good man." Following Lincoln's election, Lane had offered to provide a bodyguard of Kansans for the President-elect on his journey to Washington.[32] Now, by his dramatic action of raising and commanding the Frontier Guards, Lane firmly established himself in the regard and confidence of the President. Henceforth he enjoyed special consideration from Lincoln and possessed remarkable influence with him. Thus, by the end of April, Lane was handing applications for appointments to Lincoln, who in turn was endorsing them without even reading them.[33] Pomeroy, in contrast, obtained only a comparatively minor share of the patronage, and Conway practically none. It was soon apparent to all Kansas politicians, as it was to one disgruntled office seeker, that Lincoln "evidently thinks that Lane is the man for the times" and that "Lane gets anything of the President that he asks for while others go begging."[34]

Lane, it scarcely need be said, took full advantage of his near monopoly of Washington patronage to build up his political strength in Kansas. Every available place he filled with men who had supported him in the past and on whom, so beholden, he could count to support him in the future. Delahay and "Chet" Thomas, for instance, became respectively Surveyor General for

[32] Mary E. Delahay, "Judge Mark W. Delahay," *KHC*, X (1907–1908), 640–641; George W. Deitzler to S. N. Wood, August 18, 1860, Wood Papers; Speer, *Life of Lane*, p. 240.
[33] Clarke, "Lane of Kansas," Kansas City *Journal*, September 14, 1879.
[34] A. J. Chipman to S. N. Wood, August 20, 1861, Wood Papers.

Kansas and Mail Agent of Kansas—both jobs of great political leverage. When Lane returned to Kansas early in May, he asked confidently, "Doesn't Jim Lane look after his friends?" [35] By then he was well on the way to complete control of the Republican Party organization in Kansas, and consequently the political domination of the state.

[35] Leavenworth *Daily Times*, April 28, 1861; *Kansas State Record* (Topeka), April 30, May 4, 1861; *Topeka Tribune*, June 1, 1861.

# III

## *The Jayhawkers*

THE last territorial Governor of Kansas, George M. Beebe, proposed shortly before the achievement of statehood that if the nation were rent asunder by civil war Kansas should espouse neither the North nor the South, but instead "establish, under a Constitution of her own creation, a Government to be separate and independent among the Nations." [1] Kansans greeted Beebe's recommendation with scorn and derision. The origin, nature, and politics of the overwhelming majority of its citizens assured that Kansas would side with the North in a sectional conflict. The only major disagreement in the state concerning the secession crisis during the winter and spring of 1861 was over the best method of coping with it. The radical Republicans opposed making any concessions to the South whatsoever; the conservatives, more in harmony with their party nationally, were willing to support a "reasonable" compromise, although they were against any concession on the slavery-expansion issue.[2] Kansas

[1] Wilder, *Annals*, p. 308.

[2] *Kansas State Record* (Topeka), January 17, 1861; Leavenworth *Daily Times*, January 31, 1861; *Lawrence Republican*, February 14, 1861; Leavenworth *Daily Conservative*, February 13, March 7, 1861; *Kansas State Journal* (Lawrence), February 21, 1861; *Freedom's Champion* (Atchison), February 2, March 2, April 20, 1861.

Democrats, for their part, advocated compromise, but in spite of
the fears and accusations of some, most of them went along with
Stephen A. Douglas in proclaiming that in the great national crisis
party must be subordinated to patriotism and that Democrats
would support the Lincoln Administration insofar as its policies
tended to preserve the Union.[3]

Following Fort Sumter and Lincoln's call for 75,000 militia
to suppress the Southern "combinations," public sentiment in
Kansas became, in the words of a contemporary, "very strongly
patriotic." [4] Sentiment among the members of the legislature,
reported the Topeka correspondent of the Atchison *Champion*,
was unanimously "in favor of rigid enforcement of the laws at
all hazards and at whatever cost." Thomas Ewing wrote his wife
that the conflict of North and South was between "two systems
of civilization for the mastery of the continent" and "must be
settled by the sword." [5] Sol Miller in the *Kansas Chief* announced
that "the crisis has come to a head and Southern braggadocio
must be put to the test." "A point has now been reached in the
progress of the disunion movement," affirmed the Leavenworth
*Times*, "at which longer forbearance on the part of the Federal
authorities, would be a crime rather than a virtue." The Government, continued the *Times*, was left with "no alternative—
unless it has lost its power and vitality—but to strike an effective
and decisive blow at those who have raised their hands against
it." John Speer, in the *Lawrence Republican*, declared that "this
revolt must be checked" and called on God to "defend the
Right." The Topeka *State Record* hoped that "secessionism and
secessionists [would] be taught a lesson the memory of which
will endure for generations to come, and the seeds of this most
pernicious heresy completely rooted out from our political sys-

[3] *Topeka Tribune*, February 2, 1861; *Fort Scott Democrat*, March 9,
16, 23, 30, April 6, 13, 20, 1861; Leavenworth *Daily Herald*, quoted as
being against secession by Leavenworth *Daily Conservative*, March 3,
1861.
[4] "Everett Letters," *KHQ*, VIII (November, 1939), 371.
[5] April 21, 1861, Ewing Papers, Library of Congress.

tem. Then, and not till then, can we have peace." Jacob Stotler of the Emporia *News* reacted in a prophetic vein:

The Government is on Trial. If it shall prove equal to the emergency, it will come out of the conflict stronger than ever, and continue to be, as heretofore, a beacon light to the oppressed of all nations.

Out of this war will come a substantial peace no longer to be disturbed by the warring of class or sectional interests. Out of it will come a renewed, vigorous, national life, cleaned and purified by the fiery ordeal. . . . The war will be worth fully what it costs.

The actions of Kansans were as militant as their words. Everywhere they hastily formed military companies and held nightly drills. The legislature moved to put the state on a war footing by writing and passing a militia law, by authorizing the Governor to call into service two regiments of infantry, three companies of cavalry, and two batteries of artillery, by appropriating $20,000 (in bonds) to defray the expense of these troops, and by issuing $150,000 in bonds to meet the general financial needs of the state.[6] The citizens of Leavenworth demonstrated their patriotism by forcing a pro-Southern Missouri steamboat captain to strike the "secessionist" banner atop his ship, and even the residents of the old "Border Ruffian" town of Lecompton came out unanimously in favor of the Union and the war.[7] The Leavenworth *Conservative* expressed fear of trouble between Northern and Southern adherents, but the Topeka *Times* scoffed at such apprehensions and declared that it had not seen or heard "of a single man in Kansas who was unconditionally for disunion, or a separation of the North from the South." Kansas Democrats meeting at Leavenworth went on record as regretting the existence of the war but as being devoted to the preservation of the Union.[8]

A notable feature of Kansas newspaper comment on the outbreak of the war was the almost total absence of any contention

[6] *The Laws of the State of Kansas, 1861*, pp. 104-203, 205-206, 294.
[7] Wilder, *Annals*, p. 317; Leavenworth *Daily Times*, May 8, 1861.
[8] Leavenworth *Daily Conservative*, April 16, 1861.

that its purpose was to eradicate slavery. The only crusade the editors preached was the preservation of the Union and the punishment of the "Southern fanatics." They regarded slavery as the "prime cause," but not the basic issue, of the "irrepressible conflict." Even "Web" Wilder, although declaring that "civil war will end Slavery," stated that the object of the war was "the maintenance of the Constitution and the preservation of liberty." The archradical Martin Conway was practically alone among Kansans in suggesting that the South be allowed to secede in order to rid the nation of the sin of slavery. In short, the attitude of the people of Kansas in 1861 toward slavery was not what the contemporary and historical reputation of the state would seem to indicate.[9]

One of the by-products of the propaganda that accompanied the Kansas territorial struggle was the myth that the typical Kansan of the period was a zealous abolitionist. Northern orators such as Charles Sumner and Wendell Phillips and radical journalists such as William Phillips, Richard Josiah Hinton, and William P. Tomlinson portrayed the Free State settlers as embattled crusaders fighting to prevent the "conquest of Kansas" by the wicked and repulsive myrmidons of the "Slave Power." Southern spokesmen, on the other hand, fulminated about "abolitionist hordes" pouring into Kansas to deprive slaveholders of their rights and to secure a base for further onslaughts on the institutions of the South. The putative exploits of John Brown in Kansas, and especially his Harper's Ferry raid, fired the public imagination and caused people, when they thought of Kansas, to think of "Pottawatomie" Brown, and vice versa. In fact, even to this day Brown is popularly identified with Kansas, as is so magnificently demonstrated by John Steuart Curry's famous mural in the capitol at Topeka.

Actuality, however, differed considerably from myth. As mentioned previously, very few of those who settled in Kansas during the fifties did so for idealistic antislavery reasons. Even Brown

[9] Survey of the Kansas press, April–May, 1861.

probably came to Kansas originally for no higher purpose than acquiring some land.[10] The Free State men, wrote one of them, were "not against slavery in the abstract," and hundreds of them had a "deadly terror of being termed 'abolitionist'" and were "frightened by the mere mention of that mysterious specter, 'negro equality.'" In general, Kansans at the time of the Civil War were as much anti-Negro as they were antislavery, and they were probably in large measure antislavery because they were anti-Negro; that is, they feared the social and economic consequences of the introduction of Negro slave labor into the state.[11]

In one important respect, however, Kansas deserved its reputation for extremism on the slavery question. Without exception its major political and governmental leaders were abolitionists. Thus Robinson in his message to the 1861 legislature declared that "if it is true that the continued existence of Slavery requires the destruction of the Union, it is time to ask if the existence of the Union does not require the destruction of Slavery."[12] Pomeroy and Lane, in July, 1861, called on the Senate to institute immediate, unqualified, and uncompensated emancipation. Conway was perhaps the most rabid abolitionist in the nation and late in 1862 and early in 1863 delivered sensational speeches before Congress in which he advocated what he suggested at the beginning of the war, the Wendell Phillips doctrine of granting the Confederacy independence as a means of liberating the slaves, for fear that there would be a restoration of the Union with slavery.[13] Robinson, Pomeroy, Lane, and Conway probably represented in varying degrees the views of the majority

[10] Malin, *John Brown*, pp. 7-9, 22-23.

[11] Richardson, *Beyond the Mississippi*, p. 43; Robinson, *Kansas Conflict*, pp. 176-179; Spring, *Kansas*, p. 64; Benjamin F. Simpson, "The Wyandotte Constitutional Convention," *KHC*, II (1879-1880), 175-177; *White Cloud Kansas Chief*, November 28, 1861.

[12] Robinson, *Kansas Conflict*, pp. 176-177; *Senate Journal, 1861*, p. 28.

[13] *Congressional Globe*, 37th Cong., 1st Sess., p. 142; *ibid.*, 3d Sess., pt. I, pp. 91-92; *ibid.*, Appendix, pp. 62-67; Leavenworth *Daily Conservative*, July 24, 1861.

of Kansans on slavery; with such men as the latter three serving as its national spokesmen it is little wonder that Kansas was reputed to be the "most radical of the States."

Kansas abolitionists consisted of a majority who proposed to destroy slavery by legal and political means and a small but energetic and influential minority who advocated direct action as the best and only way to overthrow the hated institution. The two most prominent members of this second group, the so-called "practical abolitionists," were James Montgomery and Charles R. Jennison. Montgomery was a forty-seven-year-old Ohioan, who, after a wandering, obscure life as a schoolteacher and Methodist "exhorter," settled near Mound City in 1854. He was tall and slender, and "his eyes had the uneasy glare peculiar to haunted men, and his laugh aroused the unpleasant suggestion of a mind diseased." In 1858 he accompanied John Brown on a slave-liberating raid into Missouri. During the winter of 1859–1860 he led a band of zealots to Pennsylvania in an abortive effort to rescue Brown from prison. After Brown's execution he succeeded him as the military agent of that group of New England militants headed by George Luther Stearns, Thomas Wentworth Higginson, F. B. Sanborn, and N. W. Thayer. Throughout late 1860 and early 1861 he and a band of armed followers in Linn County conducted the "interesting experiment" of making the Fugitive Slave Law a dead letter by abducting slaves from Missouri, defying all attempts to recover them, and either secreting the Negroes in Kansas or sending them via the "underground railroad" to Canada. He received arms and money from Stearns, and there is strong reason to believe that the New England Relief Committee, whose Kansas representative, George W. Collamore, was a close friend of Stearns, furnished him with supplies ostensibly raised and intended for the aid of drought-stricken Kansans.[14]

[14] Montgomery to G. L. Stearns, December 12, 1860, March 8, April 22, 1861, George L. Stearns Papers, KSHS; Montgomery to Stearns, June 21, 1861, James Montgomery Papers, KSHS; Leavenworth *Daily Times*, January 4, 1861.

"Doc" Jennison was an associate of Montgomery in the guerrilla warfare in southeastern Kansas. He was a mean-looking, jockey-built individual in his late twenties from New York, and his chief traits were brutality, unscrupulousness, and opportunism. Montgomery was probably a sincere antislavery fanatic, but with Jennison, fighting against slavery was mainly an excuse for banditry. Jennison's activities gained him a considerable following of reckless young men who hated slavery and loved plunder. His lieutenant was George A. Hoyt, one of John Brown's attorneys at the Harper's Ferry Trial. He and his men were known as "the Jayhawkers." [15]

The forays of Montgomery and Jennison caused intense anger and resentment in Missouri and so much turmoil in southern Kansas that the "responsible men" of the region thought of leaving the state. Kansas and Federal authorities made several attempts to suppress or restrain them, but had little or no success. Montgomery, Jennison, and their New England backers welcomed the outbreak of war as opening up new and broader fields of operations.[16]

All through the winter and spring of 1861 the major concern of Kansans, aside from the drought and the senatorial election, was Missouri. Kansans, in fact, were always most interested in the affairs of their neighbor state. However, their attitude toward Missouri was ambivalent. On the one hand many of them came from Missouri, had friends and relatives there, and engaged in much business and political intercourse. Yet, on the other hand, they bitterly remembered the invasions of the "Border Ruffians" and intensely resented the efforts of the Missourians to control

[15] Leavenworth *Daily Conservative*, October 31, 1861, July 3, 1863; Theodosius Botkin, "Among the Sovereign Squats," *KHC*, VII (1901–1903), 433; John N. Edwards, *Noted Guerrillas; or The Warfare of the Border* (St. Louis, 1877), p. 38; Andreas, *History of Kansas*, pp. 1070, 1106.

[16] George A. Crawford to Sam Smith, January 21, 1861, Charles Robinson Papers, KSHS; N. W. Thayer to Montgomery, April 16, 1861, Montgomery Papers; Montgomery to Stearns, April 22, 1861, Stearns Papers.

the land and government of Kansas. In addition, Kansans, especially those from the Northeastern states, tended to look upon Missouri as "an exceedingly dark place," whose people were "poor white trash," shiftless and inferior to themselves. Commercial rivalry was an added incentive to antagonism, with ambitious towns such as Atchison and Leavenworth striving to supplant St. Joseph and Kansas City. Missourians, for their part, inclined to dismiss Kansans as a parcel of "nigger-loving, horse-stealing Yorkers," and thus dislike bred antipathy.

Kansans watched Missouri closely during the early months of 1861 because they were concerned over the course it would pursue in the crisis between North and South. Should Missouri join the Confederacy, then Kansas would be practically cut off from the rest of the nation. Moreover, in case of war, Kansas would be exposed to attack from the Missourians, many of whom were known to be thirsting to avenge the raids of Brown and Montgomery. It was fear of invasion from Missouri, as much as anything else, that impelled Kansans to make such vigorous military preparations.[17] This same fear caused the Kansas press to urge that all Kansas troops be retained in or near the state and to argue that the contribution of Kansas to the Union war effort should be confined to the defense of its own borders.[18]

The direction Missouri would take, North or South, long remained uncertain. Although most Missourians, torn between conflicting sympathies and interests, hoped that their state could be "neutral," small but active minorities of "Unconditional Unionists" and "secessionists" maneuvered to gain the upper

[17] G. W. Collamore to G. L. Stearns, May 2, 7, 1861, Stearns Papers; Charles Robinson to Simon Cameron, April 25, 1861, *The War of the Rebellion: A Compilation of the Official Records of the Union and Confederate Armies* (Washington, 1881–1901), ser. III, I, 112–113 (hereinafter cited as *OR*); Ewing to Mrs. Ewing, Ewing Papers, Library of Congress.

[18] Leavenworth *Daily Conservative*, April 19, 1861; Leavenworth *Daily Times*, April 20, 21, 23, 1861; Oskaloosa *Independent*, April 24, 1861; *White Cloud Kansas Chief*, April 25, 1861; *Kansas State Journal* (Lawrence), April 25, 1861; *Elwood Free Press*, April 20, 1861.

hand. Finally, on May 10, Union troops in St. Louis under Nathaniel B. Lyon captured a camp of Missouri militia suspected of treasonable intentions, then killed twenty-eight members of a mob which attacked them. Pro-Southern elements in Missouri were outraged by this "Camp Jackson Massacre," and even many former Union adherents turned against the Federal Government. The Missouri legislature promptly mobilized the State Guard and placed it under the command of Sterling Price, former Governor and Mexican War general. Last-minute efforts to avert armed conflict failed, and on June 11 Lyon set his troops in motion toward Jefferson City. Pro-Confederate Governor Claiborne F. Jackson countered by issuing a proclamation calling for 50,000 men to resist the "invasion," and open and full-fledged civil war began. Price's army was too weak to stand against Lyon and retreated to the southwest corner of the state to organize and obtain the assistance of the Confederate forces in Arkansas.

Governor Robinson regarded Jackson's proclamation as tantamount to a declaration of war on Kansas. On June 17 he called on the citizens of the state not already so organized to form militia companies and to be in readiness to repel an attack. All along the border armed Kansans gathered, and in some localities people slept in cornfields while men with binoculars kept watch both by night and by day for the approach of the Missourians.[19] A new regiment, the Sixth Kansas Volunteer Cavalry, formed at Fort Scott, and the First and Second Kansas regiments joined Lyon in Missouri. Montgomery, however, was not content with a defensive policy, but believed that the best way to "keep the Missourians from our doors was to give them something to do at home." Accordingly, late in June and during July he and Jennison made a series of quick dashes across the border, fought a few skirmishes, and returned ladened with plunder and accompanied by dozens of "contrabands"—slaves who "happened to walk off on their own accord." Furthermore, through-

[19] Leavenworth *Daily Conservative*, June 18, August 4, 1861.

out the summer hundreds of West Missouri Unionists who had been driven from their homes by secessionists fled into Kansas. These refugees told of terrible outrages and hardships and begged Kansans "on bended knee" to help them recover their property and secure revenge. Many of them joined Kansas regiments or formed bands that raided into Missouri in quest of personal vengeance.[20]

The coming of war did not bring peace between Robinson and Lane. Instead, it only occasioned new conflict as the two men struggled to control the military affairs of the state. Legally, this control belonged to Robinson, who as Governor commanded the state militia and who had been authorized by Washington to raise and organize Kansas regiments intended for Federal service. But General Lane, as he was customarily called, was determined to be the war chieftain of Kansas. Military exploits had always provided the foundation of his political career, and by the summer of 1861, if not before, he was harboring presidential ambitions.[21] Moreover, the patronage question was involved, for Robinson had the power to appoint and commission all the field and staff officers of the Kansas regiments and could thereby build up a strong political machine and undercut Lane's position. Hence, if only to protect himself, Lane deemed it desirable to curtail Robinson's authority over military matters. By so doing, not only would he diminish his rival's political influence, but at the same time he would increase his own.

Lane's first move along these lines was to attempt, through his cohorts in the legislature, to deprive the Governor of the right to select the general officers of the militia and to invest it instead in the legislature.[22] Undiscouraged by the failure of this scheme,

[20] Montgomery to Stearns, June 21, 1861, Montgomery Papers; Montgomery to Stearns, June 26, July 5, 1861, Stearns Papers; Collamore to Stearns, July 10, 1861, Stearns Papers; Leavenworth *Daily Conservative*, June 8, July 11, 17, 27, 30, August 20, 1861; E. R. Smith, "How Quantrill Became an Outlaw," *KHC*, VII (1901–1902), 216.

[21] See *Topeka Tribune*, May 25, 1861.

[22] Leavenworth *Daily Conservative*, April 23, 1861.

Lane next proceeded to create the impression that he, not Robinson, was the authority on Federal military policies affecting the state and that the public should look to him for information and direction. Although it provided 650 men voluntarily, Kansas was not assigned a quota under Lincoln's first call for troops on April 15, and there was much speculation in the state as to what, if anything, the future demands of the Government would be. Toward the end of April, Lane sent word from Washington that the President intended to requisition Kansas for two regiments. But subsequent news proved this information to be false, and when Lane returned to Kansas early in May, he admitted that Lincoln had merely told him that two regiments from Kansas would be accepted if their services were tendered. Later in May official word finally came from Washington that the state's quota was to be only one regiment.[23] This news caused a flare-up of resentment against Lane for having misled and confused the people as to their military obligations.

But confusion was not yet at an end. From the wording of Secretary of War Simon Cameron's telegram accepting the first regiment, Robinson believed that the Government would accept two additional regiments. When Cameron hesitated to take any more Kansas troops, Robinson sent State Quartermaster General George W. Collamore to Washington to persuade him to order the two regiments (which were already being formed) mustered into service. Robinson evidently feared that if they were not mustered soon, Lane would either gain control of them or forestall their mustering. Collamore's mission succeeded; on June 17 Cameron informed Robinson that he would accept the two regiments. Soon afterwards Robinson scored once more against Lane when the War Department announced that it had authorized

[23] "Kansas Regiments," *Report of the Adjutant General of the State of Kansas, 1861–'65* (Topeka, 1896), p. 11; *Senate Journal, 1861*, pp. 228–230; *Topeka Tribune*, May 11, 1861; Leavenworth *Daily Conservative*, May 8, 11, 12, 1861; Simon Cameron to Charles Robinson, May 21, 1861, *OR*, ser. III, I, 221.

Frederick P. Stanton to raise troops in Kansas and New Mexico for service in the latter territory.[24] Stanton, of course, was Robinson's political alter ego.

Lane, however, was far from being outdone. He returned to Washington and on June 20 secured from the War Department a brigadier general's commission and permission to recruit two regiments in Kansas.[25] Lincoln's friendship, the beginning of warfare in Missouri, and the assistance of influential abolitionists combined to achieve this coup.[26] The President believed that Lane's services would be useful in Kansas and Missouri, and he wrote Cameron to tell Lane that "when he starts to put it through. Not be writing or telegraphing back here, but put it through."[27] Lane now had a large quantity of military patronage to dispense, which he immediately set about doing. Robinson later charged that he appointed nearly as many officers as his regiments had men.

As soon as Robinson learned of Lane's commission, he declared his Senate seat vacant on the grounds that, under the Constitution, Lane had ceased to be a Senator the moment he became a general. To replace Lane, he appointed Frederick Stanton, who was more than willing to abandon his own military projects to achieve his old goal of the Senate. Stanton journeyed posthaste to Washington and on July 12 presented his credentials to the Senate. Lane, who was on hand to defend his seat, protested strenuously that he had not yet formally accepted the commission and that therefore the move to unseat him was like trying to bury a man before he was dead. The dispute went to the Senate Judiciary Committee, which on July 29 reported in favor of Stanton. Testimony before the committee brought out the

[21] Robinson to S. N. Wood, February 2, 1864, Wood Papers; "Report of the Quartermaster-General of Kansas," *Public Documents, Kansas, 1863* (Topeka, 1863), pp. 159–160; *OR*, ser. III, I, 275; *Topeka Tribune*, June 1, 1861.

[25] Cameron to Lane, June 20, 1861, *OR*, ser. III, I, 282.

[26] Stearns, *Life of Stearns*, p. 51.

[27] Lincoln to Cameron, June 20, 1861, *OR*, ser. III, I, 280–281.

following facts: that the Secretary of War had stated that Lane had accepted the commission, that Lane had taken the requisite oath, and that he had signed himself in official public communications as "Brigadier-General." His assertion that he had not accepted the commission rested on a mere technicality—failure to file the document bearing the commission with the Adjutant General's office. Lane, by arguing that he had been unable to present his side of the case fully, won a further hearing and in this manner postponed action until August 6. On that date the Senate adjourned after consoling Stanton by voting him traveling expenses.[28]

Robinson thus failed to supplant Lane in the Senate, but did force him to drop all claims to being a regularly commissioned United States general. The skepticism of Sol Miller, who on hearing that Lane had been appointed a general and would resign from the Senate commented that he would "believe the latter when it comes to pass," [29] was well founded. Lane did not intend to give up his long-sought senatorship unless it were very much to his advantage to do so. In the meantime he would be both Senator and general. Armed with a brigadier's commission from Governor Oliver P. Morton of his native state of Indiana, Lane headed back to Kansas, determined, as he afterwards expressed it, "to bet high on small cards." [30] In the weeks to follow he became the first and probably only man ever to command large numbers of United States troops without legal authority from the Federal Government.

In spite of what had been in truth a rather sorry performance as leader of the Free State forces, Lane had a popular reputation of being a "powerful fighter." Even those who despised him personally and opposed him politically had faith in him mili-

---

[28] *Congressional Globe*, 37th Cong., 1st Sess., pp. 82, 438-441, 452, 454; *Kansas State Journal* (Lawrence), July 25, 1861; Leavenworth *Daily Conservative*, August 24, 1861.

[29] *White Cloud Kansas Chief*, June 27, 1861.

[30] Leavenworth *Daily Conservative*, August 4, October 8, 1861.

tarily.[31] On August 15 he made a speech at Leavenworth calling on Kansas to enlist in his "brigade" and stating that when the Union army marched into Missouri he would not object to seeing "an army of slaves marching out." [32] This last remark presaged an important phase of his subsequent operations. As early as April 15 the radical New Englander, N. W. Thayer, had written Montgomery expressing the hope that Lane could "get into a position where he can reach the slaves," and Lane had proclaimed to Thayer's fellow abolitionist, George Luther Stearns, that given the opportunity he would "march to New Orleans by December," stirring up slave insurrections on the way.[33]

On August 17 Lane, accompanied by his staff—four Italian veterans of Garibaldi and a young relative of Senator Pomeroy—left Leavenworth and traveled to Fort Scott to take charge of the troops assembled there. These consisted principally of the Third, Fourth, and Fifth Kansas regiments, commanded respectively by Colonels Montgomery, William Weer, and Hamilton P. Johnson, and were known as the "Kansas Brigade," otherwise "Lane's Brigade." Montgomery, who had been commissioned a colonel by Robinson in an effort to "harmonize" the various "Unionist elements" in the state, was second in command. The brigade numbered no more than 1,200 men, was part infantry and part cavalry, and had two small cannon. Discipline was nonexistent, its camp a veritable hogpen. The line officers of the Fifth were "notoriously incompetent," and the selection of officers in Montgomery's regiment had been "brought about by corrupt combinations." Some units, notably Captain John E. Stewart's cavalry company, were no better than bandits. Jennison's "Jayhawkers" also were present.[34]

[31] *White Cloud Kansas Chief,* May 16, 1861; *Kansas State Journal* (Lawrence), September 5, 1861.

[32] Leavenworth *Daily Conservative,* August 16, 1861.

[33] N. W. Thayer to Montgomery, April 16, 1861, Montgomery Papers; Stearns, *Life of Stearns,* pp. 251–252.

[34] *OR,* ser. I, III, 447; Robinson, *Kansas Conflict,* pp. 434–435; Robinson to Montgomery, May 7, 1861, Montgomery Papers; "Kansas Regi-

Lane believed that "the neighborhood of Fort Scott" was the best point from which to defend Kansas and to launch offensive operations into Missouri. But since Fort Scott was surrounded by hills and therefore difficult to hold, he moved the major portion of his command to a hastily constructed post called "Fort Lincoln" on the Little Osage River. From there he sent a flood of dispatches to Captain William E. Prince, commandant of Fort Leavenworth, asking for reinforcements and especially for more artillery. Prince, however, had none to spare, and the most he was able to do was to try to procure additional equipment from St. Louis. Lane also invited the various Kansas Indian tribes to gather at Fort Lincoln for a "big war talk," but had to abandon this project when the Office of Indian Affairs objected.[35]

Robinson, meanwhile, kept a wary eye on Lane's activities. He soon concluded that there was little peril of an invasion by Price's Missourians unless Lane provoked one. Therefore, on September 1, he wrote Major General John C. Fremont, Union commander in the West, asking him to send the government stores at Fort Scott to Fort Leavenworth and to order Lane's Brigade from the border. If he did not, there was danger "that Lane's Brigade will get up a war by going over the line, committing depredations, and then returning into our State." Should this happen, all Missourians, Unionist and secessionist alike, would turn on Kansas. Robinson offered to "guarantee Kansas from invasion from Missouri" if the supplies at Fort Scott were removed and the state "relieved" of the Lane Brigade. Price and his men, he asserted correctly, were not interested in Kansas but in gaining control of Missouri.[36]

Robinson's letter to Fremont was scarcely written before what it was intended to prevent occurred—a clash between the Missou-

ments," *Report of the Adjutant General*, pp. 111–113; Leavenworth *Daily Conservative*, July 31, 1861; C. B. Zulavsky to G. L. Stearns, July 28, 1861, Stearns Papers.

[35] *OR*, ser. I, III, 453–455, 465; Anna Heloise Abel, *The Slaveholding Indians* (Cleveland, 1915–1919), I, 229–231.

[36] *OR*, ser. I, III, 468–469.

rians and Lane's Brigade. Price, on August 10, defeated and killed Lyon at the battle of Wilson's Creek near Springfield, Missouri, then began moving toward the Missouri River. Upon hearing that the Missouri counties east of Fort Scott were "infested" with the "marauding and murdering bands" of Lane, he sent a cavalry force under Brigadier General James S. Rains to "clear them out." Rains proceeded to Stockton, Missouri, then reported back that the Kansans were too numerous for him to attack alone. Price thereupon marched to Rains's support with the rest of his Army. Late in the afternoon of September 2 a small advance guard of Missourians encountered a detachment of Lane's Brigade at Drywood Creek. The two forces skirmished for about an hour, then Lane's men retreated rapidly, followed by the Missourians, who discontinued their pursuit only with the coming of darkness. In a report written two days later, Price referred to the engagement as a "trifle" and stated that he did not follow up his success because he had learned that Fort Scott had been abandoned. He added that he did not want to invade Kansas "unless her citizens shall provoke me to do so by committing renewed outrages. . . . In that event I shall not only cross the border, but will lay waste the farms and utterly destroy the cities and villages of that State." Content with thus "chastising" Lane, Price moved northward to Lexington on the Missouri River.[37]

For his part, Lane reported that he repulsed Rains but was forced to fall back to Fort Lincoln because of Price's superior numbers. His casualties were light, consisting of only a few men killed and wounded and the loss of Colonel Weer's mules. Jennison's men, whom he had left behind at Fort Scott "to amuse the enemy," instead amused themselves by pillaging the town, which had been evacuated by all its residents except a couple of women. Immediately after the "battle" Lane sent word to Fort Leavenworth that he was in danger of being surrounded and was badly in need of reinforcements, but that he was entrenching and

[37] *Ibid.*, pp. 162, 185; *ibid.*, LIII, 435–436; Elwood *Free Press*, September 24, 1861.

"could only try again." He refused to credit information from a Confederate deserter that Price was marching for Lexington, but insisted that Price was moving to his rear "for the purpose of crossing over to the north side of the Osage . . . to attack Barnesville, this post, and Fort Scott in detail." He remarked that if this should happen, he would be placed "in rather an awkward position," but that he hoped to "extricate" himself and defeat the enemy. Apparently not until well after Price was on his way toward the Missouri River did Lane feel secure. He then sent Colonel Johnson and Jennison in pursuit. These commanders followed Price at a discreet distance as far as Papinsville, Missouri, than returned with 200 cattle and a number of "contrabands." [38]

On September 10, "with a smart little army of about 1,500," Lane started northward along the Missouri line. His avowed objective, however, was not to pursue Price, but to "clear out" the valley of the Osage and to "pitch into" the towns of Butler, Harrisonville, Osceola, and Clinton in Missouri. By the morning of September 12 he reached Trading Post, Kansas, and from there turned eastward into Missouri. As soon as they crossed the border his men began to plunder, burn, and perhaps murder and rape. Far from restraining them, Lane urged them on. "Everything disloyal," he cried, "from a Durham cow to a Shanghai chicken, must be cleaned out." Even the chaplains shared in the looting. One of them became so notorious for his "pious zeal" in acquiring the "spoils of ungodly altars" that on one occasion Lane halted his column, pointed in "solemn mirth" to a distant church spire, and exclaimed: "See that steeple yonder? If we go there the chaplain will try to steal it, and we will never get home in the world." [39] As they marched along Lane's followers sang, to the tune of an old Methodist hymn:

> I am a soldier of the boss,
> A follower of Jim Lane,

[38] *OR*, ser. I, III, 163–164, 475; *Fort Scott Democrat*, September 21, 1861.
[39] *OR*, ser. I, III, 485, 490; Robinson, *Kansas Conflict*, p. 447; String-fellow, "Jim Lane," *Lippincott's Magazine*, V (March, 1879), 274.

> And shall I fear to steal a hoss,
> Or blush to ride the same?

The answer to the last refrain, was, of course, a resounding "No!"

The climax of Lane's march occurred at Osceola on September 23. After exchanging a few shots with some Confederates on the outskirts, his men entered the town and proceeded to ransack it. They robbed the bank, pillaged stores and private homes, and looted the courthouse. Captain Thomas Moonlight bombarded this last building with a cannon, and others set fire to the town, almost totally destroying it. Many of the Kansans got so drunk that when it came time to leave they were unable to march and had to ride in wagons and carriages. They carried off with them a tremendous load of plunder, including as Lane's personal share a piano and a quantity of silk dresses.[40]

Lane and his friends justified the sacking of Osceola on the grounds of military necessity and merited retaliation for a recent Confederate raid on Humboldt, Kansas.[41] A newspaper correspondent [42] who accompanied the Lane Brigade on its march related that Colonel Weer did not want to burn the town, but was overruled by the other officers for the following reasons: Osceola was "traitorous to the cause; that the enemy intended

[40] *OR*, ser. I, III, 196; *Kansas State Journal* (Lawrence), November 28, 1861; *White Cloud Kansas Chief*, October 6, 1864; St. Louis *Republican*, August 30, 1862, quoted in Robinson, *Kansas Conflict*, pp. 452–454; Henry E. Palmer, "The Black-Flag Character of War on the Border," *KHC*, IX (1905–1906), 457; W. S. Drought, "James Montgomery," *ibid.*, VI (1897–1900), 243; John Speer, "The Burning of Osceola, Mo., by Lane, and the Quantrill Massacre Contrasted," *ibid.*, pp. 306–308; William E. Connelley, *Quantrill and the Border Wars* (Cedar Rapids, Iowa, 1910), pp. 199–200.

[41] On September 8 a band of Missourians and Indians led by a Kansas Indian trader named John Mathews raided Humboldt, taking property but not killing or burning. A force of Kansas home guards pursued and killed Mathews.

[42] Probably Chaplain H. H. Moore of Montgomery's regiment, who was coeditor of Speer's *Lawrence Republican* and supplied that paper with laudatory accounts of Lane's operations.

to make the town during the winter a military post; that it was a strong position, and could be easily fortified"; and that since it could not be permanently occupied it should be rendered uninhabitable.[43] All these reasons are specious and beside the point, for they could have applied just as well to nearly every town in that section of Missouri. Equally absurd is the story, also put out by Lane's apologists, that all the houses of Osceola were stocked with gunpowder intended for Price's army and that the destruction of the town prevented the Missouri commander from using it as a winter base.[44] Price had no such quantities of powder to leave in a defenseless town, and during the winter of 1861–1862 his army experienced little difficulty in remaining along the Osage River in the vicinity of Osceola. Lane's own report contradicts all the above explanations, as he stated that the enemy "took refuge in the buildings of the town" and that he was "compelled to shell them out . . . and the place was burned to ashes." [45] The truth of the matter is that Lane's Brigade was an irresponsible mob which looted and burned Osceola out of a wanton lust for plunder and a self-righteous desire to injure the Missourians. The "Sack of Osceola" was henceforth to be a prime cause of bitter hatred of Lane and all things Kansan on the part of the people of western Missouri.

The self-proclaimed purpose of Lane's expedition was to suppress secessionist sentiment in Missouri and hamper Price's operations. But his actual objective, besides plunder, was to give a practical demonstration of what he had told the Senate in July—that slavery could not survive the march of the Union armies. By the time the brigade completed its march, scores of Negroes were present in its ranks as teamsters and cooks and even as soldiers. Later, in November, Chaplains H. H. Moore and H. D.

---

[43] Leavenworth *Daily Conservative*, October 16, 1861.

[44] See *ibid.*, September 28, 29, October 16, 1861; B. Rush Plumly to Colonel Thomas A. Scott, October 3, 1861, *OR*, ser. I, III, 516; Speer, "Osceola," *KHC*, VI (1897–1900), 306–308.

[45] *OR*, ser. I, III, 196.

Fisher conducted a "Black Brigade" of 160 wagons filled with Negroes into Kansas. There they distributed the ex-slaves as laborers among the farms and towns of the southern part of the state.[46]

On September 18 Fremont ordered Lane to move to Kansas City and from that point co-operate with Brigadier General Samuel D. Sturgis against Price, who was besieging the Union garrison at Lexington. Lane did not receive, or at least did not answer, the order until September 24. He then replied that he would march to Kansas City and join Sturgis, although Lexington had fallen since Fremont sent the order and there were rumors of a Confederate advance on southern Kansas, in which event "God only knows what is to become of Kansas when we move on Kansas City." Lane arrived in Kansas City on the twenty-ninth and immediately got into a dispute with Sturgis over respective rank. Before this quarrel could be settled, he and Sturgis received, on October 4, an order from Fremont, dated September 29, to retreat to Fort Leavenworth. Since they had just reliably ascertained that Price was falling back to the south, they rightly ignored the order. Two days later Fremont countermanded it and directed Lane and Sturgis to join him at Warsaw, Missouri, in pursuit of Price.[47]

Having some political matters to attend to in Kansas, Lane did not leave Kansas City until October 18. "Our march through Missouri," later wrote James G. Blunt, commander of Lane's cavalry, "was noted for nothing very remarkable except that our trail was marked by the feathers of 'secesh' poultry and the debris of disloyal beegums." The brigade arrived at Springfield on November 1, but advanced no further. Fremont, although he vastly outnumbered Price, failed to attack him or do anything else. On November 2, because of his incompetency, Lincoln re-

---

[46] *Congressional Globe*, 37th Cong., 1st Sess., p. 187; Montgomery to Stearns, July 26, 1861, Stearns Papers; Leavenworth *Daily Conservative*, September 20, October 8, 9, November 21, 1861.

[47] *OR*, ser. I, III, 500, 505–506, 515–516, 520–522.

placed him with Major General David Hunter. Ten days later the Union army dispersed to defensive positions, and Lane and his men headed back to Fort Scott, accompanied by 600 Negroes collected in the Springfield region.[48] Thus ended the garish career of the Lane Brigade.

Sometime in July or August, Governor Robinson gave "Doc" Jennison a letter to Fremont in which he asked that the Jayhawker be commissioned a colonel and authorized to raise a regiment of cavalry. Robinson afterwards attempted to explain and excuse this otherwise inexplicable and inexcusable act by stating that he hoped that if Jennison were given a legitimate outlet for his warlike propensities he would cease to rob and slay and be of service to the state and the Union cause. In any event, Jennison received the commission, and posters appeared in the towns of Kansas urging men to join the "Independent Mounted Kansas Jayhawkers." [49]

Jennison did not have a complete regiment until November 7. Many of his men were Missourians, and several units came from Illinois. The most notable company, however, came from Ashtabula County, Ohio, and was commanded by John Brown, Jr., the son of "Osawatomie." Its members were all fanatical abolitionists. In the evening they would stand in a circle around their captain's tent and "listen to the deep utterances of some impassioned orator." The speaker always closed with "Do you swear to avenge the death of John Brown?" and the response would come, low and fierce, "We will, we will." Then they would sing the John Brown song, at first slowly and solemnly, then in accelerated time, ending with "Then three cheers for John Brown, Jr." The entire regiment would gather to watch this strange but awesome ceremony.

48 *Ibid.*, pp. 559, 748; James G. Blunt, "General Blunt's Account of His Civil War Experiences," *KHQ*, I (May, 1932), 216–217.

49 Simon M. Fox, "The Story of the Seventh Kansas," *KHC*, VIII (1903–1904), 16, 27; Leavenworth *Daily Conservative*, August 21, 1861; Robinson, *Kansas Conflict*, pp. 434–435.

Another organization of more than passing interest, and in
stark contrast to the Ashtabula County contingent, was Company H, which consisted mostly of criminals and ruffians. Its
leader was Captain Marshall Cleveland, an ex-convict and a professional jayhawker. During the summer he had committed a
series of murders and robberies in Missouri border towns. He
resigned his commission, however, on November 1 following a
quarrel with D. R. Anthony, who was lieutenant colonel of the
Seventh Kansas, as Jennison's regiment was officially designated.
Some of the other officers of the regiment were hardly better
than Cleveland, but none of them was a greater rogue than its
colonel, or less competent. Jennison's conception of discipline
was expressed by him as follows: "When we're in camp, we're
all boys together, but when in the field, it's generally understood
that I run the machine." And this was a specimen of one of his
military orders: "Hello, there, you, Mr. Man! Take a squad of
men, and go down to yonder house, and burn it to the ground,
as quick as the devil will let you!"[50]

After exercising their martial prowess in sacking the saloons
of Leavenworth, the Jayhawkers crossed into Missouri at Kansas
City on November 11. Their ostensible purpose was to protect
Union supply trains in Jackson County, put down "rebels," and
"loyalize" the people of that section. Company H rode one-
fourth mile ahead of the main column as the advance guard. Its
movements were marked by the flames of burning houses and
outbuildings and by the flight of women and children into the
woods. Near the Little Blue, three companies commanded by
Anthony encountered a band of armed Missouri irregulars under
the "notorious" Upton Hayes. After a sharp fight, in which he
lost nine killed, Anthony drove Hayes's men from their camp and
then withdrew. Following a raid by Anthony on Independence, where "the citizens were given a little touch of the mis-

---

[50] Fox, "Seventh Kansas," *KHC*, VIII (1903-1904), 19-23, 26; Leavenworth *Daily Conservative*, September 20, 1861; *White Cloud Kansas Chief*,
January 2, 1862.

fortunes of war," the Jayhawkers marched back to Kansas City, carrying much plunder and accompanied by many Negroes.[51]

Late in November, Brigadier General James W. Denver, commander of the District of Kansas, received reports that Price once more was advancing, with Kansas as his objective. Denver forthwith ordered Montgomery, in command at Fort Scott, to defend that place if able and, if not, to retreat to West Point. At the same time he instructed Jennison to move to West Point and form a junction with Colonel H. W. Wessel's Eighth Kansas. Jennison complied, and his march to West Point followed the pattern of his earlier operations. "Every house along our line of march but one was burned," wrote a member of the John Brown, Jr., company, "and off on our left flank for miles, columns of smoke from burning houses and barns could be seen." Although Price's invasion failed to materialize, the Jayhawkers remained in the vicinity of West Point well into January. Commanded by Anthony, sections of the regiment plundered Pleasant Hill, Morristown, and Rose Hill and burned Dayton and Columbus. General Hunter "read with surprise" Anthony's reports on the destruction of these villages and wrote him that he found no evidence in them "of a state of facts sufficient to warrant these extreme measures."[52]

Eventually the Seventh Kansas left Missouri and went to Humboldt, Kansas, where it remained until March 25. It then moved to Fort Riley by way of Lawrence and Topeka, then back to Fort Leavenworth. From there it proceeded by steam-

---

[51] War Diary of Fletcher Pomeroy (typewritten copy of the original MS, KSHS), p. 15 (Pomeroy was a member of Company D, Seventh Kansas; this section of the diary was written in a summary fashion and not under chronological headings); Leavenworth *Daily Conservative*, October 15, 16, November 10, 12, 13, 19, 1861; "Kansas Regiments," *Report of the Adjutant General*, p. 93; William L. Webb, *Battles and Biographies of Missourians* (Kansas City, Mo., 1900), pp. 324-325.

[52] Pomeroy Diary, p. 18; *OR*, ser. I, VIII, 45-46, 392-394, 400, 403, 407, 423, 425, 481, 508; Fox, "Seventh Kansas," *KHC*, VIII (1903-1904), 29-30.

boat to Tennessee and during the next two years served east of the Mississippi. But while still in Kansas, Jennison resigned as its commander in a huff over not being promoted to brigadier general. Just before resigning he made an "intemperate speech" in which he practically urged his men to desert. A number of them, mainly from Company H, took this advice. Actually he had exercised little direct command over the regiment but had occupied himself with "playing poker over at Squiresville" and auctioning off loot collected during the raids into Missouri. Anthony was in effective charge most of the time the Seventh was in the field and therefore must share at least equal blame with Jennison for its marauding.

When he heard of Jennison's efforts to wreck the Seventh, General Hunter had him and his friend Hoyt, who had seconded him, arrested and confined in the military prison at St. Louis. Pressures from influential abolitionists, to whom Jennison and Hoyt were heroes, and perhaps blackmail threats on their part, prevented a court-martial and secured their release. Jennison then entered the "live stock" business in Leavenworth, an enterprise which gave rise to the saying that the horses of Kansas were mostly "out of Missouri, by Jennison." He and Hoyt stood as the leaders of the ultraradical elements in the state.[53]

Kansans generally approved the forays of Lane and Montgomery, of Jennison and Anthony, through the border counties of Missouri.[54] Their growing antislavery fervor caused them to applaud the slave-liberating aspect of these operations, especially since the freed Negroes relieved the labor shortage in Kansas. Moreover, reports, true, exaggerated, and false, of outrages suffered by Kansas and other Union adherents along the border at the hands of Missouri secessionists seemed to warrant retaliation

[53] Fox, "Seventh Kansas," *KHC*, VIII (1903–1904), 24, 27–30; Pomeroy Diary, p. 34; Jennison to Stearns, April 21, 1862, Stearns Papers; Leavenworth *Daily Conservative*, January 12, April 8, 30, June 3, 25, November 7, 1862, February 8, 1863.

[54] The following discussion is based on a survey of the Kansas press of the period and of other contemporary records.

in kind. In addition, the people of Kansas had a distorted concept of the object and nature of the activities of Lane and Jennison. They believed that their campaigns were designed to put down "treason" and guard against invasion, and the newspaper correspondents who accompanied Lane's Brigade and the Seventh Kansas wrote up the supposedly heroic exploits of these commands and either ignored or glossed over the looting and killing. Finally, there was a rather sizable element in Kansas who out of economic and moral poverty were quite willing to advocate and practice the plundering of the farmers of western Missouri, who had "a dangerous reputation for wealth."

The majority of Kansans tended to classify all Missourians, at least those living in the border counties, as "rebels." This viewpoint ran counter to the facts and largely reflected prejudice, ignorance, and a desire to rationalize the depredations in Missouri. Probably from one-third to over one-half of the people residing in western Missouri were in 1861 loyal to the Union or at least neutral.[55] One of the main results of the raids of Lane and Jennison was to turn many of these Unionists and neutralists into Confederates. By the end of 1861 Major General Henry W. Halleck, then in command of the Department of the West, was of the opinion that a few more such raids would make Missouri "as Confederate as Eastern Virginia." In January, Halleck, angered by "almost daily complaints of outrages" committed by Jennison, threatened to drive the Jayhawkers out of Missouri if they did not return to Kansas immediately and to "disarm and hold them prisoners" should they resist. On the Confederate side, General Ben McCulloch informed his government that Lane's Brigade "greatly injured" the Union cause in Missouri "by taking Negroes belonging to Union men." In view of Lincoln's desire to conciliate Missouri and other border states, it is hard to understand why he was so tolerant of Lane and Jenni-

[55] Wiley Britton, *Memoirs of the Rebellion on the Border—1863* (Chicago, 1882), pp. 114–118; Britton, *The Civil War on the Border* (New York, 1899), I, 147–148; Webb, *Battles and Biographies*, p. 263.

son's jayhawking operations and merely commented on a letter of Halleck's criticizing Lane, "I am sorry General Halleck is so unfavorably impressed with General Lane." [56]

Another serious consequence of the Lane-Jennison incursions was that they transformed the already-existent animosity of the people of western Missouri toward Kansas into an embittered and impassioned hatred. This feeling was not confined to pro-Confederate Missourians, but also affected pro-Unionists. Thus George C. Bingham, the famous Missouri artist, resented the pillaging of Kansas troops so intensely that while serving as a Union officer he refused to co-operate with them in operations against Price. And on at least one occasion Missouri State Militia in Federal service warned that they would fire on Kansas soldiers if they did not stay on their side of the line.[57] By the spring of 1862 the situation along the border was so tense that Brigadier General John M. Schofield, commander of the Department of Missouri, wrote Secretary of War Stanton that it was absolutely necessary to keep Kansas units out of Missouri and Missouri units out of Kansas. Unless this were done, it would be "difficult to prevent open hostility between the Union troops of Kansas and Missouri." Schofield further recommended that both states be included in the same military district in order that the movements of their respective troops could be co-ordinated so as to keep them apart. The chief obstacle to the "speedy pacification of Missouri," added Schofield, lay in the "lawless bands of border men" who exploited "the bitter feeling existing between the border people, which feeling is the result of old feuds, and involves very little, if at all, the question of Union or disunion." [58]

Scores, perhaps hundreds, of Missourians in the country devastated by Lane, Jennison, and Anthony formed guerrilla bands or joined the Confederate army. The force under Upton Hayes

---

[56] *OR*, ser. I, VIII, 449–450, 507–508, 819; *ibid.*, III, 742–743.

[57] *OR*, ser. I, III, 433–435, 457–461, 467–468; *ibid.*, XXII, pt. 1, 796–801, 808, 824; Webb, *Battles and Biographies*, p. 251.

[58] *OR*, ser. I, XXII, pt. 1, 386–387.

which Anthony encountered on the Little Blue in November had been raised in the locality to defend it against Jennison. Hayes was a freighter engaged in the Santa Fe trade when the war began, operating out of the town of Little Santa Fe near Kansas City. He turned guerrilla after the Jayhawkers captured one of his wagon trains, burned his house, and took his cattle, horses, carriages, and slaves. Far from stamping out such bands as Hayes's, the marches of Lane and Jennison served only to increase their number, strength, and determination.[59]

The Missourians were not slow in striking back. On October 14, late in the afternoon, 300 cavalry led by Colonel Talbott dashed into Humboldt, taking its garrison of 100 home guards completely by surprise. Talbott's troopers rounded up most of the male inhabitants, then put the torch to all the houses and buildings after first assisting the women and children to remove valuables and furniture. Later in the month a party of Missourians under "Sheriff Clem" raided into Linn County, killing three men and pillaging several houses. In December, Clem once more crossed into Kansas to sack and loot houses and stores near Potosi. As a result of these incursions many Kansan settlers along the border abandoned their farms and moved to the interior. Following the Potosi raid, 700 cavalry and infantry under Major H. H. Williams of Montgomery's command entered Missouri where they burned the towns of Papinsville and Butler and "laid waste the houses and farms of the Secesh."[60] In this manner a maelstrom of retaliation and counterretaliation built up, and the

[59] Webb, *Battles and Biographies*, p. 324; Leavenworth *Daily Conservative*, November 13, 26, 1861; Miller, *Missouri's Memorable Decade*, pp. 76, 89; A. Birdsall, *The History of Jackson County, Missouri* (Kansas City, Mo., 1881), pp. 271–273; W. Z. Hickman, *History of Jackson County, Missouri* (Topeka, Kansas, and Cleveland, Ohio, 1920), pp. 208–209, 214, 299; Pomeroy Diary, p. 16; George Caleb Bingham to James S. Rollins, *Missouri Historical Review*, XXXIII (October, 1938), 46.

[60] Andreas, *History of Kansas*, p. 669, 1106–1107; Leavenworth *Daily Conservative*, November 5, December 20, 1861; Wilder, *Annals*, pp. 325, 328; Samuel J. Reader to His Half-Brother Frank, December 1, 1861, *KHQ*, IX (February, 1940), 49–50.

consequences should not have been hard to foresee. Early in the spring of 1862 a gang of guerrillas made an unusually brutal raid on the little village of Aubry in Johnson County, Kansas. Not merely did the raiders take horses and other property; they also shot down helpless civilians in cold blood. Their leader had a strange, sinister-sounding name—Quantrill.[61]

[61] *OR*, ser. I, VIII, 335–336. The "sinister affect" of the name "Quantrill" (or "Quantrell" as it was sometimes spelled) on the people of Kansas at this time is mentioned in Shalor Winchell Eldridge, *Recollections of Early Days in Kansas* (Topeka, 1920), p. 182.

# IV

## *The Triumph of Lane*

IN the midst of the campaign against Price, Lane took out time from military warfare to resume his political battle with Robinson. He was angered by the efforts of Robinson to restrict the operations of the Kansas Brigade and to supplant him in the Senate, and he was now determined to crush his "hereditary foe" once and for all. The time for doing so was opportune, for he had won fresh laurels as "the saviour of Kansas from Price," and Robinson was vulnerable to attack on several fronts.

Leaving his command at Kansas City, Lane journeyed to Leavenworth and on October 8 made the most sensational speech of his career.[1] Before a capacity audience in Stockton Hall, he accused Robinson of conspiring with disloyal army officers at Fort Leavenworth, Captain Prince in particular, to wreck his brigade. He claimed that their machinations had deprived him of the artillery he needed to defeat Price at Drywood Creek and so avert the fall of Lexington and "the shedding of rivers of blood." Robinson and Prince, he declared, were "guilty of treason baser than that of Price," and he called Prince "a dirty puppy" and Robinson "that still dirtier creature." As for being labeled

[1] Speech printed in the Leavenworth *Daily Conservative*, October 9, 1861, and in most of the other newspapers of the state. The *Conservative* distributed over 10,000 copies of the speech.

a "Jayhawker" by his enemies, he gloried in the name, for jay-hawking consisted in freeing slaves from rebel masters and confiscating rebel property for the use of the Government. He defended the record of his brigade and gave a bombastic account of its military feats in defending Kansas against Price and the guerrillas. He concluded this phase of his speech by asserting that Robinson was in league with Claiborne Jackson and that if given the chance the Kansas Brigade would capture Price, even if that general "had Robinson and Prince to help him."

The remainder of Lane's harangue was devoted to urging the desirability of a separate Department of Kansas, with headquarters at Leavenworth and with himself as commander. Thus far Kansas had been part of the same military area as Missouri. From the strategic viewpoint this was as it should be, for the two states formed a natural theater of operations.[2] But there were other viewpoints, one being Lane's, with his military ambitions, and the other being that of the merchants and farmers of Kansas. As long as Kansas was in the same department as Missouri, the center for contracts and commissions to supply the troops of the department would be St. Louis, and the Missourians would tend to monopolize the business. But if Fort Leavenworth became a departmental headquarters, Kansans would then obtain a greater share of the profits of war. As the Lawrence *Journal* frankly remarked, a Department of Kansas "would be money in the pockets of our people." Sentiment throughout the state was unanimous in favor of such a department, and Lane by taking the lead in expressing it was allying himself to a popular cause which would aid him in his fight on Robinson and his desire to control the army organization in Kansas. Following Lane's address, the Stockton Hall meeting adopted a resolution calling for a Department of Kansas with Lane as its commander. The Leavenworth papers, the Lawrence press, and other journals took up the demand.

[2] See Halleck to McClellan, March 10, 1862, *OR*, ser. I, VIII, 602.

In addition to castigating his enemies and arguing the merits of dividing Kansas militarily from Missouri, Lane throughout his speech made a strong appeal to abolitionist sentiment. Here again he attached himself to the popular tide, for there was a great upsurge of antislavery feeling in the state during the fall of 1861. As Albert D. Richardson pointed out, Lane's invariable tactic was to claim that he embodied "some great principle" and to make the "sincere, the honest, and the earnest, his enthusiastic supporters." [3] With Lane this "great principle" had now come to be abolitionism, despite the fact that when he first arrived in Kansas he stated "that he would rather see Kansas a slave State, in preference to seeing it an abolition State." [4] By his zealous, at times brilliant, advocacy of abolitionist policies, Lane clasped to himself large numbers of radical Kansans, who supported him no matter what his personal failings or the means he employed to gain his objectives. At the same time, however, he was careful not to offend the anti-Negro prejudices of the majority of his constituents. He decried any effort to achieve equality between the races and proposed deportation or colonization as the best means of solving the problem of the Negro.[5]

Robinson was the last man in Kansas to avoid a quarrel, especially if it were with the detested General Lane. He counter-attacked at once. In a public communication dated October 9, he expressed his utter scorn for Lane and his charges against Captain Prince and himself. He scoffed at Lane's claim of having saved Kansas from invasion and predicted that if Kansas ever were invaded it would be in retaliation for Lane's jayhawking in Missouri. The citizens of Leavenworth, he bluntly asserted, were endorsing thievery when they endorsed Lane, and he criticized the President for countenancing Lane and his activities. Lincoln,

---

[3] Richardson, *Beyond the Mississippi*, p. 45.

[4] Quoted in Malin, "Notes on General Histories," *KHQ*, XXI (Fall, 1954), 206.

[5] Leavenworth *Daily Conservative*, November 8, 17, 1861, July 3, 1863; *Congressional Globe*, 38th Cong., 1st Sess., pp. 672–675.

he had been told, believed nothing in regard to Kansas unless it came from Lane. Should this be true, then the "honest men" of Kansas "would gladly exchange some of the instruments and appointees of President Lincoln for those of ex-President Pierce or Buchanan." [6]

Pro-Lane papers, led by Wilder's Leavenworth *Conservative*, set up a howl over Robinson's letter. By warping its meaning and quoting sections of it out of context, they pilloried Robinson as a friend and abettor of treason, as a malignant politician who would rather see the state devastated than help Lane defend it, and as a man who had basely insulted and slandered the President. The *Conservative* professed the state to be dishonored by such a Governor and declared that the people were hanging their heads in shame. Even Sol Miller, normally no political friend of Lane, joined in the outcry against Robinson. Like many other Kansans, Miller accepted Lane's claim of having saved Kansas from Price at face value and so was angered by what he deemed the spiteful efforts of Robinson to hamper the operations of the Kansas Brigade.

Lane's Stockton Hall speech was only the verbal preliminary of a campaign to deprive Robinson of the governorship. Section one of the state constitution specified that the state officers "shall be chosen by the electors of the State at the time and place of voting for members of the legislature, and shall hold their offices for the term of two years from the second Monday in January next after election and until their successors are elected and qualified." Under this provision, if interpreted literally, the terms of Robinson, the other state officers, and the members of the Senate, who had all been elected in 1859, would expire at the beginning of 1862, notwithstanding the fact that they would

[6] *Kansas State Journal* (Lawrence), October 17, 1861. Lane had written a letter to Lincoln repeating his charges against Robinson and Prince. Robinson also wrote Lincoln, denying Lane's attacks and demanding that Lane's conduct as commander of the Kansas Brigade be investigated. Lincoln did not reply to either communication (*OR*, ser. I, III, 529–530; Robinson Scrapbooks, III, 157–158).

have actually served but one of the two years for which they had been elected. The 1861 legislature took note of this anomaly and passed an act setting November 4, 1862, as the time for the next regular election of all state officers and Senators, thus allowing the incumbents to serve out their full terms. Lane and his followers now discovered suddenly that this law was unconstitutional and that a new Governor, as well as other officials, should be elected in November, 1861. Accordingly the Republican State Central Committee, which was controlled by the Lane faction, met at Topeka and selected a ticket headed by George A. Crawford of Fort Scott for Governor. Crawford was a leading Democrat, and his nomination was designed to gain Democratic support for the movement to supplant Robinson.[7]

Crawford based his election campaign on elaborate presentations of the constitutional technicalities that supposedly warranted his candidacy and buttressed it by advocating a separate Department of Kansas and promotion for all officers of the Kansas regiments. His candidacy, however, aroused little enthusiasm outside the columns of the *Conservative,* the *Republican,* and other Lane mouthpieces. The prevailing view was that his election would be of dubious legality and debatable expediency. When the citizens went to the polls on November 5 to elect the members of the lower house of the next legislature, many of them did not bother to vote for Crawford, and in some precincts election officials refused to receive his ballots or to count and return them after they were cast.[8]

But since Crawford ran unopposed, he naturally was "elected." The State Election Board, however, refused to count his votes. He thereupon applied to the State Supreme Court for a writ of mandamus compelling the board to tally them and to certify

[7] Leavenworth *Daily Conservative,* October 15, 1861; *Kansas State Journal* (Lawrence), October 24, 1861; *White Cloud Kansas Chief,* October 24, 1861.

[8] Leavenworth *Daily Conservative,* October 22, November 5, 10, 1861; *Kansas State Journal* (Lawrence), October 31, 1861; *White Cloud Kansas Chief,* October 31, November 7, 1861.

his election as Governor.[9] This brought Chief Justice Thomas Ewing, Jr., into the picture. He and Robinson were no longer friends, having quarreled over business and patronage matters. Moreover, he had shifted to the Lane camp in the expectation that in return for breaking with Robinson he would obtain "the support of Genl. Lane and his friends" for the Senate. An election for that post was in prospect since Lane had promised to resign if he became a major general in command of the Department of Kansas. Robinson, consequently, feared a deal between Ewing and Lane resulting in a court decision favorable to Crawford's claim to the governorship.[10] But although ambitious, Ewing was not dishonest. He judged Crawford's suit strictly according to its merits, with the result that the Court denied both the writ of mandamus and the claim to the governorship. Its decision, which was written by Ewing, upheld the constitutionality of the legislative act setting November 4, 1862, as the date for electing the next Governor and other state officers and pointed out that if Crawford's reasoning in the case were accepted it would mean that the lower house of the 1861 legislature, also elected in 1859, had lacked legal existence and consequently all its acts had been illegal—including, Ewing might have added, the election of Lane to the Senate.[11]

Crawford and his backers were greatly disappointed by the Court's stand. "After the adjournment of the Court," wrote Sol Miller, "we saw one sorrowful looking individual have Judge Ewing by the buttonhole, out in the snow, for a long time trying to convince him that he had decided wrongly, and to reason him into reversing the decision." [12] But Lane, despite this setback, remained implacably resolved to force Robinson from

[9] *White Cloud Kansas Chief,* January 22, 1862.

[10] Ewing to Charles S. Stone, December 20, 1861, to H. Miles Moore, December 23, 1861, to Stone, December 31, 1861, Ewing Papers, KSHS; Robinson to S. N. Wood, October 19, 1861, Robinson Papers, KSHS.

[11] Decision of court, published in Leavenworth *Daily Conservative,* January 21, 1862.

[12] *White Cloud Kansas Chief,* January 22, 1862.

the dingy little rooms constituting the "executive offices" of Kansas. Blocked in one direction he would try another. This time it would be impeachment.

In the spring of 1861 the legislature voted two bond issues, one known as the "war bonds," the other as the "seven per cent bonds." The war bonds were for the purpose of obtaining money with which to equip and maintain the state troops until they were taken into Federal service. The executive department was authorized to sell $20,000 of them. The question at once arose, however, whether this $20,000 limit referred to their par value or actual value. Since on the market they could only fetch less than one-half of their par value, Governor Robinson and State Treasurer H. R. Dutton decided to issue $40,000 of the bonds, on the assumption that the object of the act authorizing their issuance was to raise $20,000 actual cash. Dutton then sold $31,000 of the bonds to Robert S. Stevens, who took them to Washington and resold them to the Interior Department for ninety-five cents of par value, realizing a tidy little profit of $14,300 for himself, which was considerably more than the state received out of the transaction. Stevens was a close friend of Robinson, and the two men were partners in the Lawrence Bank. Robinson, consequently, was chargeable on two counts in connection with the war bonds: of exceeding his authority in issuing $40,000 of them and of being personally interested in their sale.[13]

The 7 per cent bonds involved a much greater sum, and their history was much more complex. By an act of May 1, 1861, the legislature empowered Austin M. Clark and James C. Stone, Leavenworth businessmen, to negotiate the sale of $150,000 of these bonds, which had been voted for the purpose of defraying the current expenses of the state government. Clark and Stone

[13] *Proceedings in the Cases of the Impeachments of Charles Robinson, Governor, John W. Robinson, Secretary of State, George S. Hillyer, Auditor of State, of Kansas* (Lawrence, 1862), pp. 16, 18, 256. Hereafter this document will be cited as *Impeachment Proceedings*.

soon reported that they were unable to dispose of the bonds at an advantageous price. The legislature thereupon passed a supplementary act, by which Governor Robinson, Secretary of State John W. Robinson (no relation), and Auditor George S. Hillyer, or any two of them, were authorized to sell the bonds, provided that "no Bonds shall be sold for less than seventy cents on the dollar, and proceeds arising from the sale thereof shall be paid directly into the Treasury of the State." [14]

All efforts during the summer and fall to sell the 7 per cent bonds on these terms failed. Eastern bankers not unnaturally deemed Kansas a bad risk. Then Stevens once more came upon the bond scene. He informed Secretary Robinson and Auditor Hillyer that he could sell the 7 per cent bonds to the Interior Department also. These two officials thereupon delivered to Stevens $50,000 of the bonds at a price of forty cents on the dollar and another $37,000 at seventy cents. Since this transaction was of doubtful legality, Governor Robinson refused to approve it, although admitting that the state might do worse.

Now appeared another party interested in the bonds—Senator Pomeroy. He wrote Secretary Robinson that he could secure the sale of all the bonds and asked that they be brought to him in Washington. In response, both Secretary Robinson and Auditor Hillyer journeyed to Washington, taking with them all the bonds they could collect. Once there, however, Pomeroy spoke in pessimistic terms; then he advised that they secure the assistance of Stevens. Robinson and Hillyer accordingly sent for Stevens, who arrived in Washington on November 30. Two days later Stevens and Pomeroy, in a meeting at Pomeroy's home, persuaded Hillyer and Robinson to sign a contract giving Stevens "full powers and authority to negotiate, dispose of, and sell the entire issue" of the 7 per cent bonds. In addition to his own signature, Secretary Robinson affixed to the contract the name of Governor Robinson. The Governor had previously agreed to

[14] *Senate Journal, 1861*, pp. 237–238; *Laws of Kansas, 1861*, pp. 102–104; Leavenworth *Daily Conservative*, July 28, 1864.

approve "any arrangement for the sale of the bonds" that the auditor and secretary "might make *according to law*," but had not empowered them to use his name. Hence Secretary Robinson exceeded his authority.

Stevens proceeded to offer Secretary of the Interior Caleb B. Smith the bonds at the price of eighty-five cents on the dollar, to be purchased with Indian trust funds held by the Interior Department. Smith tentatively accepted the proposition and on December 14 requested the President to approve it. Lincoln replied that he would, provided the Kansas congressional delegation acquiesced. This brought in Lane, who by this time had returned to Washington. Lane was highly suspicious of Stevens' connection with the transaction. Not only was Stevens the friend and partner of Governor Robinson; he was also a prospective candidate for the Senate seat that Lane was proposing to relinquish upon becoming a major general. Lane feared that Stevens would obtain a large sum of money from the sale of the bonds and then use it to buy enough members of the legislature to be elected Senator. Consequently, although Pomeroy and Conway signed a letter to the President expressing their approval of the Stevens-Smith agreement, Lane refused to attach his signature. Without it, the deal could not go through.

What happened next is uncertain. All that is known positively is that a signature purporting to be that of Lane appeared on the letter to Lincoln previously endorsed by Pomeroy and Conway. Lane later claimed that either it was forged or he had signed by mistake. A more likely explanation was provided by Stevens and Thomas Corwin of Ohio, who acted as Stevens' go-between with the Secretary of the Interior (who was Corwin's brother-in-law). They testified that Stevens procured Lane's signature through George A. Reynolds, Lane's private secretary, by paying Reynolds $1,000. According to Corwin, Stevens told him that Reynolds was "a toady of Lane" and that to give the money to him "was equivalent to paying it to Lane." Both Lane and Reynolds denied being bribed, but their explanations of why

Lane's signature appeared on the letter to Lincoln were weak and contradictory.

No matter how obtained, Lane's signature secured Lincoln's final approval, and on December 19 Stevens, acting as the agent of Kansas, concluded an agreement with Smith for the sale of $150,000 of the 7 per cent bonds to the Interior Department for eighty-five cents on the dollar. This did not mean, however, that Kansas received eighty-five cents on the dollar for the bonds. A day or two prior to the contract with Smith, Stevens made another agreement with Secretary Robinson and Auditor Hillyer under which he was to have whatever he could realize for the bonds above sixty cents on the dollar. Thus, as things turned out, and Stevens no doubt knew all along how they were going to turn out, Kansas received only sixty cents of the eighty-five cents paid by the Interior Department for the bonds, leaving Stevens to pocket the twenty-five-cent difference as the reward for his services. Hillyer and Robinson were reluctant to enter into this arrangement with Stevens and did so only after he threatened to drop the entire business and Pomeroy advised them that the bonds could be sold only to the Interior Department and only through Stevens and that if they did not sell them now they never would. Pomeroy's assertions were especially persuasive, for both officials already felt that the Interior Department was their last chance to dispose of the bonds and obtain money for the state. Apparently neither of them were aware that the Interior Department was willing to pay eighty-five cents.[15]

Stevens was not the sole person to profit from the bonds at the expense of the state. Corwin found compensation for his endeavors, and Pomeroy secured "a commission which amounted to several thousand dollars" for exercising "his influence" on Secretary Smith. The other principals, Hillyer and John Robinson, obtained special consideration also, getting seventy cents

[15] *Impeachment Proceedings*, pp. 16–18, 20–24, 28–30, 45, 150–159, 173–179, 189–190, 200–202, 256–261, 267, 377–386. See also Caleb Smith to Ewing, February 27, 1862, Ewing Papers, Library of Congress.

on the dollar for some state bonds held personally by them.[16] Perhaps this was an added reason for their anxiety to negotiate the bonds, although there is no evidence to indicate deliberate complicity on their part with Stevens, Corwin, and Pomeroy. Instead, they were in all likelihood the dupes of these last-named individuals. As for Governor Robinson, there is nothing whatsoever to show that he had any financial share in the deal. But he was nevertheless vulnerable, along with Hillyer and Secretary Robinson, to the accusation that he had violated the law regulating the disposal of the bonds. His signature appeared on the contract empowering Stevens to act as the agent of the state, and he gave his tacit approval to the second agreement with Stevens by not protesting against it when it became known to him. Furthermore, as mentioned already, it could be held that he had exceeded his authority in issuing more than $20,000 of the war bonds.

Lane's role in the whole affair was, to say the least, questionable, but that did not prevent him from using the "Bond Scandal" to strike at Robinson. Late in January he returned to Kansas and immediately set to work in Topeka, where the legislature was in session, "intriguing, wire-working and corrupting." On January 30 the House of Representatives passed a resolution to investigate the actions of the state executive in disposing of the bonds, and Speaker M. S. Adams, a Lane man, appointed a committee consisting entirely of Lane supporters to conduct the investigation. The committee heard the testimony of Governor Robinson, Hillyer, Secretary Robinson, Lane, Stevens, and others who had a hand in negotiating the bonds. It spent much of its time, though, "in secret conclave with a certain U.S. Senator." On February 12 the committee reported a resolution impeaching

---

[16] *Impeachment Proceedings*, pp. 11–13, 16, 19–20, 159, 166–167, 202, 260–261, 264, 384–386; Theodore to Thaddeus Hyatt, March 7, 1862, Theodore Hyatt Letter Book, Hyatt Papers. The bonds held by Secretary Robinson and Hillyer had been received by them in lieu of salary, the state government having no cash on hand to pay its officials.

Governor Robinson, Secretary Robinson, and Auditor Hillyer
for "high misdemeanors in office." The House adopted the resolution 65 to 0 and then appointed an impeachment committee
which on February 26 reported articles of impeachment against
the three officials. These the House promptly adopted by unanimous vote, except in the case of Governor Robinson. Seven
members, including Sol Miller, refused to concur in the charges
against the Governor, although, as one of them later recalled,
it "required greater courage to vote 'no' . . . than it did to face
an army in battle array." [17]

Owing to delay in obtaining evidence from outside the state,
the Court of Impeachment, which was constituted by the State
Senate, did not convene until June 2. It first tried the cases of
Secretary Robinson and Auditor Hillyer. The prosecution indicted both men on eight identical counts, but in the end the
court, by a 17 to 4 vote, declared them guilty of only one charge,
consenting to the state's being defrauded of the money due it
from the 7 per cent bonds and betraying their trust as state
officers. The court then, by a vote of 18 to 3, removed them
from office, but by a 20 to 1 vote refused to disqualify them
from holding office in the future. This last vote is a strong in-
dication that the court did not believe Hillyer and Robinson
morally culpable, a belief that is sustained by the evidence, which
merely points to a lack of intelligence, not of honesty, on the
part of these men.

The trial of Governor Robinson proved anticlimactic. It began on the afternoon of June 16 and closed on the evening of the
same day. The proceedings were listless, almost as if everyone
concerned had lost all interest. George W. Collamore testified
that Robinson had disregarded an offer by him to procure the
sale of the war bonds at par, but the evidence he presented to
support this allegation was vague. The prosecution endeavored

[17] Leavenworth *Daily Conservative*, January 28, 1862; *White Cloud
Kansas Chief*, February 20, 27, July 17, 1862; *House Journal, 1862*, pp.
119, 245–248, 367.

to link Robinson to the sale of the seven per centers, but failed to provide any tangible proof. Robinson's attorney, former territorial Governor Wilson Shannon, declared that the prosecution merely demonstrated "that the governor was not engaged in the transaction." In the end the court acquitted Robinson by an 18 to 2 vote on the charge of exceeding his authority in issuing the war bonds and by 20 to 0 on all the counts relating to the 7 per cent bonds.

Lane's drive to depose Robinson from office was thus again blocked. Nevertheless the impeachment trial marked the final and nearly total victory of Lane in his long and bitter rivalry with Robinson. Although resoundingly acquitted by the court, Robinson was not fully exonerated in the eyes of the public, and his reputation never wholly recovered from the besmirching it received as a result of the "Bond Swindle." Following his retirement from the governorship in January, 1863, he ceased to be a major political figure. He continued to exercise influence, but not power, and during the immediately succeeding years was more of a liability than an asset to any political movement of which he was a member. Henceforth, as "Web" Wilder afterwards expressed it, "in politics Lane was the King." [18]

Lane's campaign to have Kansas constituted a separate military department with himself in command achieved only half success. On November 13, 1861, Washington announced that a Department of Kansas had been established, to include the Indian Territory, Colorado, and Nebraska, but, instead of Lane, its commander was to be Major General David H. Hunter. Lincoln had been advised by Governor Hamilton R. Gamble of Missouri that if Lane headed the new department public opinion in his state would be adversely affected. Lincoln thought that in naming Hunter he would soothe Lane's disappointment at not getting the post, for Hunter and Lane had been associated in con-

[18] *Impeachment Proceedings*, pp. 57–62, 64, 84, 107–112, 344–349, 392, 411; Leavenworth *Daily Conservative*, June 12, 1862; Wilder, *Annals*, pp. 378, 438.

nection with the Frontier Guards, and the two were commonly regarded as personal friends. Indeed, Lane's Leavenworth mouthpiece, the *Conservative*, hailed Hunter's appointment as being the next best thing to Lane himself and declared that if Lane had been asked to name the department head his selection would have been Hunter.[19]

Actually, however, the appointment of Hunter was not at all to Lane's liking. From the very beginning of the war Lane had contemplated a grand "Southern Expedition" through the Indian Territory into Texas, the main feature of which would be the liberation and arming of Negro slaves. With his keen political intuition, he had early sensed that the first man to enlist and use colored soldiers would become the hero of the radicals and abolitionists, whose support might well carry him to the White House. Lane hoped to be that man and therefore wanted to lead this "great jayhawking expedition" in person. Hunter's appointment, consequently, was regarded by Lane as presenting an obstacle to this ambition.

Late in November, soon after Hunter took command in Kansas, Lane journeyed to Washington. There he succeeded in selling the idea of a Texas expedition to Lincoln, Secretary of War Stanton, and General George B. McClellan, who at that time was the commander of all Union armies. Lane told them that Hunter enthusiastically approved of the expedition and had no objection to his leading it. Both these assertions, however, were false. Lane had not consulted Hunter on the matter, and Hunter, far from favoring offensive operations, was worried about defending Kansas and the rest of his "immense wilderness of a department" with the scant forces available to him. The first inkling that Hunter received of Lane's plan was a communication from the Adjutant General, Lorenzo Thomas, stating that McClellan thought that "an expedition might be made to advantage from your department west of Arkansas against Northwestern Texas."

[19] Leavenworth *Daily Conservative*, November 13, 1861; Gamble to O. C. Cates, November 21, 1861, *OR*, ser. I, XVII, pt. 2, 92.

The astonished Hunter at once protested that he would be fortunate to prevent Kansas from being overrun by the Confederates, much less mount an invasion of Texas. McClellan telegraphed back that he was surprised by Hunter's attitude, which he ascribed to "momentary irritation," and said that he was sending to Kansas several regiments of reinforcements which would be only the "commencement" of the troops to be supplied for the expedition. This information calmed Hunter down somewhat, but he remained doubtful concerning the practicality of the expedition. On December 19 he warned McClellan that he needed at least 20,000 men in addition to those already in or on their way to Kansas, besides a large wagon train to enable this host to cross the 440 miles of "entirely destitute" country lying between Kansas and Texas.

Although the newspapers reported that Lane was to be a major general and to command all Kansas troops, Hunter had no firsthand information concerning the Kansas Senator's connection with the Texas campaign until January 3. On that date he received a telegram from Lane himself, which stated: "It is the intention of the Government to order me to report to you for an active winter's campaign." Three weeks later this rather cryptic message was confirmed and amplified by a communication from the War Department which conveyed the news that seven cavalry regiments, three batteries of artillery, and four regiments of infantry were on their way to Kansas "to operate under General Lane," who in addition would "raise about 8,000 to 10,000 Kansas troops and organize 4,000 Indians." The dispatch further stated that McClellan "desires it to be understood that a command independent of you is not given to General Lane, but he is to operate to all proper extent under your supervision and control, and if you deem proper you may yourself command the expedition undertaken." [20]

Hunter did not waste any time in deciding that it would indeed be "proper" for him to take command of the Southern

[20] *OR*, ser. I, VIII, 379, 428–429, 450–451, 482, 525, 829–831.

Expedition. Accordingly, when Lane arrived in Leavenworth from Washington on January 28, he found the following proclamation published in the local press:

#1. In the expedition about to go south from this department, called in the newspapers General Lane's Expedition, it is the intention of the major-general commanding the department to command in person, unless otherwise expressly ordered by the Government.

#2. Transportation not having been supplied, we must go without it. All tents, trunks, chests, chairs, camp-tables, camp-stools, &c., must be at once stored or abandoned. The general-commanding takes in his valise one shirt, one pair drawers, one pair socks, and one handkerchief, and no officer or soldier will carry more. The surplus room in the knapsack must be reserved for ammunition and provisions. Every officer and soldier will carry his own clothing and bedding.[21]

The proclamation not only barred the door to Lane's military ambitions, but burlesqued the entire Southern Expedition and by intimation made Lane out to be a fool. The "Great Jayhawker" was infuriated. He at once launched desperate efforts to retrieve the situation by pressuring Lincoln to counterorder Hunter's assumption of command. Lincoln, who had been under the impression that Lane would be satisfied to serve under Hunter, instead wrote a letter to both men stating that unless they could reach "an amicable understanding" Lane would have to "report to General Hunter for duty . . . or decline the service." Lane thereupon abandoned his plans and informed the legislature that it was his "sad yet simple duty . . . to announce to you, and through you the people of Kansas, my purpose to return to my seat in the United States Senate." On his way back to Washington he was reported by Sol Miller to have been "very bitter in his denunciations of Lincoln, pronouncing him a 'd—d liar, a demagogue, and a scoundrel' " and declaring that the President had broken his promises to make him a major general,

---

[21] Leavenworth *Daily Conservative*, January 28, 1862.

"leaving him (Lane) before the public in the light of a braggart, a fool and a humbug." [22]

The following month, March, Kansas became part of the Department of the Mississippi under the command of General Halleck, with headquarters at St. Louis. Hunter, who was senior to Halleck, was relieved of the, to him, distasteful post at Fort Leavenworth and transferred to the East. As Hunter's replacement in the new District of Kansas, Halleck named Brigadier General James W. Denver. Halleck believed that since Kansas was not in an active theater of war the qualifications required of the head of that district were administrative rather than military. Since Denver was thoroughly familiar with Kansas from past experience as its territorial Governor, Halleck felt that "a better selection could not have been made." He also believed that Denver would preserve peace on the Kansas-Missouri border, thus enabling the Kansas troops to get into the field "where they might be of some use." [23]

But from the very special standpoint of Senator James H. Lane, Halleck could hardly have named a worse person to head the District of Kansas, unless it were Charles Robinson himself. In the first place, Lane had a passionate personal antipathy for Denver. In the second place, with Denver in charge at Fort Leavenworth, all of Lane's hopes of controlling military matters in Kansas would be completely blasted. Therefore, as soon as he learned of Denver's appointment, Lane, seconded by Pomeroy, hastened to Lincoln in protest. Lincoln listened sympathetically and on March 21 telegraphed Halleck to suspend his order putting Denver in command.

Halleck reluctantly complied with the presidential directive. On March 30 he replaced Denver with Brigadier General Sam-

---

[22] *OR*, ser. I, VIII, 530, 534, 538, 551, 576, 831; Caleb Smith to Ewing, February 27, 1862, Ewing Papers, Library of Congress; Leavenworth *Daily Conservative*, February 28, 1862; *White Cloud Kansas Chief*, July 3, 1862.

[23] Halleck to Stanton, March 28, 1862, *OR*, ser. I, VIII, 647–648.

uel D. Sturgis. This was another unwise choice. Sturgis was highly unpopular with Kansans because he had once ordered some Kansas volunteers flogged for plundering.[24] Moreover, he was a stern and conscientious regular army officer, and Lane and his crowd knew that he would not countenance any irregular activity. Lane's preference for commander in Kansas was Brigadier General Thomas A. Davies, a relative of his. Secretary of War Stanton, however, threatened to resign if Davies were appointed. But on the same day, April 10, that Sturgis assumed command at Fort Leavenworth, Halleck left St. Louis to take charge of the Tennessee campaign. This necessitated another revamping of the Union military establishment in the West, with the result that on May 2 the War Department restored Kansas as a separate department, relieved Sturgis, and placed in his stead Brigadier General James G. Blunt.[25]

The selection of Blunt came as a perplexing shock to most Kansans. He was not at all well known, and there was little in his background or record which seemed to justify either his rank or his post. Thirty-five years old and commonly referred to as "the fat boy," he was a resident of Greeley, Kansas, and by profession a doctor. The only thing approaching military experience in his prewar career had been a few years spent as a sailor while a youth in Maine and membership on the militia committee of the Wyandotte Constitutional Convention of 1859, to which he had been a delegate. When the war began he enlisted as a private, but soon became lieutenant colonel of Montgomery's regiment and then the commander of the cavalry contingent of Lane's Brigade. His main military achievement was the tracking down and killing of a small band of Missourians and Indians which had raided Humboldt in September.[26] Politically, he was

[24] *Ibid.*, pp. 832–833; *ibid.*, LIII, 517, 519, 647; *Lawrence Republican*, July 18, 1861.
[25] Robinson, *Kansas Conflict*, p. 446; *OR*, ser. I, VIII, 368–370, 661, 832–833.
[26] Leavenworth *Daily Conservative*, April 12, 1862; Emporia *News*,

a rabid abolitionist with close connections among the leading radicals of southern Kansas. In personal character he was resolute and self-confident, but coarse and unscrupulous. During his later campaigns in Arkansas and the Indian Territory he took "female servants" along with him in the field and drank so much and was so "very licentious" that he gained "a worse reputation than even Lane himself."[27] Mentally and emotionally he probably already was tainted with the disease that led to his confinement in an insane asylum in 1879.

Blunt owed his quick rise to Lane—no one had any illusions on that score. Lane, through his influence with Lincoln and by exerting pressure elsewhere in Washington, obtained for him a brigadier's commission and the command of the Department of Kansas although there were several other Kansas soldiers much more deserving of these coveted honors.[28] Most importantly, by making Blunt commander in Kansas, Lane finally solved the dilemma which had plagued him from the beginning of the war —how to be a Senator and a general simultaneously. Since he could not be both in person, from now on he would be both in essence. Henceforth, where military matters were concerned, Blunt was to all intents and purposes merely Lane in a different body and under a different name. Thus by the spring of 1862 Lane achieved the two goals he had set for himself in the fall of 1861: the defeat of Robinson and the military control of Kansas.

By accomplishing the latter, Lane placed himself in a position not only to exercise increased influence on military patronage in the state, but also to profit from the immense and lucrative

April 19, 1862; *Kansas State Journal* (Lawrence), April 17, 1862; Charles Robinson to Mrs. Robinson, April 14, 1862, Robinson Papers, KSHS; Andreas, *History of Kansas*, p. 302.

27 Blunt to Major H. Z. Curtis, August 10, 1863, Thomas Moonlight Papers, KSHS; James Hanway to Parents, December 9, 1863; James and John Hanway Papers, KSHS.

28 *Lawrence Republican*, April 17, 1862; *Kansas State Journal* (Lawrence), April 17, 1862.

supply and freighting business that had come into being with
the stationing of large numbers of troops in Kansas and adjoining
regions. Most of this business centered at Fort Leavenworth.
From there, for example, during the year ending June 30, 1863,
over 8,000,000 pounds of stores were transported to Forts Scott
and Gibson alone, and another 12,505,844 pounds went to other
posts, such as Fort Laramie and Fort Larned. Although most of
these supplies, of necessity, came from the East, a considerable
portion, particularly grain, fodder, and livestock, was purchased
by the Government from Kansas farmers. In addition, Kansas
provided most of the wagons, teams, and teamsters which hauled
the supplies to the various forts and armies. Indeed, so numerous
were the Kansans engaged in selling and freighting military
stores and provisions that it might be said that in Kansas during
the Civil War the country lived off the army.[29]

Naturally, certain enterprising individuals made large sums of
money from army supply contracts, and many others hoped and
endeavored to do the same. These contracts were let out by officers in the quartermaster and commissary bureaus under the
supervision of the commanding generals. A person who had con-
tacts or understandings with these officers or who could dictate
their acts was able to make great sums of money. This is exactly
what Lane and the "legion of army contractors who follow in
his wake" did following Blunt's assumption of command. Most
of these "army contractors" were Leavenworth merchants,
freighters, and speculators. They cut Lane in on their profits in
return for his using his influence with Blunt and other army
officers to obtain contracts for them. Blunt also shared in this
graft, as did many of the quartermaster and commissary officers
who were appointed by Lane via Blunt or who were amenable
to Lane's bribes and other inducements. Lane, moreover, received the political backing of the Leavenworth "ring" of con-

tractors and army officers whose corrupt incomes depended on his continuance in power. Like "Web" Wilder of the *Conservative*, they felt that it paid to "stick" to the "Grim Chieftain." [30]

Having once gained control of military affairs in Kansas, with all the political and pecuniary rewards stemming therefrom, Lane was resolved—desperately so—to retain it. Supporting him in this determination were most of the army contractors and officers of the state, a formidable combination. The history of the next three years cannot be understood unless these two closely allied facts are kept always in mind.

[30] Hunter to Halleck, February 8, 1862, *OR*, ser. I, VIII, 831. The above discussion of the Lane-headed corruption in the supply service of the Union army in the Trans-Mississippi is based upon the following sources: Francis E. Adams to Lane, October 4, 1864, and M. H. Insley to Lane, December 3, 1864, James H. Lane Collection, University of Kansas; James Hanway to His Parents, December 9, 1863, Hanway Papers; Lieutenant Colonel W. T. Campbell to Major General John M. Schofield, November 24, 1863, *OR*, ser. I, XXII, pt. 2, 714; Report of Major General Francis J. Herron on conditions at Fort Smith, Ark., November 11, 1864, quoted in Boston *Commonwealth*, June 23, 1866, Robinson Scrapbooks, II, 1–2; *White Cloud Kansas Chief*, September 8, October 13, 1864; *Kansas State Journal* (Lawrence), August 4, 1864; Oskaloosa *Independent*, November 20, 1864; *Olathe Mirror*, February 13, 20, 1864. Other evidence, indirect, general, and circumstantial, could also be adduced. The reference to Wilder is from the *White Cloud Kansas Chief*, September 1, 1864.

# V

# *King Lane and General Blunt*

ONCE more the indefatigable Senator Lane was back in Kansas. He came this time not as a general, but as "commissioner for recruiting in the Department of Kansas." He opened up an "office of recruiting" in Leavenworth on August 4 and that night held a "Great War Meeting" in front of the Planters' House. The theme of his speech was that the state was in imminent danger of Confederate invasion, that it could not expect help from the Federal Government, and that it thus would have to rely upon its own men and resources for defense. General Blunt followed Lane to the platform and asserted that the state would soon be overrun by forty or fifty thousand Confederates from Arkansas and Texas if its male inhabitants did not hasten to enlist in the regiments being recruited by Commissioner Lane. Marcus Parrott injected a disharmonious note, however. He scoffed at the idea of the state being in danger and commented on how remarkable it was that a certain "illustrious military personage" always "arrived here at the very moment of peril." But before he could say more he was shouted down with cries of "Traitor!" and "Secesh!" from Lane's friends—most of whom had appointments or promises of appointments as officers in the regiments Lane proposed to raise.[1]

During the ensuing weeks the final battle between Robinson and Lane over the control of military patronage took place. This time, however, more was involved than merely the personal rivalry of the Senator and the Governor. At issue were the respective powers and spheres of the Federal and state governments. Lane's recruiting authority came from the War Department, and his "powers in the premises were full." Moreover, he instructed his agents that "all officers will be commissioned under the direction of the Secretary of War" and that "no application to the Governor of the State, for commissions in the new regiments, will be tolerated." Lane's authority and these instructions were diametrically counter to Robinson's right, under the various enactments of Congress and the regulations of the army, to appoint and commission the officers of regiments raised in Kansas. Hence Kansas was the exception to Professor Fred A. Shannon's generalization that "from the beginning of the war to its close recruiting in the north was in the hands of the governors of the states." [2]

Robinson promptly let it be known that he would disregard Lane's appointees and not issue commissions to them. Lane, thereupon, apprised Secretary of War Stanton of Robinson's intentions and received in reply a letter stating that the War Department would request Robinson to commission the officers named by Lane and that upon his refusal the President would issue the commissions.[3] Meanwhile, Robinson sent a friend, Major T. C. Eldridge, to see Stanton and inform him concerning "the true condition of affairs in this department." Eldridge carried

---

[1] Leavenworth *Daily Conservative*, August 5, 1862; Leavenworth *Daily Times*, August 5, 1862.

[2] *OR*, ser. III, I, 483–484, 489, 495–496, 818, 898; *ibid.*, II, 959; *White Cloud Kansas Chief*, July 28, 1864; Fred Albert Shannon, *The Organization and Administration of the Union Army, 1861–1865* (Cleveland, 1928), II, 160.

[3] *OR*, ser. III, II, 494.

with him a letter from Robinson to Stanton in which Robinson asked what was the precise nature of Lane's recruiting powers and what was "desired of the State Executive, if anything." On August 25 Eldridge wrote from Washington that "the Lord (of the Department) is not on our side" and that Lane had full authority to recruit. This was confirmed by a letter from Stanton of the same date, in which was enclosed a copy of Lane's commission.[4]

Deeply angered, Robinson replied to Stanton in a simmering eight-page letter.[5] He told of Lane's opposition to the executive of Kansas and his efforts to destroy it and then listed various misdeeds committed by Blunt since his assumption of command. These, he wrote, were but "a few of the transactions in this department" and provided "only a faint idea of the despotism and terrorism attempted and practiced here." Referring to a statement by Stanton to the effect that the War Department wished to see harmony restored in Kansas, he asked:

What would you have me do? Shall I quietly submit to see this State insulted in every manner possible and favor the parties giving the insult? Shall I say to the people who elected Genl. Lane U.S. Senator and myself Governor that Genl. Lane is both Senator and Governor by consent? I readily concede that you have the power to subvert for the time being the State Government of Kansas, but you have not the power to get my approval of the act.

Robinson was as good as his word. When, on October 4, he received a formal request from Lane, backed by Stanton's letter, to commission the officers of the regiments raised by Lane, he unqualifiedly rejected it. "The letter of the Secretary of War," he answered, "can only be regarded in the light of dictation, and a threat to the prerogatives of the State, in case his dictation is dis-

---

[4] Robinson to Stanton, August 20, 1862, Eldridge to Robinson, August 28, 1862, William E. Connelley Collection, Public Library, Kansas City, Kansas; *OR*, ser. III, II, 479.
[5] Robinson to Stanton, sometime shortly after August 26, 1862, William E. Connelley Collection, Public Library, Kansas City, Kansas.

regarded." He then referred the whole matter to Major General Samuel R. Curtis, commander of the Department of Missouri (of which Kansas was again a part by this time). Curtis, however, was friendly to the radical faction and therefore sustained Lane. In the end, with a few exceptions, the officers appointed by Lane were commissioned from Washington.[6]

Lane's recruiting activities resulted in the raising of four regiments. The first three of these were designated the Eleventh, Twelfth, and Thirteenth Kansas Volunteers. The colonel of the Eleventh was Thomas Ewing, Jr., who on September 13 resigned as Chief Justice. Ewing proved an excellent commander, and the Eleventh was one of the better Kansas regiments. The colonel of the Twelfth was Charles W. Adams, whose main qualification for the post was in being Lane's son-in-law. The Thirteenth was enlisted principally by Cyrus Leland, Sr., a Lane politico, but Thomas M. Bowen became its colonel, as Leland preferred the less distinguished but more lucrative position of quartermaster.

"There was," commented Sol Miller, "a good deal of humbug resorted to" in raising these regiments. By the summer of 1862 all the "footloose men" were already in the army, and those who remained were "men of families, farmers and mechanics, all poor and mostly just fairly getting a firm foothold in the state of their adoption"—either that or too profitably engaged in selling and hauling supplies to the army to have much desire to serve in it. Moreover, the military enthusiasm of the spring and summer of 1861 had long since subsided, and war weariness was beginning to set in. Defeats in the East had caused "great gloom and despondency," and Kansans felt that their state already had provided more than its just share of troops and that all the Government should rightly ask of them was to help defend their own

[6] Governor's Correspondence (Charles Robinson), 1861–1863, Military Affairs, November, 1861–1862, State Archives, KSHS; *Kansas State Journal* (Lawrence), October 9, 1862; *Congressional Globe*, 38th Cong., 1st Sess., pp. 872–873.

soil. Because of this attitude and because there was much opposition to his recruiting endeavors, Lane resorted to some rather dubious and highhanded devices to obtain men for his regiments. Not only did he create an unfounded apprehension that Kansas was in danger of invasion; he also falsely told prospective recruits that they would serve only nine months and not leave the state, and threatened to have "any person found discouraging and preventing enlistments" court-martialed and imprisoned.[7]

His most effective expedient was to warn Kansans that they would be drafted unless they enlisted. The foundation for this threat was a War Department order of August 4 stipulating that should a state fail to fulfill its quota under the President's July 2 call for 300,000 three-year volunteers the deficiency would be supplied by a "draft" under the provisions of the national Militia Act. Although Kansas was in no danger of a draft unless it failed to meet its quota of 1,771 men, Lane gave the impression that a draft was already in effect and that the only way to escape such a "disgrace" was to join one of the new regiments. Had it not been for this device and the other pressures and inducements used by Lane, it is doubtful whether Kansas would have, as was the case, exceeded its quota under the July 2 call by 1,165 men or that Lane would have filled his regiments as rapidly as he did.[8]

The fourth regiment recruited by Lane consisted of Negroes. From the very start of the war one of the pet projects of the abolitionists was the employment of Negroes as soldiers. Nothing, they claimed, would strike a deadlier blow at slavery or do more to subdue the South than the spectacle of black men in blue uniforms. By the summer of 1862 this view had achieved ascendancy in Congress, which on July 17 passed an act author-

[7] "Kansas Regiments," *Report of the Adjutant General*, pp. 198–199, 220, 223; *White Cloud Kansas Chief*, March 12, 1863; *Kansas State Journal* (Lawrence), September 4, 1862.

[8] Leavenworth *Daily Conservative*, August 13, 1862; *White Cloud Kansas Chief*, September 25, 1862.

izing the President "to employ as many persons of African descent as he may deem necessary and proper for the suppression of this rebellion."

Lane moved quickly to take advantage of the act. According to two of his henchmen, John Speer and H. D. Fisher, he obtained a verbal promise from Lincoln that he would have the tacit and informal sanction of the Government in recruiting Negro troops in Kansas.[9] All the available evidence tends to confirm Speer and Fisher. Again and again the War Department informed Lane that Negro regiments could not be raised except by "the express and special authority of the President" and that the colored regiments that he was recruiting "cannot be accepted into the service." Yet Lane went blithely ahead recruiting them, made no attempt to conceal the fact, and telegraphed the War Department such messages as the following: "Recruiting opens up beautifully. Good for four regiments of whites and two of blacks." [10]

Sentiment in Kansas toward enlisting Negroes as soldiers generally was hostile. Lane himself admitted as much when he subsequently told the Senate that it required four months of propaganda to prepare the "anti-slavery" people of his state.for the great innovation of armed Negroes and that the prejudice against the colored troops was so intense that they had to be kept out of sight and drilled in seclusion. The Fort Scott *Bulletin*, when it learned of Lane's plan to recruit Negroes, advised him to keep them away from the "Kansas troops in the field," for "with one exception, there is not a Kansas regiment from which they would not have as much to fear as from the rebels." The main argument used in favor of Negro troops was along utili-

[9] Speer, *Life of Lane*, pp. 261–262; Leavenworth *Daily Conservative*, July 10, 1863. See also "Journal of Abelard Guthrie," in W. E. Connelley, ed., *The Provisional Government of Nebraska Territory* (Lincoln, Neb., 1899), p. 151.

[10] *OR*, ser. III, II, 294, 311–312, 417, 431, 445; Leavenworth *Daily Conservative*, September 4, 1862.

tarian, not altruistic, lines. Thus the Emporia *News* maintained that if the South insisted on using Negroes "to shoot down our brave boys, ought we not to retaliate by using them to subdue the enemies of the Government?" And the Leavenworth *Conservative* asserted that Negro soldiers were needed to help defend the state's long frontiers against guerrillas and Indians. Lane's argument in favor of Negro troops was equally unidealistic. The Negro, he said, might "just as well become food for powder" as the white man. If, as George Collamore of Lawrence wrote to an Eastern friend, the willingness of Kansans to have Negroes serve in the army had "wonderfully increased" by the summer of 1862, it was mainly for reasons identical to those above and not out of any Garrisonian zeal to "elevate" the colored man by putting a musket in his hands.[11]

Indications are that the Negroes themselves were not particularly anxious to become soldiers. In his recruiting speech at Leavenworth on August 4 Lane felt called on to declare that "the negroes are mistaken if they think white men can fight for them while they stay at home. We have opened the pathway. We don't want to threaten, but we have been saying that you would fight, and if you won't fight we will make you." [12] The reluctance of the Negroes, who were mostly refugees from Missouri, to enlist stemmed mainly from a fear that they would be badly treated by the white troops and by the Government and from concern over the welfare of their families. Furthermore, the terms offered by Lane to Negro recruits—ten dollars a month and a "certificate of Freedom"—were deemed "unjust and unfair" by Negro leaders, who pointed out that the white soldier received more pay and who argued that the certificate was of no value since Negroes in Kansas were free anyway. Additional obstacles to Negro re-

---

[11] *Congressional Globe*, 38th Cong., 1st Sess., pp. 163, 873; Fort Scott *Bulletin*, July 26, 1862; Emporia *News*, December 21, 1861; Leavenworth *Daily Conservative*, January 21, July 17, 19, 1862; Collamore to Stearns, July 21, 1862, Stearns Papers.

[12] Leavenworth *Daily Conservative*, August 6, 1862.

cruitment came from the unexpected quarter of those two arch-abolitionists, Jennison and Hoyt, who resented Lane's being in charge of it. Lane conciliated them for awhile by appointing Jennison a recruiting commissioner for Negroes, but aroused their opposition again when he refused to make Jennison colonel of the Negro regiment. Calling Lane a "great humbug," Jennison and Hoyt tried to break up the encampment of the Negro recruits near Wyandotte, with the result that 200 of them deserted. Their white officers followed and arrested them and also forced Negroes who had not yet enlisted to join up.[13]

Lane's agents resorted to kidnaping as another means of filling the ranks of the Negro regiment. On August 22 a gang of fifteen men under "Lieutenant Swain," alias "Jeff Davis," a notorious jayhawker, crossed over from Wyandotte to Kansas City to "make converts" among the colored population there. They collected twenty-five Negroes and forty horses, but before they could recross the river they were intercepted by a force of Missouri State Militia, which captured eight of the band, wounded one, and recovered the Negroes and horses. Missourians living in the Kansas City region were greatly alarmed by the affair and petitioned Lincoln to disband the Negro troops and to punish Lane and Jennison for raising them. Otherwise, there would be the "most serious difficulties" between Kansas and Missouri.[14]

On October 28 a detachment of Lane's Negro soldiers fought the first action of the Civil War involving colored troops when it beat off a force of Confederate irregulars at Butler, Missouri, where it had gone to raise additional recruits. About a month later five companies of Negroes re-entered Missouri and near Island Mound had another battle with Confederates, after which they captured "a large amount of stock" and marched on to Fort Scott. Here, early in 1863, the Negro regiment was mustered

---

[13] *Ibid.*, July 8, August 6, 27, November 9, 15, 20, 1862; Hoyt to Robinson, August 12, 1862, Jennison to Robinson, August 22, 1862, Montgomery to Robinson, August 3, 1862, Robinson Papers, KSHS.

[14] *OR*, ser. I, XIII, 618–619; Andreas, *History of Kansas*, p. 1232.

into Federal service under the designation of the First Kansas Colored Volunteers. It was the fourth colored regiment to enter the Union army, three Negro regiments having been enrolled by Ben Butler at New Orleans in the fall of 1862. Kansas, however, could rightly claim to be the first Northern state to enlist Negroes. Personal honors in this regard must go to Hunter, who while in command in South Carolina anticipated his old friend by about four months. Jennison, it might be added, was reported by a Missourian to have had an entire company of Negro soldiers, under a Negro officer, during his raid through Jackson County in November, 1861.[15]

Lane manifested his political power during the 1862 electoral campaign by, in effect, selecting both the next Governor and the new representative to Congress. His choice for Governor was Thomas Carney, a Leavenworth merchant. Politically, Carney was a little-known newcomer. Personally, he was a thirty-five-year-old Ohioan, of slight formal education, but of much enterprise and ambition. His chief distinction was in being the richest man in Kansas. Lane's candidate for Congress was another citizen of Leavenworth, A. Carter Wilder, brother of "Web," chairman of the Republican State Central Committee, former commissary of the Lane Brigade, and a rabid abolitionist. Carney and Wilder were nominated at the Republican convention in Topeka on September 18–19. Lane controlled this convention—or, as Sol Miller expressed it, "bought the ticket" —largely through the patronage available to him from the regiments he was raising. Before the convention met, political observers generally expected that its gubernatorial nominee would

[15] "Kansas Regiments," *Report of the Adjutant General*, pp. 247–248; Leavenworth *Daily Conservative*, September 21, 1861, November 10, 1862; *OR*, ser. III, II, 29–31; Dudley T. Cornish, "Kansas Negro Regiments in the Civil War," *KHQ*, XX (May, 1953), 417–418; George C. Bingham to J. S. Rollins and W. A. Hall, February 12, 1862, *Missouri Historical Review*, XXXIII (October, 1938), 52.

be George Crawford. The Leavenworth *Times* and Speer's *Lawrence Republican* were about the only papers to boost Carney. At the convention Jennison accused Carney of bribing delegates, a charge which "Web" Wilder echoed in the *Conservative*. It was mainly to placate "Web" and the other Leavenworth radicals that Lane arranged to have Carter Wilder chosen as the congressional candidate instead of the incumbent Martin Conway. At any rate, following the convention the *Conservative* did a complete turnabout and spoke of the "universal esteem" in which Carney was held. Conway bitterly denounced Lane for having "sold him out" and since he no longer had a political future to consider threw off all restraints and made sensational speeches in Congress advocating recognition of the Confederacy as the only way to rid the nation of slavery.[16]

Lane so completely dominated the state's political scene that the election was fought out solely along pro-Lane and anti-Lane lines. Since the Lane forces controlled the regular Republican organization, the anti-Lane faction, calling itself the "Union Party," held a separate convention at Lawrence on September 29–30 and nominated William R. Wagstaff for Governor, John Ingalls for Lieutenant Governor, and Mark Parrott for Congress. Wagstaff was a Democrat and had gained what little prominence he possessed by serving as the chief prosecutor at the impeachment trials. His candidacy was designed by the Union Party to get Democratic support and to protect itself from being labeled a Robinson movement. But the Democrats, although they found it "inexpedient" to nominate a state ticket of their own, refused to combine with the anti-Lane Republicans for fear of losing their identity as a party. Instead they held a pathetic little convention at Topeka on October 1 and adopted a resolution advocating the "restoration of the Union as it was"—that is, with slavery. Such a stand was political suicide. By the fall of

[16] Leavenworth *Daily Conservative*, September 3, 18, 20, 1862; Leavenworth *Daily Times*, November 3, 1862.

1862 antislavery sentiment was so intense and pervasive in the state that a correspondent of the New York *Times* declared that "all" Kansans were abolitionists.[17]

The election took place on November 4 and resulted in an overwhelming victory for the Regular Republicans. Carney received 10,012 votes to Wagstaff's 5,467, and Wilder's majority over Parrott was nearly as large. This outcome had been a foregone conclusion from the moment Lane dictated the Republican slate at Topeka. Under the impetus of war, Kansans were already forming their inveterate habit of voting straight Republican no matter who were the candidates or what the issues. Lane was now at the height of his power, and Sol Miller was absolutely correct when he called the election a "Lane triumph."[18]

Kansas was a part of the largest and least important military theater of the Civil War—the Trans-Mississippi. The Northern high command regarded this area, and the forces operating in it, as the extreme right wing of the Union army, to be in a sense "refused" or even sacrificed, if need be, while the main war effort was concentrated in the drive down the Mississippi and toward Richmond. The theory behind this strategy was sound. Should the Union armies win in the East, the Confederate Trans-Mississippi would inevitably fall, while on the other hand no success west of the Mississippi could compensate for failure east of that river. Consequently Union operations in the West were primarily of a holding nature. There was no all-out attempt to conquer Arkansas or to penetrate into western Louisiana or into Texas. The offensive campaigns that were undertaken were limited both in scale and objective and sharply circumscribed by the difficult nature of the country in which they took place. Geography, in fact, dominated the warfare in

[17] Leavenworth *Daily Conservative*, August 24, September 30, October 1, 1862; *Kansas State Journal* (Lawrence), October 2, 16, 1862; *White Cloud Kansas Chief*, September 25, 1862; *Freedom's Champion* (Atchison), October 4, 11, 1862; *Topeka Tribune*, October 4, 1862.

[18] Leavenworth *Daily Conservative*, November 15, 25, December 7, 1862; *White Cloud Kansas Chief*, November 13, 1862.

the West, for in combination with the lack of communications
and the sparseness of settlement, it prevented either side from
maintaining advanced positions or from permanently occupying any sizable extent of the enemy's territory. Thus the war
on the border was indecisive, the armies of both North and
South constantly swaying back and forth between the Missouri
and the Arkansas rivers, first one, then the other, on the
offensive. Yet these campaigns should not be dismissed as possessing no interest. What they lacked in strategical significance
they made up for in dramatic content. The story of the Civil
War in the West has yet to be well and fully told, but when so
recounted should prove fascinating.

What part Kansas troops would play in Northern military
operations was for some time indeterminate. Kansans were inclined to feel that they should be employed in or near their own
state, yet some of the Kansas regiments saw most of their
service in Tennessee and Georgia. During the winter and spring
of 1861–1862, Kansas troops, principally Lane's Brigade, were
in such poor condition that Halleck contemptuously dismissed
them all with the word "humbug." Plans to use them to reinforce the Union army in Arkansas failed to materialize, and a
proposed expedition from Fort Riley to New Mexico was abandoned when Halleck, early in May, requested that the regiments
intended for it be sent to bolster Grant's army in Mississippi.[19]

Not until June, 1862, did an operation of any consequence
involving Kansas units get under way. This was an expedition
under Colonel Weer into the Indian Territory. Weer's force
consisted of the Second, Sixth, and Ninth Kansas cavalry regiments, the Tenth Kansas Infantry, the Ninth Wisconsin Infantry, the Second Ohio Cavalry, the First and Second Indiana
batteries, and two Indian regiments, numbering in all 6,000 ef-
fectives. The purpose of the campaign was to reassert Federal
authority over the Indian Territory, to protect the southern borders of Kansas and Missouri from Confederate Indian troops

[19] *OR*, ser. I, VIII, 594, 598, 602, 661.

in the area, and to restore Unionist Indian refugees to their homes. By the summer of 1862 thousands of these refugees had congregated in the southern part of the state, where they presented a serious problem both to the settlers and to the Government, which had to feed and take care of them. What little money Congress appropriated for their relief had been quickly squandered, and many had died of exposure, hunger, and disease. The Indians were desperately anxious to return to their homes and joined with alacrity the two regiments into which they were formed.[20]

Confederate troops in the Indian Territory were unable to offer any resistance to Weer's column, which had little difficulty in occupying Tahlequah, capital of the Cherokee Nation. Weer planned next to capture Fort Gibson on the Arkansas River, but before he could undertake this operation, his army mutinied and Colonel Frederick Salomon of the Ninth Wisconsin usurped command. Salomon and the other officers accused Weer of gross incompetency, drunkenness, insanity, and of exposing the army to destruction. Although there was no danger from the Confederates, Salomon promptly marched back toward Fort Scott with all the white units, leaving behind only the Indian regiments. Blunt first learned of the mutiny in a letter of explanation from Salomon. Flabbergasted, but relieved that the Indian Territory had not been totally evacuated, he ordered Salomon to halt and send back two of the Kansas regiments in order to reinforce the Indian units. When Blunt arrived at Fort Scott on the way to take personal command of the expedition, he found Salomon and all the white troops there already, even though his order had reached them at Baxter Springs. He thereupon sent back the reinforcements himself and convened a general court-martial to investigate the mutiny. Nothing came of the court-martial, however, for too many officers were involved and there were insufficient time and means to deal with them.

[20] Blunt, "Civil War Experiences," pp. 220–224; Abel, *Slaveholding Indians*, I, 254–261; *ibid.*, II, 85–107.

Yet, in spite of Salomon's mutiny and retreat, Weer's expedition resulted in the permanent occupation of the upper portion of the Indian Territory by Federal forces.[21]

On September 24 Kansas again became part of the Department of the Missouri under the command of Major General Samuel R. Curtis, victor of the Battle of Pea Ridge. Blunt remained in charge of the now District of Kansas, but instead of staying at Fort Leavenworth he took the field at the head of the "Army of the Frontier," as the troops of his district were designated. On October 1 his army joined the forces of Schofield in southwestern Missouri in a campaign to forestall a Confederate invasion from Arkansas. Marching in advance of the rest of Schofield's army, Blunt pushed into northwestern Arkansas and the adjoining Indian country. On October 22 he fought a successful engagement at Old Fort Wayne, and on November 28 he once more forced the small Confederate army facing him to fall back in a battle at Cane Hill.

Blunt was unable to follow up this victory, however, for a superior Confederate army under Major General T. C. Hindman was now advancing toward him. Hindman had hastily formed this army in a desperate effort to save Arkansas from being overrun by the Union forces and was hoping to deliver a quick, crushing blow at either Blunt or Brigadier General Francis J. Herron, commander of the other wing of Schofield's army. Instead of withdrawing northward to gain Herron's support, as he should have, Blunt remained at Cane Hill and awaited Herron to join him there, in expectation that Hindman would attack him first. But Hindman forced his way through a mountain pass which Blunt had failed to protect adequately and moved around Blunt's left flank to strike Herron. Blunt, who had been completely fooled by Hindman's maneuver, was "sound asleep, or sitting up with some female hangers-on," when he first heard the sound of firing off to the northeast. "What was that?" he

[21] *OR*, ser. I, XIII, 138, 473, 475–478, 484–485, 512, 521–522, 531–532; Blunt, "Civil War Experiences," pp. 232–234.

cried, and then blurted out, "My God, they're in my rear!" [22]
Yet Blunt did not lose control of himself or of the situation,
but set his army in a pell-mell rush toward "the sound of the
guns" to aid the embattled Herron, he himself bounding along
on horseback far ahead of his army. Herron, with a superiority
of artillery fire power that compensated for his inferiority in
numbers, was holding Hindman at Prairie Grove when Blunt's
men streamed on the field. The Kansas troops aided materially
in beating back Hindman's frantic thrusts, but it is debatable
whether they "saved the day" as Blunt later claimed. Frenzied
and bloody fighting continued until after dark, with neither side
gaining a clear-cut advantage. In the morning, under the cover
of a truce, Hindman retreated with his badly battered army,
much to the relief of Herron and Blunt.[23]

Nearly three weeks elapsed before Blunt and Herron pursued
Hindman, who had retired to Van Buren. They made a rapid
march to that town and drove a rear guard of Texas cavalry to
the other side of the Arkansas River, where Hindman's main
force stood. The two armies waged an artillery duel across
the river, but Blunt and Herron did not attempt to follow the
Confederates when they resumed their retreat. The next day,
after a night of drunken plundering and burning, the Union
army marched back to Cane Hill, from where it dispersed into
winter quarters.[24] For the time being Confederate power north
of the Arkansas was destroyed.

The Kansas press, at least the pro-Lane portion thereof, hailed
Blunt as a great general and hero.[25] He, too, thought very highly
of his performance and began to plume himself as a military
leader, especially of cavalry. In truth he had displayed many of

[22] *Kansas State Journal* (Lawrence), February 12, 1863, quoting letter
from a soldier in Blunt's army; Prentis, *Kansas Miscellanies*, pp. 27, 31–32.

[23] *OR*, ser. I, XXII, pt. 1, 60–84, 138–146. During the Prairie Grove
Campaign, Schofield was ill and so unable to exercise personal or direct
command.

[24] *Ibid.*, pp. 167–170.

[25] Leavenworth *Daily Conservative*, January 13, 1863.

the attributes of a successful commander—courage, aggressiveness, promptness, confidence, and, above all, luck. Nevertheless he probably owed his victories more to the weakness of the Confederates than to his own strength.[26] Most of the commanders he opposed were either drunk or incompetent or both, and the troops they led were miserably equipped and poor in morale— at Prairie Grove entire regiments of Arkansas conscripts surrendered en masse. Furthermore, there is some reason to doubt whether he deserved full credit even for what he apparently did well. Many years after the war his chief of staff, Thomas Moonlight, a former soldier in the regular army, asserted that had it not been for his advice "Blunt would not stand in history with the same military victories attached to him," in particular Old Fort Wayne, Cane Hill, Prairie Grove, and Van Buren.[27] Yet at the time Blunt was well regarded by his soldiers, the general public, and Congress, which in May promoted him to major general.

[26] John M. Schofield, *Forty-six Years in the Army* (New York, 1897), p. 63, stated that Blunt was "unfit in any respect for command of a division of troops against a disciplined enemy."

[27] Moonlight to Patrick H. Coney, September 20, 1898, *KHQ*, I (May, 1932), 212. See also Ewing to Mrs. Ewing, December 27, 1862, Ewing Papers, Library of Congress, criticizing the "blundering" of Blunt.

# VI

## *The Bushwhackers*

WILLIAM CLARKE QUANTRILL became the most famous and feared of the Missouri guerrillas. Yet he was not a Missourian, but had been born in Ohio in 1837 and had spent most of his adult life in Kansas. He came to Kansas in the spring of 1857 and for a while worked on a farm near Stanton in Johnson County. In 1858 he joined an army expedition to Utah as a teamster. Then, after a period in the gold fields about Pike's Peak, he returned to Kansas and taught school briefly at Osawatomie. Next he went to Lawrence, where under the assumed name of Charley Hart he joined up with a band of jayhawkers and engaged in horse stealing, burglary, and the kidnapping of Negroes. Eventually the Douglas County authorities indicted him for his crimes, but were unable to arrest him.

Quantrill achieved his first real notoriety in December, 1860. He persuaded five Kansas "practical abolitionists" to accompany him on a raid into Missouri for the purpose of "liberating" the slaves of Morgan Walker, a prominent Jackson County farmer. Prior to the raid, however, he forewarned Walker, with the result that the five abolitionists walked into a trap in which three of them were killed and from which the other two barely escaped. Quantrill remained in Jackson County the rest of the winter, during which he gained the sympathy of the Missourians by telling them that he had engineered the Morgan Walker affair in order to revenge the killing of his elder brother by Kansas jayhawkers. Late in March he returned to Kansas, only to be captured by a posse and placed in a jail at Paola. But some of the numerous Southern sympathizers in the region quickly secured his release on a writ of habeas corpus, and he rode back to Jackson County just ahead of a posse from Lawrence.[1]

Following the outbreak of hostilities in Missouri, Quantrill joined a band of guerrillas led by Andrew Walker in attacking raiding parties of Kansans. In December he formed a small band of his own and on March 7, 1862, sacked the little village of Aubry, Kansas. Two weeks later a detachment of the Second Kansas Cavalry surprised and surrounded his gang in a house near Little Santa Fe, but after a desperate revolver fight he and most of his men were able to escape. On August 10 he joined other Confederate guerrillas and irregulars in a successful assault on the Union garrison at Independence. Nearly a month afterward he made his largest raid yet, striking at Olathe in retaliation for the execution of one of his followers at Fort Leavenworth. His 150 men killed ten Kansans on the way to Olathe, captured the 125 soldiers stationed there without a shot, then remained all day and night plundering and shooting down citizens "like so many hogs." In the morning they departed, taking the soldiers with them for several miles and then turning them loose after killing only one. The Tenth Kansas pursued the band and on September 19 overtook it north of Pleasant Hill, Missouri, scattered it, and recovered most of the loot from Olathe. The Kansas troops burned a dozen houses in the

---

[1] Leavenworth *Daily Conservative*, March 29, 1861; Connelley, *Quantrill*, pp. 17-195 *passim*. Connelley's work contains the fullest account of Quantrill's career and is especially valuable for the recollections of ex-guerrillas and other participants in the border wars. It should be used with extreme caution, however, owing to the uncritical and prejudiced views of the author.

neighborhood which had sheltered Quantrill's men and marched back with "upward of 60 loyal colored persons, tired of the rule of rebel masters." This setback did not seriously injure Quantrill, and on October 17 he returned to Kansas to raid and burn Shawneetown, where his followers murdered seven civilians and fifteen soldiers. With the approach of cold weather, which stripped the trees and brush bare of their concealing leaves, Quantrill and most of the other guerrillas left Missouri and passed the winter in Arkansas. By now he was the most notorious of the "bushwhackers," and people in Kansas spoke of him as a "second Nero" and a "fiend."[2]

The strength of Quantrill's gang fluctuated greatly, ranging from less than thirty to more than 300, depending on circumstances and the scale of the enterprise undertaken. Its members were of two basic types: first, young Missouri farmers turned guerrilla because of Southern sympathies, persecution by Missouri Unionists and Federal troops, and resentment against Kansas jayhawking raids and, second, border ruffians, outlaws, and outcasts, men driven by a lust for loot and excitement. Representative of the first class were such men as Cole and Jim Younger, William Gregg, and Frank and Jesse James. Cole Younger became a guerrilla after jayhawkers burned his home and killed his father; prior to these outrages he and his family had been pro-Union. Jesse James turned bushwhacker at the age of seventeen, having been preceded by Frank, because Missouri Unionist militia tortured his stepfather and imprisoned his mother and his sister. The raids of Jennison and Anthony caused Gregg to "take to the bush," as they did many other Jackson County youths.[3]

[2] Leavenworth *Daily Conservative*, March 13, September 9, 1862; *OR*, ser. I, VIII, 335-336, 346-347; *ibid.*, XIII, 267-268, 779, 803; Connelley, *Quantrill*, pp. 196-275; "Letters of Julia Louise Lovejoy," *KHQ*, XVI (May, 1948), 184-185.

[3] Leavenworth *Daily Conservative*, April 5, 1862; Henry E. Palmer, "The Black-Flag Character of the War on the Border," *KHC*, IX (1905-1906), 284; Birdsall, *History of Jackson County*, pp. 208-209; Edwards, *Noted Guerrillas*, pp. 54-55, 167-168; Connelley, *Quantrill*, pp. 167, 221.

George Todd and Bill Anderson were notable examples of the second type of guerrilla. Todd was an illiterate, murderous brute, probably the cruelest of all of Quantrill's followers and eventually supplanting him as leader. A Canadian by birth, he was eighteen before he came to Missouri in 1859 to work as a stonemason in Kansas City. No one could ever explain why he turned bushwhacker.[4] "Bloody Bill" Anderson, like Quantrill, was nominally a Kansan, although originally from Missouri. Along with his father and brother he had committed a number of robberies in the vicinity of Rock Creek and Council Grove before the war. In time he headed his own gang, the "Kansas First Guerrillas," which he claimed consisted mainly of Kansans.[5] Quantrill himself belonged to the same category as Todd and Anderson. Despite his story to the contrary, he did not become a guerrilla out of personal grievances, and although he was without doubt pro-Confederate, it is equally certain that his main interest was simply plunder. Essentially he was, like Jennison, Anthony, Hoyt, Stewart, Cleveland, and other jayhawkers, a product of border strife and frontier turbulence.[6]

Whatever their original character or motivation, the majority of Quantrill's men became, in the words of a Confederate general, only a "shade better than highwaymen," killers who regarded "the life of a man less than that . . . of a sheep-killing dog."[7] The Confederate military authorities felt that their forays did more harm than good and therefore endeavored to get them to join the regular service. They did participate, it

[4] Daniel Geary, "War Incidents at Kansas City," *KHC*, XI (1909-1910), 284.

[5] Andreas, *History of Kansas*, p. 800; *OR*, ser. I, XLI, pt. 2, 75-77.

[6] Quantrill gained the sympathy and confidence of the Missourians by telling them that Lane's jayhawkers killed his elder brother and wounded Quantrill while they were passing through Kansas in 1856 on their way to California. Quantrill did not have an elder brother, was not in Kansas in 1856, and, instead of being attacked by jayhawkers, was in fact a jayhawker himself. But the Missourians believed him, and the story, with many elaborations, became part of the Quantrill legend, still prevalent in western Missouri.

[7] *OR*, ser. I, XXXIV, pt. 2, 542.

is supposed, in the battle of Prairie Grove, but until the Price Raid of 1864, that was the extent of their direct contribution to the Confederate war effort.[8] The reason that they refused to join the regular Southern army, as assigned by Confederate General Henry E. McCulloch, was because many of them were deserters and because such service would not "pay men who fight for plunder." [9] An added source of their unwillingness was that many of them were more interested in defending their homes against jayhawkers and in avenging themselves on Missouri Unionists and the Kansans than in fighting for the Confederate cause as such.

Quantrill and his men received both moral and material support from the people of western Missouri. A pro-Confederate or, more accurately, a pro-Southern sentiment dominated this area, which provided such leading Missouri Confederates as Sterling Price of Keytesville and Joseph O. Shelby of Waverly. This feeling stemmed only in part from slaveholding. Very few West Missourians owned slaves, and not many of these possessed large numbers of them. Most of these slaves, moreover, were domestic servants, not field hands. The main reason why the people of West Missouri sympathized with the South was that their culture and family ties were Southern. Yet in spite of this the majority of them had been pro-Union until the Lincoln Administration instituted a policy of "coercion" and hostilities broke out between the state government and the United States military. Guerrilla activity began at the same time, but did not occur on a large or serious scale until prompted and stimulated by the incursions of Lane and Jennison.[10]

[8] *Ibid.*, XXII, pt. 2, 855; Connelley, *Quantrill*, p. 280.

[9] *OR*, ser. I, XXXIV, pt. 2, 942.

[10] Miller, *Memorable Decade*, p. 36; John G. Haskell, "The Passing of Slavery in Western Missouri," *KHC*, VII (1901–1902), 31; James C. Malin, *Background of the Kansas-Nebraska Question* (Lawrence, 1954), pp. 27–32; Britton, *Memoirs of the Rebellion*, pp. 128–137; R. I. Holcombe, comp., *History of Vernon County, Missouri* (St. Louis, 1887), p. 272.

Jayhawking, however, was not the sole cause of bushwhacking. The intense ill-feeling and strife between pro-Union and pro-Confederate Missourians was an equally important factor. Early in 1862 the Union state authorities ordered a general enrollment of all able-bodied men into the militia and authorized the United States military commander to call this "enrolled militia" into Federal service. Upon the announcement of this order thousands of Southern sympathizers, otherwise dormant, fled to the South or became guerrillas, rather than serve in the Union army against friends and relatives in the Confederate army. Partly as a consequence the enrolled militia regiments were composed mainly of radical Unionists implacable and bitter in their hatred of the "secesh." These regiments were often poorly disciplined and scarcely distinguishable in appearance from bushwhackers, being without any uniform except a rosette pinned to their hats. They sometimes conducted pillaging expeditions through entire counties, in the course of which they robbed and even killed suspected secessionists. The guerrillas then struck back by attacking the militia and driving Union men and their families from their homes. This in turn enraged the Unionists, who countered with parallel outrages upon the families of bushwhackers and Confederate soldiers. Many a man turned guerrilla because of terroristic acts committed by "Feds," in particular former members of Price's army who had returned home intending to be loyal and peaceable, but who were harried and persecuted by suspicious Unionist neighbors and the militia.[11]

The combination of jayhawking and Unionist oppression caused most of the people of West Missouri to loathe the Kansas "Yorkers" and the Missouri "Bluebellies" with murderous passion and to look upon the bushwhackers as defenders and revengers. The young men of the region "took to the bush" to join established outfits like Quantrill's or to form bands of their own. The

[11] *OR*, ser. I, XIII, 7–15; *ibid.*, XLI, pt. 1, 416–417; *ibid.*, pt. 2, p. 87; Lucien E. Carr, *Missouri: A Bone of Contention* (Boston and New York, 1888), pp. 343–356; Holcombe, comp., *Vernon County*, p. 311.

older men, the women, and even the children provided the bush-whackers with ammunition, food, clothing, shelter, and medical care and acted as spies and sentinels. Loyal Union men also helped the guerrillas, either out of regard for the claims of kinship or because they feared the consequences if they refused. As a result the Union forces stationed in West Missouri were in effect op-posed by an entire people.

During the summer of 1862 guerrilla activity mounted to such a high peak of intensity that the Federal authorities feared a "gen-eral insurrection." In July and August large numbers of Confed-erates, led by J. A. Poindexter and Joseph C. Porter, formed north of the Missouri River with the intention of marching southward to link with Price. General Schofield, then in command in Mis-souri, blockaded the river and sent all available troops against them. After much bloody fighting he dispersed them, although for a while he complained that they gathered recruits faster than they could be killed. In Jackson County the bushwhackers, in-cluding Quantrill, combined with the Confederate semiregulars of Colonel John T. Hughes and captured the Union garrison at Independence on August 11. Next they joined a brigade of Con-federate cavalry from Arkansas and on August 16 attacked and defeated 800 Union troops at Lone Jack. Then Blunt, who had been pursuing the column from Arkansas, came up and forced the victors to retreat southward. Although he followed them closely for several days deep into southern Missouri, he could not bring them to bay. His energetic conduct, however, probably saved Kansas from a devastating raid.[12]

Notwithstanding the general success of Union operations dur-ing the summer, the bushwhackers remained active and dangerous well into the fall. Quantrill in particular continued his forays across the border, driving the Black Bob and Shawnee Indians from their reservations, sacking Shawneetown, and burning

[12] OR, ser. I, XIII, 15, 225–230, 235–239, 513–519, 535, 557–558; Britton, Memoirs of the Rebellion, pp. 136–139; Miller, Memorable Decade, pp. 81–83.

Pottawatomie. Hundreds of Kansans living along the border became panic-stricken and either moved back into the interior, abandoning crops and homes, or else left the state altogether.[13] Aroused by their pleas for protection and by the persistent incursions of the guerrillas, Governor Robinson endeavored to mobilize a force of militia for border duty. In doing so he was severely handicapped by the inadequate provisions that the legislature had made for raising and maintaining state troops. The Militia Act of 1861 lacked effective means whereby the state authorities could organize the militia, and neither the 1861 or 1862 legislatures appropriated funds for paying and equipping the militiamen when brought into service. In his message to the 1862 legislature Robinson pointed to these deficiencies and asked that they be remedied. "It is for the legislature," he affirmed, "to decide whether, in any emergency, the Executive shall have the means to protect the State, or whether it shall be left powerless as during the past year." The legislature, however, dominated as it was by Lane adherents, refused to comply with Robinson's request, fearing or professing to fear that to do so would give him increased patronage power and desiring also to make him unpopular in the border counties by having it appear that he was unable and unwilling to take measures for defense against the guerrillas. As a result of the legislature's failure to act, there were toward the end of 1862 less than ten companies of militia in the entire state in organized condition.[14]

So long as General Curtis commanded the Department of the Missouri, Lane was content that Kansas was not a separate department, especially since the District of Kansas was under Blunt. Curtis was a former Republican Congressman from Iowa and, although a West Pointer, was more of a politician than a general.

[13] *OR*, ser. I, XIII, 801–805; Leavenworth *Daily Conservative*, October 19, 1862; Abel, *Slaveholding Indians*, II, 204–205.

[14] *Kansas State Journal* (Lawrence), January 23, March 13, 1862; Leavenworth *Daily Conservative*, October 10, 1862; Charles Chadwick, Adjutant General of Kansas, to Major General John A. Halderman, September 22, 1862, John A. Halderman Papers, KSHS.

His military and administrative policies were highly favorable to the radical faction of the Republican Party in Missouri and Kansas. Naturally the Missouri Conservatives, headed by Governor Gamble, angrily and vocally resented this favoritism to their opponents. By May of 1863 their criticism of Curtis became so intense and virulent that Lincoln, who himself was dissatisfied with him, decided to remove him from command in Missouri. To replace him Lincoln selected Major General Schofield, who was a professional soldier and thoroughly familiar with the Missouri situation. Lincoln instructed Schofield to stay clear of the "pestilent factional quarrel" in Missouri and set up this criterion for his guidance: "If both factions, or neither, shall abuse you, you will, probably, be about right. Beware of being assailed by one and praised by the other." [15]

Schofield's appointment greatly alarmed Lane. He considered that general a friend of the conservatives and an enemy of himself and the radicals. Furthermore, with Curtis out his influence in St. Louis was gone, and he feared that Schofield would interfere with Blunt and so threaten his politically and financially profitable control of military affairs in Kansas. Therefore, as soon as it became known that Schofield would supersede Curtis, the Leavenworth *Conservative* began agitating for the creation of a "Frontier Department" under the command of Blunt, to be "free from Schofield and Gamble." Speer's Lawrence *Tribune*, successor to the *Republican,* and the Rosses' Topeka *Record* took up the cry, and Lane tried unsuccessfully to induce the National Union League to adopt a resolution urging Lincoln not to name Schofield commander of the Department of the Missouri. The Missouri radical press likewise denounced Schofield, declaring that he was "soft" toward rebels and a tool of the Copperheads.[16]

[15] Lincoln to Schofield, May 27, 1863, *OR,* ser. I, XXII, pt. 2, 277.
[16] Leavenworth *Daily Conservative,* May 6, 1863; *Kansas Weekly Tribune* (Lawrence), May 23, 1863; *Kansas State Record* (Topeka), May 23, 1863; Union League of America, *Proceedings of the National Convention* (Washington, 1863), pp. 11–12.

It was at once apparent that the neutral role that Lincoln had assigned Schofield was not only going to be difficult, but virtually impossible.

Lane's apprehensions were quickly realized. On June 9 Schofield divided the District of Kansas into two sections. One, the "District of the Frontier," consisted of Kansas below the thirty-eighth parallel, the Indian Territory, and the western tier of counties in Missouri and Arkansas south of the thirty-eighth parallel. Blunt remained in charge of this area, which corresponded to the lower half of the now defunct District of Kansas, with headquarters at Fort Scott. The other division, the "District of the Border," included all of Kansas above the thirty-eighth parallel and the two western tiers of counties in Missouri north of the parallel and south of the Missouri River. Its headquarters was Kansas City, its commander Brigadier General Thomas Ewing, Jr.[17]

This reorganization was a severe blow to Lane. It deprived him of direct control of the quartermaster and commissary depots at Fort Leavenworth and shunted Blunt off to a remote corner with only a "colonel's command." He lost no time in trying to retrieve the situation. Seconded by Carter Wilder and the Leavenworth army contractors, he hastened to Washington and attempted to induce Stanton to reconstitute Kansas as a separate department with Blunt in charge. Schofield learned of Lane's machinations and at once protested to Halleck, now commander in chief of the Union army, "that peace cannot be restored and preserved near the border of Kansas and Missouri unless the country on both sides of the line be under the same command." Halleck fully agreed and for the time being completely frustrated Lane's efforts.[18]

Soon after taking command Ewing made a much-discussed speech at Olathe in which he denounced "men in Kansas who are

[17] *OR*, ser. I, XXII, pt. 1, 15; *ibid.*, pt. 2, p. 315.
[18] Leavenworth *Daily Conservative*, July 3, August 1, 1863; *OR*, ser. I, XXII, pt. 2, 351.

stealing themselves rich in the name of liberty" and those who
had arrogated "to themselves and their sympathizers, all the radical antislaveryism and genuine loyalty in Kansas." These persons, declared Ewing, "who are influential by reason of boldness,
position or talent, have long been engaged in distorting the honest
sentiment of the State, and giving respectability to robbery when
committed on any whom they declare disloyal." Ewing signaled
out for particular condemnation an organization of jayhawkers
and outlaws known as the Red Legs, a name derived from the red
leather leggings they wore. The Red Legs operated primarily in
the border districts of Missouri, but also robbed and molested
Kansans whom they claimed were proslavery and pro-Southern.
In both personnel and character they were nearly identical with
Jennison's old Jayhawkers, and their leader was Jennison's friend
and lieutenant, George Hoyt. Their main headquarters was Six-
Mile House, an inn on the road between Wyandotte and Leavenworth. Most of the cattle and horses that they stole in their forays
they sold in Leavenworth or Lawrence. Perhaps more than anything else, they helped to keep alive the bitterness and resentment
of the Missourians against Kansas and to provide a cause and excuse for bushwhacking. Ewing warned them to abandon their
ways and get into the army or else be put down "with a rough
hand." [19]

Ewing's Olathe speech, however, was more than a condemnation of the Red Legs. It was also, as every informed Kansan knew,
a covert yet clear attack on the Leavenworth ultraradicals associated with Lane, of whom the more conspicuous were the Wilders
and D. R. Anthony. Through the columns of the *Conservative*
this coterie had for some time been "giving respectability to robbery," "distorting the honest sentiment of the State," and claiming
a monopoly on "all the radical anti-slaveryism and genuine loy-

[19] Leavenworth *Daily Conservative*, July 2, 1863; Oskaloosa *Independent*, July 25, 1863; C. M. Chase to the Sycamore, Ill., *True Republican and
Sentinel*, August 10, 1863, Chase Letters; *OR*, ser. I, XIII, 478; *ibid.*, XXII,
pt. 2, 125; Connelley, *Quantrill*, pp. 411–417; Spring, *Kansas*, pp. 285–286.

alty in Kansas." Thus the April 23 issue of the paper had contained a fervent eulogy of the Red Legs and Hoyt, and the June 30 edition had posted the names of Jennison and Wendell Phillips as candidates for President and Vice-President, at the same time challenging any other newspaper to surpass it in radicalism. "Web" Wilder, in his editorials, made it a regular practice to label anyone who disagreed with him a "copperhead" or "secessionist," and he never tired of praising Lane and Blunt. A person from another state who read "Kansas's Leading Newspaper" could have formed no other impression than that its citizens indeed were ready to vote for Jennison and Phillips.

It was not long before Ewing clashed directly with the Leavenworth radicals. On July 19 he placed that town under martial law. This drastic measure was necessary, he averred, because the mayor was interfering with efforts to rout out the illegal trade in stolen livestock centering in the town. The mayor was none other than Anthony, who had been elected to the office in April. His administration was arbitrary and inefficient, and he did nothing to suppress the Red Legs and their unlawful traffic. He protested vehemently against Ewing's imposition of martial law and demanded that it be lifted at once. "Web" Wilder backed him with billingsgate tirades in the *Conservative* and got up a petition to rescind martial law. The *Times*, on the other hand, defended Ewing and produced a counterpetition. Ewing ignored Anthony's protests and Wilder's petition and wrote to Schofield that he would not revoke martial law in Leavenworth until Anthony left office.[20]

Thomas Carney was Governor only a brief time before he made it quite evident that although elected as a "Lane man" he was determined to be a "Carney man." He insisted on his official prerogatives as stubbornly as Robinson ever did and, with his political ambition fired by the governorship, began maneuvering

[20] *OR*, ser. I, XXII, pt. 2, 388–392; Oskaloosa *Independent*, July 25, 1863; Leavenworth *Daily Conservative*, July 21, 22, 31, August 2, 1863; Leavenworth *Daily Times*, July 21, August 4, 1863.

secretly to succeed Lane as Senator. Lane quickly became suspicious of Carney's intentions and was irritated when Carney refused to comply with his wishes in regard to matters of military patronage. For the time being, however, Lane did not break openly with Carney, but watched him closely and did everything possible to prevent him from gaining in political strength. With his large personal fortune, Carney was a formidable rival, especially in a senatorial contest to be decided by the impecunious and none-too-scrupulous members of the legislature.

Carney and Lane first clashed in March, 1863, when Carney refused to commission James Williams colonel of the First Colored Regiment. Carney had his own candidate for the post, R. C. Anderson. But the other officers of the regiment, all Lane appointees, "combined together" against Anderson and threatened to shoot him if he tried to take command. Lane and Blunt also supported Williams, Lane reportedly sending him blank commissions with instructions to fill them out and to muster no one who had been commissioned by the Governor without Williams' approval. The War Department sided with Lane, and when Carney insisted on Anderson, Stanton issued the commission to Williams.[21]

Late in March, following the adjournment of the legislature, Carney went to Washington to see Lane, Stanton, and the President and to look after the disposal of the state bonds. On March 27 he wrote his close friend, James L. McDowell of Leavenworth: "I met Lane here & he promised Everything. Expressed a willingness to do something for me. Says that Blunt shall not attempt any more to give trouble, but shall be my friend and all that sort of thing—all of which you & I understand." He then described a "highly satisfactory" interview with Stanton and Lincoln, in which both told him that "no more irregular work

[21] *Kansas State Journal* (Lawrence), March 20, 1863; Asa Reynard to R. C. Anderson, March 10, 1863, Governors' Correspondence (Thomas Carney), 1863–1865, Military Affairs, Kansas State Archives.

shall be done in Kansas—that Kansas shall be treated as Ohio, Penn., etc." [22]

Having obtained these comforting assurances, Carney undertook next to dispose of the bonds. At his urging the 1863 legislature had authorized the issuance of $54,000 of 7 per cent bonds. These were to meet the obligations of the state arising from the war bonds of 1861 and to complete the Interior Department contract negotiated by Stevens. This contract remained in effect notwithstanding the impeachments, the only change being that the state was to get the full 85 per cent instead of 60 per cent as arranged by Stevens. Carney, after investigating the matter, decided that he could obtain more than 85 per cent on the bonds held by the Interior Department and therefore induced Secretary of the Interior J. P. Usher to release the state from the contract. He then sold the 1863 bond issue of $54,000 and $1,000 of the 1861 issue at ninety-three cents on the dollar in New York; he later disposed of $26,000 of the 1861 issue to Usher at par and obtained the cancellation of a like amount of the war bonds held by the Interior Department. At the same time he sold another $4,000 of the 7 per cent 1861 bonds on the open market at ninety-five cents on the dollar. These transactions were not in strict accordance with the law authorizing him to act as agent of the state in negotiating the bonds, but since he had been able to realize much better terms than that law contemplated, he was confident the legislature would ratify his actions. It did so in 1864.[23]

In making the above arrangements, Carney not only "put the State on a cash basis," but secured a private profit for himself and his friend McDowell. While in the midst of negotiating the bonds he instructed McDowell to buy "State Bonds held by private in-

[22] Carney to McDowell, March 27, 1863, James L. McDowell Papers, KSHS; Carney to Lincoln, July 19, 1863, Governors' Correspondence (Thomas Carney), General, 1863, 1864, Kansas State Archives.

[23] *Laws of Kansas, 1863*, pp. 32–35; *Senate Journal, 1864*, p. 17; *Senate Journal, 1866*, pp. 447–448; *Kansas State Journal* (Lawrence), January 22, 1863; Leavenworth *Daily Conservative*, May 15, 1863, July 28, 1864.

dividuals that no doubt can be bought at from 70 to 80¢." The bonds, he informed McDowell, could be sold "at from 93 to 95¢ in New York so that you can at a glance see what you can do." In case McDowell was able to purchase more bonds than he had money available to pay for them, he was authorized to draw on Carney's own account, after which they would divide the proceeds.[24] Somebody, it seems, was destined to make money from the bonds of Kansas, and in the end it was the state's second Governor and James L. McDowell.

When Carney returned to Kansas in May, he was faced with a severe crisis arising from the renewed guerrilla raids. The worst and most startling of these was made by a gang of Quantrill's men led by Dick Yeager. With several dozen companions Yeager rode 130 miles into the interior of the state, struck the village of Diamond Springs, then headed back to Missouri, robbing stagecoaches, burning houses, shooting settlers, and looting Rock Springs, Black Jack, Gardner, and Shawnee on the way. McDowell, acting in his capacity of major general of the militia, hastily collected a posse of sixty men and pursued Yeager, but although ten of Yeager's followers were captured, McDowell could not bring him to bay. Simultaneously with Yeager's foray other guerrilla bands committed depredations around Mound City and Fort Scott. By May 21 the Lawrence *Journal* was reporting that all the border counties from the Kaw to Fort Scott were nearly depopulated.[25]

The Yeager and other raids caused great excitement and indignation. Carney received many letters demanding better protection, criticizing Blunt, and warning that large numbers of settlers planned to leave the state.[26] Carney shared the feeling of

[24] Carney to McDowell, April 19, 1863, McDowell Papers.

[25] *Council Grove Press*, May 11, 1863; Leavenworth *Daily Conservative*, May 7, 30, 1863; Leavenworth *Daily Times*, August 30, 1863; OR, ser. I, XXII, pt. 2, 274.

[26] Various letters of May, 1863, in Governors' Correspondence (Thomas Carney), General, 1863, 1864, Kansas State Archives.

alarm and was aware of the political consequences of a failure to cope with the situation. On May 9 he requested leave from the War Department to raise a regiment of home guards, to be maintained and equipped by the Federal Government, for the defense of the Kansas border. In spite of Carney's statement that "a portion of the State will be depopulated unless protection is given," Stanton refused to authorize such a regiment and also rejected an additional proposal to recruit several Negro regiments for general service.[27]

Meanwhile Carney visited the stricken border counties in person. After conferring with the settlers, he raised a body of 150 mounted men, whom he paid out of his own pocket. He instructed this force to patrol the border, fill gaps in the defenses maintained by the regular troops, and co-operate with the Federal officers in the area. He also had the border county sheriffs form posses to guard against bushwhackers and suppress banditry.[28]

Carney, however, deemed these measures to be at best only temporary and makeshift. Therefore later in May he sent State Senator W. H. M. Fishback of Olathe to Washington with a petition from the citizens of Johnson County asking that the state government be allowed to organize a home guard regiment on the basis previously proposed. Fishback endeavored to get Lane's support for the petition, but the Senator adamantly refused to have anything to do with it. He told Fishback that the petition would injure Blunt with the War Department by making it appear that he was neglecting to provide adequate protection against the guerrillas and that Carney would derive too much political patronage from raising the regiment. He also questioned Fishback as to whether Carney planned to run for the Senate and vowed that "if Carney gets in my way, he shall feel my power." Fishback then turned to Pomeroy, who on June 4 recommended

[27] Telegrams, Carney to Stanton, May 9, 1863, and Stanton to Carney, May 11, 1863, Thomas C. Stevens Papers, KSHS.
[28] *Senate Journal, 1864,* p. 117.

to Stanton that Carney be authorized to raise the regiment. Stanton agreed, provided Schofield approved.[29]

Meanwhile, Lane moved to block Carney and to strengthen his own control over military affairs. On June 5, the very day after Stanton's promise to Pomeroy, the War Department appointed Blunt special recruiting commissioner for Kansas, with authority to enlist a regiment of white cavalry and one of Negro infantry. It also empowered him to name the officers of these regiments. Those of the white regiment would be commissioned by the Governor of Kansas on Blunt's application, those of the Negro regiment by the Secretary of War.[30]

The terms of Blunt's commission not only challenged Carney's authority as Governor, but also presented a check to his political ambitions. By using the military patronage of the two new regiments made available, Lane could exercise a commanding influence over the 1863 election and so acquire control of the 1864 legislature. He then would be in a position to hamstring Carney's administration as he had Robinson's and to foil Carney by having himself re-elected to the Senate. Although normally the legislature would not choose a Senator until 1865, when Lane's term expired, Lane in all likelihood was plotting to advance the election to 1864. Should this occur, Carney's hopes for the senatorship might well be blasted. Carney was aware of Lane's scheme and placed no reliance on his assurance that he would not try to get himself re-elected "next winter." [31]

As soon as Carney learned of Blunt's appointment, he hastened to Washington, intent, as he announced to friend McDowell, on "running Blunt out [of Kansas] or completely shelving him" and having Ewing placed in command of the entire state. En route he stopped at St. Louis and obtained Schofield's approval of his plan to raise a home guard regiment to be supported by the

---

[29] Leavenworth *Daily Times*, September 12, 1863, containing letter by Fishback.
[30] Leavenworth *Daily Conservative*, June 14, 1863; *OR*, ser. III, III, 322.
[31] Carney to McDowell, March 27, 1863, McDowell Papers.

Federal Government.[32] Once in Washington he addressed, on June 25, a letter to Lincoln in which he complained about Blunt's being permitted to appoint officers and declared that he was not being treated in this respect as were the other governors. He concluded the letter with a request that Blunt's military authority in Kansas be "absolutely suspended" and that Blunt's power to nominate officers be revoked.[33]

Carney's protest resulted in a modification of Blunt's instructions. On June 26 the War Department informed Blunt that henceforth he was not to nominate officers for the Fourteenth Kansas, as the white regiment was designated, that instead all the officers would be elected by the regiment itself and then commissioned by the Governor. Carney was less successful, however, in regard to the home guard regiment. Despite his promise to Pomeroy, Stanton again refused to authorize it, even though Schofield had approved it. He did so, probably, in order to placate Lane, who had brought his potent influence to bear on the matter.[34]

Carney remained in Washington until July 18 trying to achieve the other objective of his mission. On July 17 Lincoln wrote Stanton that he believed it to be "proper, on principle, that the Governor of Kansas should stand on the same ground as the other loyal governors, in giving original commissions" and that therefore equal treatment should hereafter be accorded Carney unless there was "some substantial reason to the contrary." Stanton, however, successfully opposed Carney's efforts to obtain the right to name and commission the officers of the Negro regiment. This authority, he pointed out, belonged to the Federal Govern-

[32] Carney to McDowell, June 15, June 16, 1863, McDowell Papers.

[33] Carney to Lincoln, June 25, 1863, Governors' Correspondence (Thomas Carney), General, 1863, 1864, Kansas State Archives.

[34] Order of June 26, 1863, from War Department to Blunt, Moonlight Papers; Special Orders no. 162, Department of the Missouri, Stevens Papers; Carney to McDowell, June 26, 1863, McDowell Papers; Leavenworth *Daily Times*, September 11, 1863; *White Cloud Kansas Chief*, February 18, 1864.

ment, which had taken complete charge of organizing all Negro troops. And Lincoln was noncommittal about extending Ewing's district to include all Kansas, thereby confining Blunt to the Indian Territory. When Carney returned to Kansas, he was still dissatisfied and also miffed at Lincoln's failure to keep an appointment.[35] The Blunt-Lane combination retained the patronage of the Negro regiment, whose officers were all white. Blunt also derived political advantage from the Fourteenth Regiment by manipulating its elections for officers.

Carney, however, did achieve one definite success during his Washington trip—authority to raise a cavalry regiment. Ostensibly this regiment, the Fifteenth Kansas, was intended for regular service and not subject to restrictions concerning its location and use. In actuality, by virtue of an informal agreement between Carney and Schofield, it was to be assigned exclusively to border defense. In this way Carney circumvented Stanton and Lane and obtained, in effect, a home guard regiment which would be equipped and maintained by the Federal Government.[36]

Carney arrived back in Topeka on July 28 and immediately set to work organizing the regiment. As its colonel and lieutenant colonel he appointed, respectively, Jennison and Hoyt. These two gentlemen had been at odds with Lane ever since he refused to make Jennison colonel of the first Negro regiment. In return for their commissions they promised to use their influence in southern Kansas and among the radical element in favor of Carney against Lane.[37] Carney also selected the other officers of the regiment with a view to their political usefulness.[38] In short, he at-

[35] Roy P. Basler, ed., *The Collected Works of Abraham Lincoln* (New Brunswick, N.J., 1953), VI, 335; Lincoln to Carney, July 21, 1863, and Carney to Lincoln, July 19, 1863, Governors' Correspondence (Thomas Carney), General, 1863, 1864, Kansas State Archives.

[36] *Senate Journal, 1864,* p. 30.

[37] *Kansas State Record* (Topeka), July 29, August 5, 1863; Carney to McDowell, February 18, 1864, and McDowell to Carney, February 28, 1864, Governors' Correspondence (Thomas Carney), General, 1863, 1864, Kansas State Archives.

[38] This statement is based on a survey of various letters in Governors' Correspondence (Thomas Carney), General, 1863, 1864; Governors'

tempted to turn Lane's principal political weapon, military patronage, against him. By placing men like Jennison and Hoyt in high commands he demonstrated himself to be just as unscrupulous in its use as Lane. Whether he would be equally successful remained to be seen.

Ewing had a twofold responsibility as commander of the District of the Border: suppressing the bushwhackers in Missouri and preventing them from raiding Kansas. Of these two tasks, Ewing rightly considered the first to be the main one, for if successfully performed the other would cease to exist. Therefore he did his utmost, during the months of June and July, to put down bushwhacking in Jackson County and adjacent areas. His efforts, however, were severely handicapped by a lack of troops. He had but 2,500 men in his entire district, and a sizable portion of them were stationed in western Kansas or along the state line. Then, too, many of these troops were poorly equipped and badly officered or were infantry and so of little use against the well-mounted guerrillas.[39] Consequently the bushwhackers were as active as before, if not more so. Every day brought to Ewing's headquarters at Kansas City word of another raid, ambush, or outrage on Union adherents.[40]

In August, Ewing concluded that unless his forces were tripled the only possible way he could uproot the bushwhackers was to adopt drastic measures against their families. Two-thirds of the families in western Missouri, he estimated, were kin to the bushwhackers and were "actively and heartily engaged in feed-

Correspondence (Thomas Carney), Military Affairs, 1863–1865; Kansas Adjutant General's Correspondence, Fifteenth Kansas Volunteer Cavalry —all in Kansas State Archives, KSHS. See in particular, in the last-named depository, an undated memorial from the soldiers of Company K, Fifteenth Kansas, to Carney accusing him of depriving them of the right to elect their officers and of "low contemptable [sic] demagogue tricks" in order to control the regiment for political purposes.

[39] *OR*, ser. I, XXII, pt. 2, 322–323, 416.

[40] For events in the District of the Border during the summer of 1863, see *ibid.*, pt. 1, pp. 319–461; *ibid.*, pt. 2, pp. 589–590; Kansas City *Western Journal of Commerce*, June 6–August 25, 1863; Miller, *Memorable Decade*, pp. 94–96.

ing, clothing, and sustaining them." Hence, on August 3, he recommended to Schofield that the families of several hundred of the worst guerrillas be transported to Arkansas. This, he reasoned, would not only deprive the guerrillas of their aid, but would cause those whose families had been removed to follow them out of the state. Terms then would be offered to the less offensive ones remaining.[41]

On August 14 Schofield approved Ewing's plan, but cautioned him to be very careful in its execution. Four days later Ewing promulgated General Order No. 10. It instructed officers commanding companies and detachments in the District of the Border to arrest and send to the provost marshal, with a written statement as to their guilt, all men and women not heads of families who were willfully aiding and encouraging the bushwhackers. The officers were to discriminate carefully between those who aided the guerrillas under compulsion and those who aided them from "disloyal motives." Wives and children of known bushwhackers and women who were heads of families and who voluntarily assisted them were to be ordered to remove themselves "forthwith" from the district and from Missouri. These people were to be permitted to take with them their stock, provisions, and household goods. Those failing to depart promptly were to be taken to Kansas City for shipment south. Guerrillas who voluntarily surrendered would be protected by the military until banished with their families. Troops carrying out the order were enjoined not to "burn or destroy any buildings, fences, crops, or other property," excepting furnaces and blacksmith shops. Officers and men of Kansas military units, both organized and unorganized, were forbidden to enter Missouri without written permission from some commanding officer or other authority.[42]

While thus combating directly the guerrilla menace, Ewing did not neglect the protection of Kansas. For this purpose he established a cordon of posts and patrols along the border from Westport to Mound City. When completed, this defense system

[41] *OR*, ser. I, XXII, pt. 2, 428–429.          [42] *Ibid.*, pp. 450–451, 460–461.

ran as follows: at Westport, four companies of cavalry; at Little Santa Fe, three companies of cavalry; at Olathe, one company of infantry; at Aubry, two cavalry companies; at Coldwater Grove, one cavalry company; at Paola, one company of infantry; and at Mound City, one infantry company.[43] The major and more mobile portion of these forces, it will be observed, was concentrated between Westport and Aubry, in a position to cover the Santa Fe Trail and the country where all of Quantrill's previous raids had occurred.

Ewing probably did not expect this line of border posts to prevent guerrilla forays altogether, but apparently was confident that it would be sufficient to provide timely warning when they were attempted, so that troops could be rushed to the threatened area and the countryside alerted. Toward the middle of August he advised Carney that his special force of state troops no longer was required and that he could disband it. This Carney accordingly did, no doubt gladly since it had cost him over $10,000.[44] There had been no raids of any consequence into Kansas since May, and fear of the bushwhackers had generally subsided throughout the state. The people of Lawrence in particular felt secure. Affirmed the *Journal* on August 6: "Mr. Quantrill is not invited to do bloody and infamous deeds upon unarmed men in any part of this State; but we venture to say that his chance of escaping punishment after trying on Lawrence just once are indeed slim—perhaps more so than in an other town of the state."

[43] *Ibid.*, pp. 419–420.
[44] *Senate Journal, 1864*, p. 30. The 1864 legislature, however, refunded this sum to Carney.

# VII

## *Lawrence*

THE war had brought increased prosperity to Lawrence. Government spending, in the form either of soldier's pay or of contracts for freighting, storage, and produce, was the main factor. The frequent passing of troops and travelers made things "lively and fresh." In spite of heavy enlistments the town's population had increased to over 3,000, and it was now the "second city in Kansas." The buildings and houses were all "substantial," with, as one newspaper man noted, "not a cottonwood among them." The citizens confidently expected even better times when the bridge across the Kaw was completed and the railroad constructed from Wyandotte.[1]

From the very beginning of the war Lawrence had considered itself in special danger of an attack by the Missourians. Three times already, in the stormy days of 1855 and 1856, they had marched on the town and on one of these occasions had sacked it. They were known to regard Lawrence as the citadel of "Kansas abolitionism" and to harbor a grudge against it for its part in the territorial struggle. Refugee Negroes all testified that their former masters frequently talked of going to Lawrence and

[1] Leavenworth *Daily Conservative*, April 15, 1863; *Kansas State Journal* (Lawrence), August 6, 1863.

"wiping it out." Consequently, whenever there was a report or rumor that the bushwhackers were coming, the whole town and surrounding countryside flew into a near panic. But as the war went on and the bushwhackers never came, the people of Lawrence gradually began to feel that the probability of a raid was not so great as first imagined. After all, the town was nearly fifty miles from the border and much too populous to be attacked by any except a very large force, which of course would be observed long before it got that far.

Lawrence relied mainly upon its local home guard companies for defense against bushwhackers. It posted details from these companies along the roads and trails leading to the town to act as sentinels. The townspeople were confident that if given "fifteen minutes notice" they could muster "over five hundred fighting men" and easily beat off any raid. But by the summer of 1863, owing to the increasing sense of security, the home guard companies were in a moribund condition, the men more often than not failing to report for duty. Newly elected Mayor George Collamore, however, still believed the guerrilla menace to be serious and therefore early in June requested Ewing to station a permanent force in the town. Ewing complied by sending "20 odd men" under Lieutenant T. J. Hadley. Collamore also reorganized the home guard and obtained better arms for it. He stored these weapons in an armory where the companies could readily obtain them in case of an emergency.[2]

On July 31 Lieutenant Hadley received a letter from his brother, a member of Ewing's staff, stating that spies reported that Quantrill planned to raid Lawrence within the next few days. Hadley showed the letter to Collamore, who at once called out the local troops, detailed pickets, and alerted the countryside. Once again the bushwhackers did not appear, and after several days of anxiety the townspeople concluded that it was just another false alarm. Collamore did not reveal the reason for the

---

[2] H. E. Lowman, *Narrative of the Lawrence Massacre* (Lawrence, 1864), pp. 10–39.

sudden preparations, and many of the citizens laughed at him and his "great scare." Despite Collamore's protests, Ewing withdrew a battery which he had sent to reinforce Hadley's detachment on learning of the threat to Lawrence. Captain Edmund Ross's company of the Eleventh Kansas marched away, too, after spending several days in the town. Hadley and his men stopped scouting the countryside and withdrew to the north bank of the Kansas River. Discouraged by the apathy of his fellow citizens, Collamore made no effort to revive the local picket system.

On the night of August 20, following a railroad meeting at the Eldridge House, the people of Lawrence went to bed, feeling, as John Speer expressed it two weeks previously in the *Tribune,* that there was no "special danger." [3]

Possibly Quantrill had contemplated a raid on Lawrence ever since he returned to Missouri from Texas early in May. During the summer he sent spies into Lawrence, and according to one rather dubious account he himself spent a few days surveying the adjacent country. About August 10 he held a council of the various guerrilla captains and made definite arrangements for the raid. A week later nearly 300 bushwhackers gathered at a farmhouse on the Blackwater River in Johnson County, Missouri, some fifty miles from the Kansas line. Quantrill took command and told the men of their destination, offering to excuse anyone who did not care to go. On August 19 he marched westward along the south side of the Blue, passing through Chapel Hill and stopping for the night on the middle branch of the Grand River. During the day he was joined by a hundred Confederate recruits under Colonel John D. Holt, who accidentally encountered the guerrillas and were invited to come along and be "christened." On the morning of the twentieth his strength was further augmented by fifty bushwhackers from the Grand and Osage River

---

[3] *Ibid.,* pp. 38–42; *Kansas State Journal* (Lawrence), August 6, 1863; *Kansas Weekly Tribune* (Lawrence), August 6, 13, 1863; Leavenworth *Daily Conservative,* August 4, 1863; O. W. McAllaster, "My Experience in the Lawrence Massacre," *KHC,* XII (1911–1912), 402.

region.[4] This gave him in all approximately 450 men, the largest such force assembled under one command during the Civil War.

At about 6 P.M., August 20, Quantrill and his men rode into Kansas south of the village of Aubry. There are two versions of their entry. One, contained in the official report of Ewing, which was based on the reports of subordinates, has it that they passed five miles from Aubry and that the officer in charge there, Captain J. A. Pike, was not aware of their passage until 7 P.M., when he received word from one of his scouts to that effect. The other version is contained in a statement made over forty years later by William Gregg, one of Quantrill's lieutenants. According to Gregg the guerrillas crossed into Kansas only one and a half miles from Aubry and in full view of Pike, who drew up his company on the prairie as if to give battle. But instead of fighting, he allowed the guerrillas to ride on unmolested. Quantrill, for his part, ordered his men to "make no attack unless fired upon." [5]

Both accounts agree that Pike made no effort to pursue and harass Quantrill, but remained at Aubry. The sole action taken by him was to forward word of Quantrill's penetration to the other stations along the line and to Kansas City. He neglected utterly to send a warning to any of the towns in the interior.[6] Quantrill doubtlessly chose to enter Kansas south of Aubry because in so doing he would outflank the heavier concentrations

[4] *OR*, ser. I, XXII, pt. 1, 320, 579–580; F. W. Hinsey, "The Lawrence Raid," Kansas City *Star*, July 19, 1903; Edwards, *Noted Guerrillas*, pp. 188–189; Connelley, *Quantrill*, pp. 311–315. Connelley had access to a manuscript, prepared by William Gregg, one of Quantrill's followers. A shorter account of the Lawrence raid by Gregg appeared in a newspaper, a clipping of which is to be found in the Oscar Eugene Learnard Collection, vol. IV, University of Kansas. This article will hereafter be cited as Gregg Statement.

[5] Gregg Statement; Connelley, *Quantrill*, pp. 315–316.

[6] *OR*, ser. I, XXII, pt. 1, 580, 583; "Statement of Captain J. A. Pike concerning the Quantrill Raid," *KHC*, XIV (1915–1918), 311–318. In this statement, Pike dealt with certain minor matters of dispute, but did not explain why he neglected to send warning westward.

of border guards to the north, but fortune had put in his way an incompetent officer.

The guerrilla column rode on across the prairies to a point two and a half miles south of Squiresville, ten miles inside of Kansas. There they halted briefly to rest and feed the horses. When darkness came, they resumed their march, turning southwest to Spring Hill and then northwest to Gardner, which they reached at 11 P.M. Three miles beyond Gardner they veered due north to the petty settlement of Hesper. There was no moon and the terrain was difficult, so they now pressed guides into service from the countryside. Quantrill was familiar with this region, but realized that a loss of direction would be fatal for his enterprise. As soon as a guide no longer was of any help or, in some cases, was recognized as being a refugee from Missouri, his men shot him. They also killed a number of other persons along the way, in particular those who were on a previously prepared list of victims. The column reached Franklin "at the first glimmer of day." The bushwhackers now broke into a gallop, for their objective was only a few miles away, and they were behind schedule. "Push on, boys," one of them, probably Quantrill, cried, "it will be daylight before we are there."

Quantrill halted his command on a summit southeast of Lawrence and sent several men ahead to reconnoiter. Some of his followers were worried and hesitant and suggested turning back. Quantrill, however, was adamant. "You can do as you please," he said. "I am going into Lawrence." Then, without waiting for the scouts to return, he ordered his men to advance.[7]

The raiders came charging down the streets of Lawrence shortly before five o'clock on the morning of Friday, August 21. Most of the townspeople were still asleep or just rising. They had received absolutely no warning that Quantrill was on the way. Although numerous persons saw the guerrillas during their march, they had assumed them to be Union cavalry and paid

[7] Lowman, *Narrative of the Lawrence Massacre*, pp. 42, 47–56; Connelley, *Quantrill*, pp. 323–328, 335–336; Andreas, *History of Kansas*, p. 321.

them no particular heed. Others who perceived their true identity and guessed their destination had for some strange reason made no effort to spread the alarm. Only one man had tried to bring word to Lawrence, and he had been thrown from his horse and killed. Thus the first inkling the town had of the presence of the bushwhackers was the sound of firing, the clatter of hoofs, and the agonized screams of the wounded and dying.[8]

Quantrill apparently had resolved to crush out by sheer terror any attempt to resist him. His followers shot down every man that they saw and fired into windows and doorways as they galloped by. Near the center of the town they came upon an encampment of twenty-two recruits of the Fourteenth Kansas, which they literally trampled into the ground, killing seventeen of the young men. They also attacked a nearby camp of colored recruits, but most of these managed to flee to safety. As soon as they reached the center of the town, they dispatched flanking parties to the east and west to cut off escape in those directions. The main body then dashed up Massachusetts Street, Quantrill in the lead. People who witnessed them as they thundered past never forgot the sight—bearded, long-haired, wild-looking men, with slouch hats and greasy, sweat-stained shirts, yelling, shooting, and riding superb horses with reckless skill. Arriving at the river, they cut the cables of the ferry, then turned back and surrounded the Eldridge House, the town's central building.

They approached the hotel cautiously. It was a four-story brick structure with iron grillwork on its lower front windows and presented a formidable appearance. But the occupants, bewildered by the sudden onslaught, possessed neither the will nor the means to defend the place. One guest, Captain A. R. Banks, waved a sheet from an open window in token of surrender and called for Quantrill. He rode forward, a slender, unshaven man with four pistols in his belt and two more in saddle holsters. "What is your intention in coming to Lawrence," cried Banks.

[8] *Kansas State Journal* (Lawrence), October 1, 1863; *OR*, ser. I, XXII, pt. I, 583.

"Plunder," replied Quantrill. "We are defenseless and at your mercy," said Banks, "the house is surrendered, but we demand protection for the inmates." Quantrill promised that they would not be harmed if they offered no resistance. He then ordered them to leave their rooms and come down to the street. As they did so, they were met by two bushwhackers who relieved them of their money and valuables. Other guerrillas went inside and pillaged the rooms. When they finished, they set the hotel on fire—the second time within ten years that the Missourians had burned it.

Some of the bushwhackers tried to kill the people from the Eldridge House once they were out on the street. Only the efforts of their guards and Quantrill's personal intervention saved them. Finally Quantrill had the prisoners conducted to the nearby City Hotel for safekeeping. During the days when he was Charley Hart he had stayed at this establishment and when sick and penniless had been befriended by the proprietor, Nathan Stone, and his family. In gratitude he now ordered his men to spare the City Hotel and not to molest its inhabitants. He set up his headquarters there, conversed with the Stones and other old acquaintances, and ate a hearty breakfast.

Meanwhile the bushwhackers dispersed in small bands to loot, burn, and murder. The town was completely in their possession. Except in a few isolated instances they encountered no resistance. Most of the killing took place in the western part of the town where Todd's band operated. Colonel Holt's recruits generally abstained from the massacre, as did some of the guerrillas. One young bushwhacker expressed regret to a Lawrence woman that he was involved in the affair and said that he had been told that they were going to Lawrence merely to retrieve stolen horses. Occasionally the raiders even helped women remove their furniture before applying the torch to their homes and advised the menfolk to stay out of sight. They did not kill or rape any women.

At first the men of Lawrence thought that the bushwhackers intended to kill only certain persons, such as soldiers, Negroes, and Red Legs. Consequently many who might have otherwise escaped remained in their homes and fell easy victims. When it became apparent that the raiders were engaged in wholesale and indiscriminate slaughter, they fled to the cornfields and woods west and east of the town or concealed themselves in the brush along the riverbank. Others, whose dwellings were surrounded before they could get away, hid in cellars, attics, barns, and gardens or even disguised themselves as women. Still others sought refuge under the board sidewalks or in a bush-covered ravine which ran through the middle of the town. And some preserved their lives by saying that they were Southerners or by advancing the claims of Masonic brotherhood.

Charles Robinson, John Speer, George Deitzler, Wilson Shannon, H. D. Fisher, and other prominent citizens managed to escape. Mayor Collamore, Josiah Trask of the *Journal*, and two of Speer's young sons were not so fortunate. Collamore was suffocated by smoke while hiding in the bottom of a well.

The bushwhackers were handicapped in their plundering by lack of transportation. Nonetheless they robbed the banks and looted all the stores and most of the houses. In particular they ransacked the saloons, yelling "Whisky! Whisky!" as they smashed into them. They forced individuals to surrender their money, watches, and jewelry and in several instances even tore wedding rings off the fingers of women. Most of them obtained fresh horses to replace their own jaded mounts or to bear additional plunder. What they could not carry off or use, they burned. They proceeded systematically from building to building, setting fire to each. The smoke swirled straight up into the sky and "stood like great black columns along the street." Soon the entire town was darkened with an overhanging cloud of smoke and ashes.

At nine o'clock the bushwhackers began to reassemble. Probably their lookouts atop Mt. Oread reported the dust of approaching troops, and Quantrill decided that it was time to begin the march back to Missouri. His men formed into a column, and as suddenly as they came, they departed. Behind they left an almost totally devastated town. The business center along Massachusetts Street was destroyed, a hundred homes were burned, and another hundred damaged by fire. Dead lay scattered along the streets, "some of them so charred that they could not be recognized, and could scarcely be taken up." Bones were visible among the embers, and "the sickening odor of burning flesh was oppressive." In some places corpses were piled in heaps, and bodies were "on the sidewalks, in the streets, among the weeds in the gardens, and in the few remaining homes." In all, an estimated 150 men had lost their lives and thirty others were wounded.[9]

At the top of Quantrill's list of those to be killed in Lawrence was the name of Jim Lane. The death of Lane was one of the prime motives and objectives of the raiders. If he were captured, Quantrill intended to take him back to Missouri and burn him at the stake. Fortunately for Lane, he had been away from Lawrence for a short period just prior to the raid, and a Negro spy reported to Quantrill that he was not in town. So, instead of making straight for Lane's home in the northwest corner of Lawrence, Quantrill did not go there until after he disposed of the Eldridge House. This gave Lane a chance to scamper, clad only in a nightshirt, to the safety of a cornfield. Mrs. Lane met

---

[9] The above account of the Lawrence Massacre is based upon the following sources: C. M. Chase to the Sycamore, Ill., *True Republican and Sentinel*, August 22, 1863, Chase Letters; R. G. Elliott, "The Quantrill Raid as Seen from the Eldridge House," in Eldridge, *Early Days in Kansas;* Cordley, *History of Lawrence;* Lowman, *Narrative of the Lawrence Massacre;* Connelley, *Quantrill;* H. D. Fisher, *The Gun and the Gospel* (4th ed.; Kansas City, Mo., 1902); Sara T. D. Robinson, "Personal Recollections of Mrs. Sara T. D. Robinson of the Quantrill Raid of August 21, 1863" (a manuscript, written about 1905, in the library of the University of Kansas). Lowman's work, written shortly after the raid from his own first hand experiences and knowledge, is the basic account, from which all the later printed sources, with the exception of Elliott's, derive to varying degrees. Contemporary newspaper accounts of the raid were also consulted.

Quantrill and a group of bushwhackers at the door and informed them that her distinguished husband was not at home to receive visitors. Since this was in accordance with what he had already been told, Quantrill made no attempt to find the Senator, but contented himself with burning his newly built and expensive brick house.

Lane acquired a pair of pants from a farmer and, astride a plow horse, galloped into Lawrence soon after the raiders left, shouting, "Let us follow them boys, let us follow them!" A dozen or so men responded to the call and set out in pursuit, armed with shotguns, old pepperbox revolvers, and corn knives. Lane's force picked up reinforcements on the way, so that by the time it reached Brooklyn, it numbered about thirty-five. At this hamlet, which was in flames, it made contact with the guerrillas and hung on their flank as far as the vicinity of Baldwin. Here it met and joined 200 Union cavalry under Major Preston B. Plumb.[10]

Plumb, "a tall and very slim young man with a pale face," later a Senator, had ridden all night in a desperate effort to overtake the raiders. He had received word at Kansas City at 12:30 A.M. of Quantrill's entry into Kansas and marched south from there shortly before 1:00 A.M. with about fifty men. Not knowing Quantrill's exact direction, he headed toward Olathe. As in the case of Pike, he made no effort to alert the towns in the interior. At daylight he reached Olathe and, learning that the raiders had gone toward Lawrence, moved in that direction also. At 10:30, six miles southeast of Lawrence, he met a force of 180 men under Captain Charles F. Coleman and Captain Pike. The latter had not attempted to pursue Quantrill until joined at Aubry by Coleman at least three hours after the guerrillas entered the state. Coleman, who was in charge of the Little Santa Fe post, had been notified of Quantrill's penetration at 8:15 P.M. by a courier from Pike. Coleman transmitted this message to Kansas City, where Plumb received it, and also to Olathe, asking the

[10] *OR*, ser. I, XXII, pt. 1, 580; Gregg Statement; Connelley, *Quantrill*, pp. 352–353, 398–399; Cordley, *History of Lawrence*, pp. 229–230.

officer in command there to pass the news westward. This officer thereupon sent a courier out along the Santa Fe Trail, but the courier, after riding only as far as Gardner, turned back upon learning that Quantrill already had passed through there. In the meantime Coleman had marched to Aubry, joined Pike, and then slowly followed Quantrill's trail through the night. Plumb assumed command of the Pike and Coleman troops and pushed on. When he saw smoke columns south of Lawrence, he realized that Quantrill had left the town and was moving in that direction. Therefore he proceeded to Baldwin where, soon after his junction with Lane, he finally came into contact with the bushwhackers.[11]

Quantrill retreated from Lawrence at a leisurely pace, sending out detachments to plunder and burn the farms along the way. At Brooklyn he turned off the Santa Fe Trail and took the Fort Scott road toward Ottawa. When Lane and Plumb began to press him, he turned a portion of his column about and made a brief stand. Plumb divided his command and tried to cut Quantrill off at a river ford. But the Federal horses were now badly jaded, and the movement failed. During a skirmish in a cornfield the bushwhackers charged Lane's followers and routed them. Once beyond the ford, Quantrill swerved east off the Fort Scott road and struck out across the prairie in the direction of Paola. His men now started to abandon much of their plunder.

Plumb maintained the pursuit through the long, hot afternoon. He was joined by additional troops, militia, and more armed civilians. His horses were so exhausted that they could move only at a slow trot. Toward evening, three miles northwest of Paola, Quantrill turned on his pursuers and forced them to fall back.

[11] *OR*, ser. I, XXII, pt. 1, 580, 589–590. Coleman claimed that the slowness of his pursuit from Aubry was caused by difficulty in following Quantrill's trail. On this point, two questions are in order: (1) Why was the trail of 450 men and horses difficult to follow on a summer night? (2) Why was it necessary to "follow their trail" anyway? Did it require unusual perception to realize that their objective was very likely Lawrence?

Then, instead of going through Paola, he swung sharply to the north, thereby avoiding a group of a hundred soldiers and civilians under Lieutenant Colonel Charles S. Clark awaiting him at the crossing of a creek south of Paola. Plumb did not follow, but went on to Paola, where he joined Clark, who took command. He and Clark decided to suspend the pursuit temporarily because, according to Clark, they did not know the exact route taken by Quantrill. The troops and their horses were now completely worn out. The majority of them had been on the march constantly for twenty-four hours and over a hundred miles. Many of the horses had collapsed, and a number of the men had died of sunstroke.

Quantrill halted five miles northeast of Paola. Then, at midnight, following a brush with some militia, he resumed his march. A force of 150 Missouri militia tried to intercept him at the state line, but he eluded them. By morning he was back in Missouri, having re-entered only a few miles south of the point where he invaded Kansas. Clark did not renew the pursuit until daybreak, and by the time he reached the Grand River in Missouri, the bushwhackers were scattered among the hills and woods. Many of them had abandoned their horses and were on foot. All of them were hungry and nearly exhausted, and they retained little of the loot from Lawrence.[12]

The pursuers likewise dispersed into detachments and began a remorseless hunt for the raiders. During the succeeding week they killed, so they claimed, approximately 100 guerrillas. They did not take any prisoners. The Kansans burned houses indiscriminately and "strung up" a number of "sympathizers." But they failed to capture or kill Quantrill, Todd, Anderson, Yeager, Gregg, or any of the other leaders, and the bushwhackers, although lying low, remained strong and dangerous.[13]

[12] *Ibid.*, pp. 580–592; *ibid.*, pt. 2, pp. 479–480; Connelley, *Quantrill*, pp. 404–405; Edwards, *Noted Guerrillas*, p. 200.

[13] Diary of Sherman Bodwell, August 23, 1863 (Bodwell was an officer in the Eleventh Kansas; his original diary is in the possession of the KSHS); Leavenworth *Daily Conservative*, August 27, 1863; *OR*, ser. I, XXII, pt. 1, 582, 619; Britton, *Memoirs of the Rebellion*, p. 163.

The Lawrence Massacre was the most atrocious act of the Civil War. Nothing else quite matched it in stark horror and melodramatic circumstances. It gave to Quantrill a somber notoriety which persists to this day and made him one of the great villains of American history. And it was the outstanding single event of the Civil War in Kansas, the bloody climax of the border strife with Missouri.

The bushwhackers in the main acted like fiends at Lawrence. Yet they were impelled by certain motives that makes their conduct understandable if not excusable. Foremost of these motives was a desire to revenge the atrocities and depredations of Kansans in Missouri. Wrote "One of the Sufferers" of Lawrence soon after the raid:

The universal testimony of all the ladies and others who talked with the butchers of the 21st ult. is that these demons claimed they were here to revenge the wrongs done their families by our men under Lane, Jennison, Anthony and Co. They said they would be more merciful than were these men when they went into Mo.[14]

As the bushwhackers rode about in Lawrence, shooting and burning, they cried: "Jennison!" "Osceola!" "Butler!"[15] And when a citizen asked Quantrill why he had come to Lawrence, he replied: ". . . to plunder and destroy the town in retaliation for Osceola."[16] Lawrence was the natural target for the vengeance of the people of West Missouri, for it symbolized to them Kansas and abolitionism.[17] Lawrence was also the town of Lane, whom they detested perhaps only less than Jennison.

The bushwhackers and their people, moreover, were full of

[14] "One of the Sufferers" to S. N. Wood, Lawrence, September 2, 1863, *Council Grove Press*, September 14, 1863.

[15] Paper copied by Amos Lawrence from a letter of Mrs. G. W. Collamore, wife of Mayor Collamore, sent him in 1863. See Amos A. Lawrence Papers, KSHS.

[16] C. M. Chase to the Sycamore, Ill., *True Republican and Sentinel*, August 22, 1863, Chase Letters.

[17] Gregg Statement; Miller, *Memorable Decade*, p. 97; Kit Dalton, *Under the Black Flag* (Memphis, Tenn., c. 1914), pp. 98-99.

bitterness for very specific reasons. In the words of a Missouri historian, Lawrence by 1863 had become "a mere fence-house for stolen property"—property stolen from Missouri.[18] It was the headquarters of the Red Legs in southern Kansas; they had free run of the place and sold their loot at public auctions held on its streets. The livery stables were packed with stolen horses, and Missourians who came there in quest of their plundered possessions were liable to be shot down on sight by Hoyt or some other Red Leg. The citizens either were unable to drive these bandits out or were indifferent to their presence.[19] When Quantrill's men rode into the town, they found a collection of board and straw shacks in a ravine across Massachusetts Street which were piled with household goods taken from Jackson County and inhabited by Negroes from the same region.[20] The raiders killed every one of the occupants of the Johnson House because this hotel was the local hangout of the Red Legs.[21]

The foregoing observations, however, are in no way intended to justify the massacre or exonerate the massacrers. What Quantrill's followers did at Lawrence merely demonstrates the truth of Edmund Burke's statement that there is no way of justly condemning an entire people. The vast majority of the people who were killed or burned out at Lawrence were but indirectly connected with the activities of Lane, Jennison, Anthony, and the Red Legs. At most they were culpable for countenancing this element and their deeds.[22] Very few, if any, of the really guilty

---

[18] Carr, *Missouri*, p. 334.

[19] Spring, *Kansas*, pp. 285–286. See also W. H. T. Wakefield to G. W. Martin, March 31, 1902, *KHC*, VII (1901–1902), 575–576; Leavenworth *Daily Conservative*, December 16, 1862.

[20] Gregg Statement.

[21] Elliott, "Quantrill Raid as Seen from the Eldridge House," in Eldridge, *Early Days in Kansas*, pp. 193–194.

[22] See paper read by Charles Robinson before the Kansas Loyal Legion in 1885, Kansas History Clippings, Scrapbook III, KSHS. Robinson tried to break up the Red Legs, but without success; some of them attempted to assassinate him (Spring, *Kansas*, p. 286). Certain writers have adduced that the Lawrence raiders were motivated by a desire to revenge a number

fell victim. Lane escaped, and Hoyt and the Red Legs were not even in town.[23] In fact, Charles Robinson was so struck by this aspect of the massacre that he wrote Amos Lawrence that "from all the circumstances I believe Gen'l. Lane & his element were in collusion through third persons with Quantrell."[24] Others voiced the same suspicion,[25] although there was no discoverable factual, and certainly very little logical, basis for it.

It is extremely unlikely, too, that men of the Quantrill-Todd-Anderson ilk were motivated more than slightly by any higher purpose than plunder and murder. In a strict sense they were not even Missourians, and their careers show that they were as ready to rob and slay Confederate adherents as they were Union. Thus in 1864 Todd and Anderson burned the Missouri towns of Lamar and Carthage as thoroughly and ruthlessly as they did Lawrence, and Quantrill's men also robbed and murdered pro-Southern people in Texas and Missouri.[26] Quantrill divided practically all the money taken at Lawrence among the members of Todd's gang, giving very little of it to the other bushwhackers and none whatsoever to needy families in Missouri, à la Robin Hood, as he had promised prior to the raid.[27] Most of the killing done at Lawrence, too, was committed by the gunslicks of Todd and Anderson.

---

of Missouri girls killed or injured in the collapse of a building used as a Federal military prison in Kansas City on August 13, 1863. Few of the raiders, however, ever gave this as a reason, and the evidence indicates that the raid was planned before the incident, which probably only intensified the wrath of the guerrillas. The same applies to Ewing's removal policy as embodied in his Order No. 10, which Schofield believed to have touched off the raid. See *OR*, ser. I, XXII, pt. 2, 471, 482.

[23] Elliott, "Quantrill Raid as Seen from Eldridge House," in Eldridge, *Early Days in Kansas*, pp. 193–194.

[24] Robinson to Amos Lawrence, October 6, 1863, Lawrence Papers.

[25] *Council Grove Press*, September 14, 1863.

[26] *OR*, ser. I, XXXIV, pt. 3, 742; *ibid.*, XLI, pt. 3, 328, 766; Connelley, *Quantrill*, pp. 438–448; W. F. Switzler, *History of Missouri* (St. Louis, 1879), p. 435.

[27] According to Gregg, in Connelley, *Quantrill*, pp. 419–420.

A number of reasons explain the impunity and success with which Quantrill marched into Kansas and destroyed Lawrence. Chief among them are the following:

(1) The small number of troops in the Department of the Missouri. During the summer of 1863 Schofield stripped the department of all available men and sent them to reinforce Grant and Rosecrans. As a result he had by August only 23,000 men in his vast command. Most of these, moreover, were Missouri militia. Thus Schofield, and in turn Ewing, simply lacked sufficient manpower to suppress the bushwhackers or to hold them completely in check.[28]

(2) Lane's politically motivated thwarting of Carney's attempts to raise a border-defense regiment. Although there is no way of proving that Quantrill would have been kept out of Kansas by such a regiment, it nevertheless seems reasonable to assume that the chances of keeping him out would have been improved had there been one.

(3) The failure of Pike at Aubry to send warning to Lawrence and to pursue and harass Quantrill. In the words of Ewing, "By Captain Pike's error of judgment in failing to follow promptly and closely, the surest means of arresting the terrible blow was thrown away, for Quantrill would never have gone as far as Lawrence, or attacked it, with 100 men close on his rear." [29]

(4) The failure of the civilians living east of Lawrence on Quantrill's route to sound the alarm.[30]

(5) The carelessness of the people of Lawrence themselves. Had they stationed a few volunteers or hired some men to patrol the roads leading to their town, they could have easily prevented the surprise and obtained an opportunity to organize a defense. Without such a warning the local militia companies were use-

---

[28] *OR*, ser. I, XXII, pt. 1, 13, 15–16; *ibid.*, pt. 2, pp. 290–291, 577.

[29] *Ibid.*, pt. 1, p. 580.

[30] This failure was criticized by Ewing, *ibid.*, p. 583, and by the Kansas City *Western Journal of Commerce*, September 1, 1863.

less, as the event proved. Several contemporary Kansas news-papers bluntly asserted that Lawrence had nobody but itself to blame for what happened.[31]

(6) The woeful lack of enterprise, intelligence, and courage on the part of the Union officers, besides Pike, along the border. They were not alert as to Quantrill's intentions or movements, and even with their small forces they could and should have done more to prevent him from concentrating his men and moving through Missouri deep into Kansas.

(7) As a positive factor, Quantrill's own skill and daring. His ability should not be overlooked because of his cruelty. From the purely tactical standpoint his raid was a masterpiece, con-sisting of a nearly perfect combination of timing and execution. He was, to be sure, aided by luck, but he did everything possible to minimize the necessity of luck. By his boldness in striking at Lawrence he confused and misled the Union military authorities and the people of Kansas, who found it almost impossible to believe that he would attempt such a feat. It was this fatuous be-lief that he could not and would not attack Lawrence that in large measure explains the absence of an effective defense for the town and the failure of the Federal officers to pursue him en-ergetically or send immediate warning to the town.

A number of critics attributed the lack of success in catching Quantrill once he started back to Missouri to the incompetence and cowardice of Major Plumb.[32] They claimed that he did not make a determined effort to overhaul the bushwhackers, but merely "escorted" them out of the state. The official reports, on the other hand, and the apologists for Plumb blamed the jaded condition of his horses for his failure to bring the raiders to bay. This last seems to be the more likely explanation, al-

---

[31] *Council Grove Press*, September 14, 1863; Oskaloosa *Independent*, September 5, 1863.

[32] *White Cloud Kansas Chief*, September 10, 1863; *Council Grove Press*, September 14, 1863; Sara Robinson, "Personal Recollections"; Spring, *Kansas*, p. 231.

though there is evidence that Plumb lost his nerve when he attempted to cut the raiders off at the ford south of Brooklyn.[33] All accounts and criticisms of the pursuit of Quantrill are based on the rather curious assumption that the Union forces needed only to catch up with the bushwhackers, after which they would easily defeat them. Yet at no time were they anywhere close to being equal to Quantrill's band in numbers, and for the most part they were decidedly inferior to it in weapons and fighting experience. If Plumb was in fact timid about engaging Quantrill, he had good reason to be. In a pitched battle the guerrillas would have cut his command to pieces. On at least two occasions Federal forces comparable in size and equipment to Plumb's were utterly destroyed by bands of bushwhackers less numerous than the one led by Quantrill as he marched away from the smoldering ruins of Lawrence.[34]

[33] *OR*, ser. I, XXII, pt. 1, 403, 580–583, 590; Connelley, *Quantrill*, p. 404.

[34] The two occasions referred to are at Baxter Springs, Kansas, October 6, 1863, and Centralia, Mo., September 27, 1864. That Quantrill's men were a formidable bunch is made evident by a letter of Confederate General McCulloch, who in complaining about the depredations of the "Captain Quantrill command" around Bonham, Texas, stated that he was unable to control them because he did not have any troops with the "physical and moral courage to arrest and disarm them" (McCulloch to Magruder, April 6, 1864, *OR*, ser. I, XXXIV, pt. 3, 742).

# VIII

## Order No. 11

THE shocking and bloody massacre at Lawrence called for action, and Ewing took it. On August 25 from his headquarters at Kansas City, he issued "General Orders, No. 11." Under its provisions the people residing in Jackson, Cass, and Bates counties and that part of Vernon County within the District of the Border, except those living within one mile of Independence, Hickman Mills, Pleasant Hill, Harrisonville, and Kansas City, were required to leave their homes by September 9. Those who by that time established their loyalty with the commanding officer of the military station nearest their place of residence would be permitted to remove to any military station in the district or to any part of Kansas "except the counties on the eastern border of the State." Persons failing to establish their loyalty were to move out of the district—an order to be enforced by military action if disobeyed.[1]

Ewing issued Order No. 11 for five distinct yet closely related reasons. The first of these was military. He regarded the order as vitally necessary for the suppression of bushwhacking and the prevention of further raids. The order was not a retaliation

[1] *OR*, ser. I, XXII, pt. 2, 473.

for the massacre. In substance it had already been presaged by Order No. 10 and was based on the same theory—that without a vast and impracticable increase in the forces operating against the guerrillas they could never be effectively combated unless something was done to deprive them of their support among the population.[2]

The second reason was to calm and reassure the people of Kansas. They were greatly alarmed by the massacre and feared that Quantrill would strike again. In Lawrence on the Sunday after the raid a veritable stampede occurred when a man, who had mistaken the smoke of a trash fire outside of the town for the return of the guerrillas, rushed through the streets crying "Quantrill is coming! Quantrill is coming!" Most of the men and practically all the women and children fled the town terror-stricken and spent the entire night in the fields in the rain. On the same day a similar panic was touched off in Topeka by a rumor that the dreaded Quantrill was marching on that town.[3] The order demonstrated to Kansans that the military authorities were instituting drastic measures to suppress the bushwhackers and so prevent future incursions.

Ewing's third purpose was to forestall mob retaliation against the people of West Missouri. Kansans not only were frightened by the massacre, but also were intensely angered and desirous of revenge. They tended to classify all the inhabitants of West Missouri as rebels and willing abettors of Quantrill. Their newspapers screamed for a "war of extermination" against the bushwhackers and advocated sweeping the border counties of Missouri with "fire and sword." Anthony and other such leaders called on the men of the state to assemble at Leavenworth and then cross into Missouri, destroy Independence, Westport, and

[2] See Chapter VI, p. 122. See also Schofield to Ewing, January 25, 1877, in Webb, *Battles and Biographies*, p. 265; Kansas City *Western Journal of Commerce*, September 5, 1863.

[3] Sara Robinson, "Personal Recollections"; Fisher, *Gun and Gospel*, pp. 214–215; Diary of Samuel J. Reader, August 23, 1863, KSHS.

Kansas City, and retrieve "stolen property." Ewing especially wished to head off this movement.[1]

Ewing's fourth motive was personal and political. He was greatly distressed by the massacre and shared the wrath of his fellow Kansans. Moreover, there was, as a result of the raid, much public dissatisfaction with his supposed "want of capacity to command." Almost the entire Kansas press severely criticized him and demanded his removal. Much of this condemnation, however, was politically inspired. The Wilder-Anthony coalition saw in Ewing's "failure" to stop Quantrill a golden opportunity to get him out of the way. Hardly had the ruins of Lawrence stopped smoking than the *Conservative* launched a vicious campaign of scathing invective against him, stopping short only of saying that he plotted the raid with Quantrill and shared in the loot. Ewing, who believed himself innocent of any negligence or blunder which might have made the raid possible, was thus prompted to issue Order No. 11 in an attempt to counter the attacks of the Kansas press and his political enemies.[5]

The fifth and final cause of the order was a desire on Ewing's part to placate Lane. Ewing and Lane met on the night of August 22 at Morristown, Missouri. Lane applied pressure on Ewing to adopt a policy along the lines of Order No. 11. He warned him that if he did not he would be "a dead dog." Ewing promised to do so, and Lane in return defended Ewing in a speech soon afterward at Lawrence. Ewing, ever ambitious, was amenable to Lane's influence because he wished to stay on good terms with Lane who, he believed, would be re-elected Senator.[6]

Whatever Ewing's personal motives might have been, some such program as Order No. 11 would have been put into effect.

[4] Leavenworth *Daily Times*, August 22, 1863; Leavenworth *Daily Conservative*, August 22, 1863; *OR*, ser. I, XXII, pt. 2, 472–473.

[5] *OR*, ser. I, XXII, pt. 2, 472–473; James Hanway to John Hanway, August 30, 1863, Hanway Papers; Leavenworth *Daily Conservative*, September 1, 1863.

[6] Schofield, *Forty-six Years*, pp. 79–80; Connelley, *Quantrill*, pp. 417–418.

For on the very same day that Ewing promulgated the order, Schofield sent him a letter (which obviously was not received until a subsequent date) enclosing a draft of an order almost identical to Order No. 11. The major difference between them was that Schofield's draft envisioned much harsher treatment of the people of West Missouri than Ewing's order. Schofield believed that "nothing short of total devastation of the districts which are made the haunts of guerrillas will be sufficient to put a stop to the evil." Therefore his draft order proposed that by a certain date all "disloyal persons" in Jackson, Cass, and Bates were to remove from the counties, after which all their "houses, barns, provisions, and the other property" were to be either confiscated or destroyed. Unlike Order No. 11, Schofield's proposal established no method of differentiating between loyal and disloyal persons. Consequently, although in theory it would have operated only against the latter, in practice it would have, like Order No. 11, affected all persons in the district. Furthermore, Schofield deemed nearly all the people of Jackson, Cass, and Bates disloyal, calling the region a "country inhabited almost solely by rebels." He was aware that "some innocent persons" would suffer under his plan, but regarded such suffering as "unavoidable." [7]

The condemnation of Schofield in Kansas following the massacre equaled if not surpassed that of Ewing. Lane, who had lost all his personal belongings in the raid except a nightshirt, hoped that as a result of this criticism Lincoln would be forced to remove Schofield and place in his stead a commander more sympathetic to the radicals and to himself. Therefore, as soon as he returned to Lawrence from the futile pursuit of Quantrill, Lane made a speech in which he sought to increase the popular fury against Schofield by pinning the blame for the massacre on that general's "copperhead" policies. For the time being, however, he did not join in the clamor against Ewing. He did so not only because of Ewing's promise to take drastic measures

[7] *OR*, ser. I, XXII, pt. 2, 471–472.

against West Missouri, but also because he did not want Ewing dismissed as commander of the District of the Border while Schofield remained in charge of the Department of the Missouri. He feared that any replacement for Ewing named by Schofield would be even less favorably disposed to his interests than was Ewing. The difficulty with this course, however, was that it brought him into conflict with his Leavenworth political allies, the Wilders and Anthony, who were too angry and impatient to proceed against Ewing via Schofield, but who were assaulting him directly and openly.[8] Consequently, following his Lawrence speech, Lane lapsed into a neutral attitude toward Ewing, neither publicly attacking nor defending him.

On August 26 Lane journeyed to Leavenworth, where in conjunction with Carter Wilder he sent the following telegram to Lincoln:

> The result of the massacre at Lawrence has excited feelings amongst our people which make a collision between them and the military probable. The imbecility and incapacity of Schofield is most deplorable. Our people unanimously demand the removal of Schofield, whose policy has opened Kansas to invasion and butchery.[9]

The following night he addressed an open-air mass meeting. Besides assailing Schofield, he called on his listeners and all the men of the state to assemble at Paola on September 8 for the purpose of carrying out the "extermination of the first tier of counties in Missouri." The audience, who had listened to Lane "with open mouths" and who were "boiling over with concentrated rage," greeted this proposal with "uproarious cheers." Anthony, Jennison, and Hoyt spoke in a similar vein.[10]

Ewing promptly reported Lane's speech to Schofield. He stated that it was intended "to scare the people of the border

[8] Schofield, *Forty-six Years*, pp. 80–81.

[9] *OR*, ser. I, XXII, pt. 2, 475.

[10] Leavenworth *Daily Conservative*, August 28, 1863; C. M. Chase to the Sycamore, Ill., *True Republican and Sentinel*, August 28, 1863, Chase Letters.

counties into a prompt compliance" with Order No. 11 and to make "political capital." He expressed confidence that he would be able "to control matters so as to prevent any considerable acts of retaliation" and promised to do everything possible to avoid a collision between the army and the citizens of Kansas. He added that he had rebuffed an offer from Lane to place the Paola expedition under his command.[11]

Upon receiving Ewing's report Schofield wrote Carney urging him to mollify the "just anger" of the people of Kansas and to use his influence to forestall Lane's proposed invasion of Missouri. He stated that he would not object to this expedition if it resulted only in the recovery of stolen property and if the vengeance it inflicted were confined to the actually guilty, but that inevitably it would involve "indiscriminate retaliation upon innocent and guilty alike." "You cannot expect me," he affirmed, "to permit anything of this sort." [12]

Two days later, August 31, Schofield left St. Louis and traveled in person to Leavenworth, arriving there on the morning of September 2. He first saw Carney and "several of his political friends." From them he learned, among other things, that Carney desired to "kill off" Ewing because he considered him "a formidable rival" for the Senate or else a supporter of Lane. Next he had a long private interview with Lane. With "apparent candor" the Kansas Senator stated that he had "bent the whole energies of his soul" to destroying Schofield, but that he now realized that he was mistaken and stood ready to atone for his past acts. He refused, however, to abandon his projected expedition from Paola. He professed that he would keep it under control and that he would be responsible for its conduct, and he pledged that it would do nothing beyond search for stolen property. He threatened to appeal to the President should Schofield deny the people of Kansas their "right" to go into Missouri.

In the evening Schofield had another conference with Carney. His object was to obtain the Governor's co-operation in pre-

[11] *OR*, ser. I, XXII, pt. 2, 490.     [12] *Ibid.*, pp. 491–492.

venting an invasion of Missouri. But Carney held back from agreeing to this. He hoped to make some political capital of his own out of the Paola movement by letting Lane go through with it, confident that it would turn out to be a "grand humbug." In his opinion Lane really "had no serious design of entering Missouri." Finally, however, he reluctantly promised to issue a proclamation asking the citizens of the state to abstain from invading Missouri.[13]

That night Lane again harangued a large crowd on the streets of Leavenworth. He urged all who could do so to meet at Paola on September 8 and then go into Missouri and ransack Jackson, Cass, and Bates counties—"extermination for revenge, desolation for security." Following the speech his followers adopted a series of resolutions which condemned Ewing and denounced any attempt to elect a United States Senator in 1864.[14] This marked the end of Lane's neutral attitude toward Ewing and inaugurated an open attack on Carney, whom so far neither he nor the Leavenworth radicals had publicly criticized. Although an open break between Carney and Lane would have occurred sooner or later, it was probably occasioned by an assertion in the Leavenworth *Times*, Carney's organ, that Lane was to blame for the Quantrill raid because of his opposition to the Governor's home guard regiment.[15] Lane's decision to open up an attack on Ewing stemmed from the pressure of the Wilders and Anthony and from Ewing's refusal to co-operate with the Paola movement. Possibly, too, Lane believed that Ewing was in league· with Carney.

In spite of his promise to Schofield, Carney did not issue the proclamation against the Paola movement, for he felt that it would be playing into Lane's hands to do so. Therefore, on September 4, Schofield published an order which warned that "armed bodies of men not belonging to the United States troops"

---

[13] Schofield, *Forty-six Years*, pp. 81–83.
[14] Leavenworth *Daily Conservative*, September 3, 1863.
[15] Leavenworth *Daily Times*, September 2, 1863.

would not be permitted "under any pretext whatever" to pass between Kansas and Missouri. Ewing reinforced this order two days later by posting a regiment at Coldwater Grove with instructions "to prevent the threatened invasion of Missouri by Kansas men not in the service of the United States." [16]

September 8 arrived, but instead of thousands of armed and vengeance-bent men, only a few hundred "blanketed, crestfallen, dripping people" assembled at Paola. After standing in a thundershower listening to "the stale and well-remembered 'Great Gods' of Jim Lane," they passed a resolution demanding the removal of Schofield and Ewing and the creation of a separate Department of Kansas. Then they went home. Not even the *Conservative* was able to conceal the fact that the "Paola camp meeting" was, in the words of Sol Miller, "a fizzle." Lane in particular came in for much ridicule in the press.[17]

On the eve of the Paola meeting what might be regarded as the side battle between Ewing and the Wilder-Anthony clique reached its climax. Some detectives in the employ of Ewing, but acting without his authority, arrested Anthony on the streets of Leavenworth, dumped him into a carriage, and drove off with him to Kansas City, his feet kicking in the air. Anthony's friends immediately petitioned Lincoln to punish or censure those responsible for this "outrage." Ewing, as soon as he learned of the arrest, ordered Anthony released. The rash action of his detectives, however, placed him in such a position that he no longer could resist the agitation against martial law in Leavenworth, and a few days later he revoked it.[18]

Lane's campaign to have Schofield superseded was part of a larger movement by the radicals of Missouri and Kansas against

[16] Schofield, *Forty-six Years*, pp. 83–84.

[17] Leavenworth *Daily Times*, September 10, 11, 12, 1863; *Freedom's Champion* (Atchison), September 17, 1863; Leavenworth *Daily Conservative*, September 10, 11, 13, 1863; *White Cloud Kansas Chief*, September 17, 1863.

[18] Leavenworth *Daily Conservative*, September 8, 11, 1863; Schofield, *Forty-six Years*, p. 84; Andreas, *History of Kansas*, p. 437.

that commander. With much cause the radicals had been angered by the action of the conservative-dominated Missouri State Convention in passing an ordinance of emancipation which postponed abolition of slavery in the state until July 4, 1876, and which exempted slave property from taxation. But with little or no cause the radicals believed and asserted that Schofield used his position to sustain the conservatives and to injure them. On September 1 they held an "Emancipation Convention" at Jefferson City and adopted resolutions complaining of Schofield's administration and calling on the President to replace him with Ben Butler or "some other suitable man." The convention, in addition, named a delegation to visit Lincoln and urge the dismissal of Schofield, assigning the Lawrence Massacre as the principal reason for such action.

The delegation, seventy strong, arrived in Washington on September 27. A small coterie of Kansas radicals accompanied it, including Lane and Carter Wilder. Lane was in charge of the whole delegation, Kansans and Missourians alike. On September 30 he conducted "his little army" into the East Room of the White House. John Hay, Lincoln's private secretary, thought that these Western radicals were more remarkable "for sincere earnestness and stubborn determination than for either high average intelligence or adroitness." Lincoln handled them with superb tact. After listening to a long memorial he discussed their grievances with them for several hours, then promised to give them a formal and final reply within a few days.[19]

While the radical delegates were in Washington, their friends in Leavenworth attempted to influence the President by sending him dispatches to the effect that Missouri "Paw-Paw" militia were driving Union men from their homes in Platte County. Schofield immediately ordered Ewing to investigate the matter. He soon learned from Ewing and other sources that the Leaven-

[19] John G. Nicolay and John Hay, *Abraham Lincoln* (New York, 1914), VIII, 209–220; Leavenworth *Daily Conservative*, October 4, December 26, 1863.

worth reports were unfounded and so informed Lincoln by telegram. He also wired the President that the radical delegation's memorial was "not only untrue in spirit, but most of it . . . literally false." Replied Lincoln: "I think you will not have just cause to complain of my action." [20]

And Schofield did not. Lincoln, on October 5, replied to the memorial with a letter upholding Schofield and his policies and refusing to dismiss him from his command. A week later Lane and the other radical delegates returned to St. Louis "very much crestfallen." Lane sent word to Schofield that he had stopped his "war" on him and intended hereafter not to oppose him unless "circumstances rendered it necessary." According to information obtained by Schofield, Lincoln had told Lane that whoever made war on Schofield made war on Lincoln. To this Lane had replied lamely that he had never warred on Schofield "except incidentally." [21]

Meanwhile, both civil and military authorities took steps to strengthen the defenses of Kansas against the guerrillas and to reassure its people, many of whom feared that Quantrill would attempt to retaliate for Order No. 11. Immediately after the massacre, Carney telegraphed Stanton to order the commanding officer at Fort Leavenworth to turn over to the state 1,000 stand of arms. This request Stanton promptly granted, at the same time offering to provide any other assistance within the power of the Government. On August 24 Carney called into active service the entire state militia, and having discovered that there were no arms at Fort Leavenworth, he wired Stanton asking him to supply the state with arms sufficient to meet the needs of the militia. Stanton replied the same day that the arms were ordered and that they would be assigned to Carney on his requisition. He ignored, however, a request by Carney for permission "to raise two new regiments for home protection."

Carney transmitted Stanton's authorization of arms for Kansas

[20] *OR*, ser. I, XXII, pt. 2, 584–591, 595, 601.
[21] Schofield, *Forty-six Years*, p. 99.

to Schofield and asked him to send enough to equip three regiments of infantry and cavalry. Schofield responded by ordering 3,000 stand of arms shipped to Kansas at once and by supplying horses for Jennison's regiment. These arms, along with 5,000 additional ones from Stanton, enabled the government of Kansas to equip its militia for the first time in the war. On September 16 Carney directed McDowell, commander of the state troops, to arm the militia of Johnson, Miami, and Linn counties. He also authorized McDowell to order into active service as many militiamen as he deemed necessary and instructed him to take care "that every portion of the border, from the Kansas River south," was "fully protected." Ewing accepted fifteen companies of the militia for garrison duty and posted two of them at Leavenworth and one each at Shawnee, Olathe, Paola, Mound City, Osawatomie, Lawrence, Topeka, Council Grove, LeRoy, Wyandotte, Atchison, Doniphan, and Marysville. He informed Schofield of this arrangement on September 19 and stated that he would not need the militia companies over six weeks or two months, by which time he expected the danger from the guerrillas to be ended and the populace calmed down.[22]

Missouri conservatives attacked Order No. 11 as "inhuman" and "barbarous."[23] But in spite of their criticism and the protests of the people affected by it, Ewing, backed by Schofield, carried out its terms implacably. By the end of September over two-thirds of the civilian population of Jackson, Cass, and Bates counties had evacuated the area. This exodus, as foreseen by Schofield, occasioned much suffering, and the Kansas troops enforcing the order were guilty of a certain amount of plundering and other outrages. There were, however, few if any such scenes as depicted by the Missouri artist George Caleb Bingham in his famous propaganda painting, "Order No. 11."[24] Although

[22] *OR*, ser. I, XXII, pt. 1, 576–578; *ibid.*, pt. 2, 467–468, 470, 537–538, 545.

[23] Kansas City *Western Journal of Commerce*, September 5, 1863, quoting the St. Louis *Republican*.

[24] Bingham's painting, executed out of personal hatred for Ewing, de-

later, during the winter, many of the evacuees managed to return, the order, in conjunction with the relentless pursuit of the
guerrillas in Missouri and the strengthened border defenses of
Kansas, forced the bushwhackers farther into the interior of Missouri and caused them to scatter into smaller bands in order to
obtain food and shelter. Never again did they raid a Kansas town.

---

picts a band of Kansas Red Legs looting and burning a Missouri farmhouse.
One of the Red Legs has just killed a young man, and another, oblivious
to the pleas of a beautiful young woman at his feet, is preparing to shoot
the elderly head of the house. Astride a horse, complacently supervising
this scene of horror, is Ewing, while near him is another Union officer
who probably is Jennison. Anyone familiar with Ewing's efforts to combat
the Red Legs realizes at once how viciously unfair this painting is.

# IX

# The Tribulations of General Blunt

NO one in the radical camp hated General Schofield more than did General Blunt. His reasons were not merely political, they were personal. Early in 1863, following the Battle of Prairie Grove, Schofield had written to Curtis that Blunt should be relieved of field command and assigned exclusively to the primarily administrative duties of the District of Kansas. Blunt's campaign against Hindman, declared Schofield, had been "a series of blunders," and his army had "narrowly escaped disaster where it should have met with complete success." Blunt learned of this letter and very naturally was incensed. He intrigued with Curtis against Schofield and through Lane's influence thwarted Schofield's confirmation as major general by the Senate.[1]

With this background, the placing of Blunt under Schofield's command in May of 1863 was bound to lead to trouble between the two generals. All that was needed was an occasion, and this was soon supplied. Schofield, by dividing the District of Kansas in half and by transferring Blunt's headquarters to Fort Scott, deprived Blunt of control over the quartermaster depot at Fort Leavenworth. This control, for reasons previously explained,

[1] *OR*, ser. I, XXII, pt. 2, 6, 94–95; Schofield, *Forty-six Years*, pp. 63–64; Blunt, "Civil War Experiences," *KHQ*, I (May, 1932), 240.

had a high pecuniary and political importance to Blunt, and he determined not to abandon it without a struggle. Therefore he claimed the right to give orders to Major L. C. Easton, chief quartermaster at Fort Leavenworth, on the grounds that General Orders, No. 48, of the Department of the Missouri appointed Easton quartermaster of several districts, including his own, the District of the Frontier. Blunt's contention, however, was totally incorrect, for Easton was subject to orders only from Schofield and the chief quartermaster of the department. Easton appealed the matter to Schofield, who sustained him and tartly reminded Blunt of his proper sphere of authority. In fact, one of the main reasons Schofield had removed Fort Leavenworth from Blunt's jurisdiction was to put an end to "irregularities and abuses" in the quartermaster service in Kansas. In notifying Halleck of his action on the matter, Schofield declared that if Blunt refused to submit to the restrictions imposed on him he saw "no way of preventing the recurrence of such abuses but by removing him from command."[2]

The foregoing controversy took place in June. Blunt did not acquiesce in its outcome, but for the time being was too preoccupied with other concerns to press his case. During July he undertook another campaign in the Indian Territory, with the objective of driving the Confederates from the Arkansas River and capturing Fort Smith. With about 3,000 men, mainly Negroes and Indians, he marched from Fort Gibson, crossed the Arkansas River, and on July 17 near Honey Springs met and defeated 6,000 poorly armed Texans and Indians under the half-drunk and totally incompetent General Douglas H. Cooper. He pursued Cooper a few miles, then returned to Fort Gibson, unable to go on because of illness and fearful that he would be overwhelmed by what he believed was a superior Confederate army at Fort Smith.

In the meantime he had learned of Schofield's intention to remove him if "abuses and irregularities" continued in his com-

[2] *OR*, ser. I, XXII, pt. 2, 326–327, 392–393.

mand. Moreover, he was aware of Carney's efforts in Washington
to have him dismissed, and he suspected that Carney and Schofield were leagued against him. Therefore, feeling that his position was stronger and his prestige enhanced by the success at
Honey Springs, he now turned, as he expressed it, from the
enemy at his front to the "secret assassins" at his rear.[3]

First, on July 25, he wrote a letter to Carney. Calling him a
"thief," he dared Carney to present the charges against him which
he understood Carney had taken to Washington, but had failed
to show to Lincoln, and to be prepared "to substantiate them."[4]
Next, on July 26, he addressed a long letter to Stanton. A "combination composed of traitors, Government peculators, and
Copperheads," he charged, was persecuting him. Schofield was
a coward and incompetent. Major Easton at Fort Leavenworth
was a traitor and corrupt. Carney was guilty of "wholesale robbery" of refugee Indians. Others, "proslavery demagogues of
Missouri and Kansas," were out to ruin him because he had "no
affinity for rebels." Working through Schofield, they all had
"determined . . . to sacrifice this command by withholding
troops for the purpose of sacrificing and getting rid of me."[5]

Finally, after resting his pen for five days, he appealed directly
to Lincoln. Stating that he had learned that Carney had filed
serious charges against him, such as sharing in the spoils of the
Red Legs, he demanded a court-martial to investigate the accusations and to establish his innocence. He then repeated his in-
dictment of Schofield, Carney, and Easton and complained of
lacking sufficient troops and supplies and of being in peril of
being crushed by the enemy. He concluded by again requesting
a court-martial, threatening, if not granted one, to challenge
Carney and Schofield to duels.[6]

Nearly three weeks passed before Lincoln replied to the irate
Kansas general:

[3] *Ibid.*, pt. 1, pp. 447–462; Blunt, "Civil War Experiences," pp. 243–245.
[4] Blunt to Carney, July 25, 1863, Moonlight Papers.
[5] *OR*, ser. I, pt. 2, 398–399.        [6] *Ibid.*, ser. 1, LIII, 565–567.

Yours of July 31 is received. Governor Carney did leave some papers with me concerning you, but they made no great impression upon me, and I believe they are not altogether such as you seem to think. As I am not proposing to act upon them, I do not now take the time to re-examine them. I regret to find you denouncing so many persons as liars, scoundrels, fools, thieves, and persecutors of yourself. Your military position looks critical, but did anybody force you into it? [7]

If there were any answers from Stanton or Carney, there is no record of them. Still so sick that he could not ride a horse, Blunt remained at Fort Gibson until late August. He called on Schofield for reinforcements so that he could resume the offensive south of the Arkansas. Schofield, however, believed this movement to be unnecessary and refused to send any. But on August 22 Blunt was able to get hold of 1,500 troops under Colonel William F. Cloud, and with his army thus increased to 4,500 he crossed the Arkansas River. A march of sixty miles in forty-eight hours brought him to the Confederate camp on the Canadian River, but the enemy had retreated at his approach. Their main body under General William Steele retired south to the Red River, while 3,000 others under General William L. Cabell went east toward Fort Smith. Blunt followed Steele's force and on the night of August 25 drove it from Perryville, which his army then burned. Feeling that it was useless to pursue Steele further, he next moved on Fort Smith. He arrived before that place on August 31 and on the following day occupied it as Cloud drove Cabell from a position atop Devil's Backbone, a nearby mountain. His health now gave way completely, and after reporting to Schofield on September 11 that "the entire Indian Territory and Western Arkansas are in my possession and under my control," he returned in a carriage to Fort Scott.[8]

Schofield was not in the least impressed by Blunt's victories.

[7] *Ibid.*, p. 567.
[8] *Ibid.*, XXII, pt. 1, 597–609; *ibid.*, pt. 2, pp. 439, 465–467, 517, 525, 534–535; Blunt, "Civil War Experiences," pp. 243–247.

In fact, he had come to the not-too-reluctant conclusion that the Kansan must be relieved of his command. Having "received, from various sources, official and unofficial, reports of fraud, corruption, and maladministration in the Department and District of Kansas, while under the command of Major-General Blunt, which seemed to demand official investigation," he had ordered a thorough inspection of military affairs in Kansas and the Indian Territory, both past and present. The inspection was completed by the end of September and revealed that "gross abuses" and "general demoralization and lack of efficiency" prevailed in the District of the Frontier. Although it uncovered no evidence directly implicating Blunt in fraud and corruption, it did make clear that he had allowed these to occur and had done nothing to correct the poor condition of his troops. On October 1 Schofield informed Halleck that he intended to replace Blunt with Brigadier General John McNeil, but before he could carry out this decision an event took place which came close to removing Blunt not only from his command but from the world itself.[9]

Late in August, Major Henry Z. Curtis, Blunt's chief of staff and a son of General Curtis, established a small military post at Baxter Springs, Kansas, a point fifty-eight miles south of Fort Scott and so near the boundary of the state that many thought that it was in the Cherokee Nation. The purpose of the post was to protect and facilitate communications between Fort Scott and Fort Gibson. Called a fort, it consisted merely of some barracks and a dirt and log embankment about four feet high. The garrison was composed of 150 Negro and white troops commanded by Lieutenant James B. Pond, "a brave and gallant officer." Pond did not arrive at the post until October 4 and, finding it too small for the additional men he brought with him, had the western end of the embankment removed so that it could be extended in that direction.

[9] *OR*, ser. I, XXII, pt. 2, 319, 586–588, 595–597.

At noon, October 6, most of Pond's men had just gathered for lunch in a cooking camp some 200 feet south of the fort; the remainder, all his serviceable cavalry, sixty in number, were away foraging. Suddenly they were startled by an outburst of revolver firing, and almost before they realized what was happening, they were beset by a large force of riders coming at them from east, west, and south. They ran pell-mell to the fort, so closely pursued that the enemy entered the enclosure nearly at the same time as they did. Grabbing their weapons, they counterattacked and drove their assailants back outside the fort and into the surrounding woods and brush. Then followed thirty minutes or so of long-range firing, after which, for no apparent reason, the enemy broke off the assault and rode away.

The soldiers of the garrison did not know it yet, but the men who had surprised them and nearly captured the post were Quantrill's. Four days previously they had assembled, about 400 strong, at their old rendezvous on the Blackwater. Order No. 11, the constant harassment of the Union troops, and the coming of cold weather had made their operations hazardous and unprofitable, and so they were on their way to Texas for the winter. They had been marching southwestwardly along the border when early on the morning of October 6 scouts reported a wagon train ahead. Quantrill, sniffing a chance for plunder, ordered his advance guard to press ahead and ascertain the nature of the train. Instead of finding the train, it discovered the cooking camp at Fort Baxter, of whose existence the bushwhackers had been ignorant. As soon as his main force came up, Quantrill had about half of his men charge the camp, while he and Todd with the rest moved around to the prairie on the north side of the fort. There he spotted a small group of wagons, accompanied by a detachment of Federal cavalry, approaching Baxter Springs along the Fort Scott Road.

By a fantastic coincidence, this column was Blunt's personal escort and headquarters' train on the way to Fort Smith. Neither

Blunt nor any of his party heard the firing at Baxter Springs, nor could they see the fort itself. When 400 yards distant from the fort he ordered a halt so as to enable the escort and wagons to close up. While this was taking place, he and some of the other officers noticed Quantrill's men coming from the east. Since they were dressed in Federal uniforms, it was at first thought that they were Pond's cavalry out drilling. Blunt, however, became suspicious and formed his escort in line of battle, at the same time sending Captain Tough, his chief of scouts, forward to reconnoiter. Tough and Major Benjamin S. Henning of Blunt's staff both reported that the approaching horsemen were enemies. Blunt now rode forward to see for himself. Hardly had he proceeded fifty yards when the bushwhackers made their true identity evident by opening fire. Blunt's escort, taken completely by surprise, fired only a few scattering, ineffectual shots and then broke into terrified flight across the prairie. The guerrillas were far better mounted and quickly overtook the panic-stricken Federals. Every soldier whom they caught they ruthlessly shot, stripped, robbed, and mutilated. In all they killed over seventy of the hundred men in Blunt's party, among them ironically, Major Curtis. Blunt himself escaped only because of the fleetness of his superb horse.

At about two o'clock Quantrill returned to the fort and demanded its surrender. Pond refused, and Quantrill, who by then was drunk and bragging about his victory over Blunt, decided not to resume the attack. Later in the afternoon he marched away, having attained the high point of his blood-soaked career. Blunt, accompanied by a handful of stragglers, came into the fort in the evening. He remained there for five or six days, then returned to Fort Scott, badly shaken by the experience through which he had just gone. The people of Kansas were greatly perturbed by this fresh outrage of Quantrill's, and anti-Lane papers sharply criticized Blunt for allowing his men to be surprised. Blunt denied that he had been negligent and placed all the blame for the massacre on the cowardice of his escort. His defense, however, was not altogether convincing, and his reputation was severely impaired.¹⁰

Blunt's near brush with death at Baxter Springs did not cause Schofield to relent in his determination to supersede him. On October 19 he issued a circular directing General McNeil to "repair to Fort Smith, Ark., and relieve Maj. Gen. James G. Blunt in command of the District of the Frontier." He instructed the latter to go to Leavenworth upon being relieved and report by letter to him "for further orders." Another section of the same circular extended the District of the Border to include all of Kansas, thus realizing Carney's desire to have the entire state under Ewing's command.

Blunt received the order deposing him on October 24 at Fort

¹⁰ The above account of the Baxter Springs Massacre was based on the following sources: Blunt's Report, October 19, 1863; Report of Lieutenant Colonel Charles W. Blair, October 15, 1863; Major Henning's Report, October 7, 1863; Lieutenant Pond's Report, October 7, 1863; and Quantrill's Report, October 13, 1863—all in *OR*, ser. I, XXII, pt. 1, 688–701. Also used were W. H. Warner, "The Battle and Massacre at Baxter Springs, October 6, 1863," in Andreas, *History of Kansas*, pp. 1152–1153; Blunt, "Civil War Experiences," pp. 247–248; and Connelley, *Quantrill*, pp. 421–434. Main, but cautious, reliance was placed on the reports of Pond, Blunt, and Henning. Other accounts, especially that of Warner, give a version which in many important respects, particularly as to the conduct of Blunt prior to Quantrill's attack on the escort, is fundamentally different from Blunt's and Henning's. Henning, however, was in an excellent position to see all that took place in connection with the attack, and he wrote his report the day after the massacre. Warner's account, on the other hand, was written over twenty years later. As nearly as can be gathered, he was a surgeon in the fort and so could not have personally witnessed the attack. Henning's report, moreover, corroborates Blunt's, which was written twelve days after Henning's. Of course Henning may have been motivated by a desire to protect Blunt from blame, but there is no way of knowing this. Insofar as possible, other reports, including Quantrill's, were used to check and countercheck Pond, Blunt, and Henning. Connelley provides material from W. H. Gregg, one of Quantrill's men, and Cyrus Leland, Jr., who related the experiences of his father. Connelley attempts to use all the sources indiscriminately, with the result that there are numerous contradictions and absurdities in his account of the massacre.

Scott. On October 28 he wrote Schofield that the order left him in doubt as to whether it was contemplated that he be relieved at Fort Scott or at Fort Smith, "although the literal reading of the order makes it imperative that I should be relieved at the latter place." For this reason and because he felt responsible for his command until "properly relieved," he would proceed to Fort Smith. As soon as he was relieved, he would report to Leavenworth "without delay."

Blunt arrived at Fort Smith on November 9 and found McNeil already in charge. Although he conducted himself in an insolent manner, he did not overtly challenge McNeil's authority. Awaiting him at Fort Smith was a commission from the War Department to organize a regiment of Negro troops at that place, and he used this as an excuse for remaining. On December 9, after completing the organization, he let loose his resentment at Schofield in a long, angry letter to Stanton. Schofield was endeavoring to destroy him and his army, he wrote. Legally, he was Schofield's superior, for Schofield's rank as a major general had never been confirmed by the Senate. Unless assigned to a field of active service he would resign from the army. In no event would he continue to serve under Schofield, and he deemed it his duty to say that he would not report to Schofield by letter from Leavenworth as ordered, "or hold any further intercourse with him, except to prefer charges against him for incompetency and cowardice." Several days later Blunt stormed into McNeil's headquarters and before a number of shocked onlookers launched into a profane tirade against Schofield, boasting of having once defeated Schofield's confirmation as major general and of his ability to do so again. Following this "vulgar display" he headed back to Kansas, a general without an army.[11]

Schofield's removal of Blunt from the command of the District of the Frontier, attended as it was by the incorporation of all of Kansas into Ewing's district, was a severe blow not only

[11] *OR*, ser. I, XXII, pt. 2, 663, 666, 681–682, 689–693, 727–728, 735–737, 742–743; Blunt, "Civil War Experiences," p. 249.

to Blunt, but also to Blunt's patron, Senator Lane. For it deprived Lane of the last vestige of the politically and financially profitable control that he had exercised via Blunt over army contracts and the organization of troops in Kansas and threatened to give this control to Carney and his circle, whom he suspected of being in league with Schofield and Ewing. Therefore he endeavored with increased intensity and added urgency to have Lincoln erect Kansas once again into a separate department and to name as its commander General Curtis. Lincoln was in a receptive mood to Lane's solicitations, for he had already come to the conclusion, based on the advice and experience of Schofield, that it was impossible for the same commander to satisfy both the people of Missouri and those of Kansas or to reconcile their differences. Therefore, on December 31, he directed Stanton "to have the Curtis department fixed at once." This the Secretary promptly did, and on January 1, 1864, the War Department officially announced that Curtis was assigned to the Department of Kansas, which was to include also Colorado, Nebraska, and the Indian Territory. Several weeks later Lincoln, in order both to placate the Missouri radicals and to satisfy Schofield's desire for a field command, replaced Schofield with Major General William S. Rosecrans.[12] Schofield then joined Sherman in Tennessee and during the succeeding months gave the lie to Blunt's allegations by his efficient handling of the Army of the Ohio in the Atlanta Campaign and by his important victory over Hood at Franklin.

The pro-Lane radical press in Kansas warmly welcomed and gleefully reported the announcement that Curtis was to command a separate Department of Kansas. Carney and his adherents, on the other hand, were downcast by the news, for they were fully aware that Lane was behind Curtis's appointment and that Curtis would favor Lane and his group to the detriment of their own aspirations. The Leavenworth *Times*

[12] Schofield, *Forty-six Years*, pp. 106–112; Nicolay and Hay, *Lincoln*, VIII, 471–474; *OR*, ser. I, XXXIV, pt. 2, 7, 757.

tried to arouse popular sentiment against Curtis by predicting that he would commit tyrannical acts under the guise of military necessity, but it is doubtful whether these forebodings created much impression. When Curtis arrived in Kansas to assume command, he was met by a clamoring swarm of contract seekers.[13]

The re-creation of the Department of Kansas left Ewing with only the Missouri portion of his District of the Border. On January 8 Schofield incorporated this remnant into the District of Central Missouri and ordered Ewing and the Kansas troops to report to Curtis for duty. The transfer was tantamount to placing Ewing under the orders of Lane: on February 28 Curtis assigned Ewing to the command of Colorado Territory, thereby completely exiling him from Kansas politics. But Ewing had too many influential friends for this arrangement to last long. On March 21 the War Department ordered him to report to Rosecrans, who in turn placed him in command of the District of St. Louis.[14]

At Lane's instance, the War Department order establishing the Department of Kansas specified that it was to include the "military post of Fort Smith." On February 23 Curtis directed Blunt to proceed to Fort Smith and "resume command" of the Indian Territory. But when Blunt reached Fort Smith on March 12, he was amazed and enraged to discover that the War Department's order had been interpreted literally, and that Brigadier General John M. Thayer of the Department of the Arkansas had taken over the town of Fort Smith, leaving only the "military post," a "stone inclosure, about 200 feet square," within the Department of Kansas. Worst of all, Blunt found that practically all the troops in the vicinity were within Thayer's line, whereas he had only a few Indian regiments scattered throughout the Indian Territory. He did, however, possess one advantage: the quarter-

---

[13] Leavenworth *Daily Conservative*, January 5, February 24, 1864; *Kansas Weekly Tribune* (Lawrence), January 8, 1864; Leavenworth *Daily Times*, December 29, 1863.

[14] *OR*, ser. I, XXXIV, pt. 2, 49, 464, 682.

master's depot and transportation were located at the post. He therefore attempted to gain control of the troops in the town by withholding rations from them, thereby forcing them to report to him or else starve.

Naturally Thayer and Colonel William Judson, who was in immediate command at Fort Smith, protested against these high-handed tactics. They appealed to Major General Frederick A. Steele, commander of the Department of the Arkansas, who in turn brought the matter to the attention of Halleck and Stanton. Halleck informed Grant, now at the head of all Union armies, of the "confusion and difficulty" at Fort Smith and asked that he approve Blunt's removal from command. This Grant did, whereupon Lincoln added his consent, and on April 17 the War Department issued an order attaching the military post of Fort Smith and the Indian Territory to Steele's department and directing Blunt to report back to Kansas and Curtis. Steele transmitted this order to Judson and instructed him to arrest "any officer" who interfered with its execution. But Blunt relinquished the post peaceably and for the second time in a matter of months returned to Leavenworth a commandless general.

On the very day that the War Department relieved Blunt, Curtis had written him that the Department of Kansas was already "better provided with generals than troops." Curtis, consequently, had considerable difficulty in reassigning Blunt. In the end he resorted to the expedient of carving out a completely new district for him, "The District of the Upper Arkansas," with headquarters at Fort Riley. Blunt assumed command of this remote and unsettled region on August 2. He had at his disposal scarcely 300 troops, a force more befitting a major than a major general.[15]

[15] *Ibid.*, pp. 408, 444–445, 537, 617–618, 621, 733, 763–764; *ibid.*, pt. 3, pp. 160–161, 192, 196–197, 200, 213–215; Blunt, "Civil War Experiences," pp. 250–251.

# X

# *Lane Embattled*

IN spite of the appointment of Curtis to command in Kansas, the early weeks of 1864 found Lane's political prospects in serious jeopardy. His popularity was badly impaired, most of the state press was hostile to him, and the newly elected legislature was "largely anti-Lane." Five main factors were responsible for the decline in his fortunes.

(1) There was widespread and intense anger over the naming, in October, 1863, of Lane's political crony, Mark Delahay, to the important post of United States District Judge for Kansas and Nebraska. Especially offended were numerous "brilliant and ambitious" lawyers, who not unjustly thought that they were better qualified for the position than Delahay. Even stanch pro-Lane men were inclined to agree with Sol Miller that the "only bench Delahay is suited for is one with a hole in it." [1]

(2) Feeling was particularly strong in the border counties that Lane was responsible for the Lawrence Massacre because of his interference with Carney's efforts to raise a home guard

[1] Hawkins Taylor, "My Year in Kansas," Topeka *Commonwealth*, December 4, 1886; Charles Robinson to Mrs. Robinson, December 27, 1863, Robinson Papers, KSHS; Troy *Kansas Chief*, February 7, 1889; Speer, *Life of Lane*, pp. 244–245; H. Griswold to S. N. Wood, October 9, 1863, Wood Papers; *White Cloud Kansas Chief*, October 19, 1863.

regiment. Many people in this region also believed that Lane had willfully neglected their railroad and other economic interests.[2]

(3) Leavenworth business elements, other than those grouped around the Wilders and Anthony, blamed Lane for the Kansas branch of the Pacific Railroad going from Wyandotte to Lawrence rather than to Leavenworth and for the defeat in the Senate of a treaty with the Delaware Indians which would have facilitated the construction of a railroad from Kansas City to Leavenworth.[3]

(4) Lane was unpopular in the northern tier of counties because of his opposition to the Henderson Amendment of the Pacific Railroad Bill of 1862, which called for giving the Kansas legislature the option of permitting the Hannibal and St. Joseph Railroad to build directly westward from St. Joseph instead of, as the bill stipulated, entering the state at Atchison.[4]

(5) Lane had lost the support of many of his erstwhile followers and allies. The break with Carney and his group was of course the prime example of this. Others had left him because they resented what they considered his shabby treatment of George Crawford. A great many of his best and most influential friends were out of the state serving in the army at posts to which he had secured their appointments. He himself had weakened his hold on the state by remaining in Washington for long periods of time and by failing to answer letters from the people back home. "Nothing is so fatal to a politician's success," observed a shrewd veteran politician, "as failure to answer letters." [5]

Three groups sought to increase the upsurge of dissatisfac-

[2] Leavenworth *Daily Times*, September 12, 1863; *Kansas Weekly Tribune* (Lawrence), February 7, 1864; *Kansas State Journal* (Lawrence), February 11, 1864.

[3] *Kansas State Journal* (Lawrence), July 30, 1863; Leavenworth *Daily Times*, November 8, 1863, February 13, 1864.

[4] *Nemaha Courier* (Seneca), February 20, 1864; *White Cloud Kansas Chief*, March 26, 1863.

[5] Taylor, "Year in Kansas," Topeka *Commonwealth*, December 4, 1886.

tion with Lane and to take political advantage of it. There were, first, the members of the old Robinson faction. These "disappointed, though perhaps deserving aspirants for place and power" were "raw from continued snubs and rebuffs" inflicted by Lane and desperately wanted revenge. They numbered in their ranks "many of the staidest, most respectable men in the State." [6]

Secondly, there were Carney and his circle, which included McDowell, Champion Vaughn and his son John, and Ward Burlingame, all of Leavenworth, and James F. Legate of Lawrence and Samuel N. Wood of Council Grove. The Leavenworth *Times*, the *Council Grove Press*, and other Carney papers filled their columns with anti-Lane material, charging him with flagrant corruption, coarse personal vices, and responsibility for the weak border defenses that resulted in the Lawrence Massacre. Carney made full use of the patronage available to him in the militia and in Jennison's regiment and campaigned to win over Lane's abolitionist following by outdoing him in professions of radicalism, going so far eventually as to advocate Negro suffrage.[7]

Pomeroy and the Atchison crowd comprised the third group. Pomeroy had come more and more to resent his colleague's superior influence with the President and the resultant near monopoly of the Federal patronage. He wished to control this patronage for himself and to supplant Lane as the political leader of Kansas.[8] In addition, he and other Atchison railroad promoters believed that Lane had favored the railroad ambitions of Leavenworth at the expense of their own.[9]

Pomeroy, in keeping with his cautious and circumspect char-

[6] Leavenworth *Daily Conservative*, July 3, 1863.

[7] *Ibid.*, January 14, 15, 1864; Schofield, *Forty-six Years*, p. 108.

[8] Troy *Kansas Chief*, February 7, 1889; reprint of article by Sol Miller, based on a conversation with Ward Burlingame, Carney's private secretary in 1863–1864, in the Topeka *Commonwealth*, April 13, 1879, with comments by John Speer, in Kansas Legislature Clippings, Scrapbook, vols. I–II, KSHS (hereafter cited as Miller-Burlingame-Speer Article).

[9] *Freedom's Champion* (Atchison), February 11, 18, 1864.

acter, did not come out openly against Lane, but proceeded against him covertly both in Washington and in Kansas. On the national level he took the lead in espousing the candidacy of Treasury Secretary Salmon P. Chase for the 1864 Republican presidential nomination. On February 20, 1864, he issued his famous "circular" stating that Lincoln could not be re-elected and that only Chase could bring Republican victory in November. He advocated Chase not because of antislavery radicalism, as most historians have assumed, but because he figured that as long as Lincoln were President he would play second fiddle to Lane patronagewise, whereas if Chase became President the situation would be reversed, especially if Chase were under obligations to him.

On the state level he encouraged Carney in his plans to have himself elected to Lane's seat in the Senate during the 1864 session of the legislature. Sometime late in 1863 he confidentially informed Carney through an intermediary that the Senate Republican leaders had held a caucus in which such powerful men as Ben Wade, "Zach" Chandler, and John Sherman had declared themselves in favor of Carney's election to the Senate in 1864 and had pledged to sustain him by holding the seat against any other man the Kansas legislature might name in 1865, when Lane's term expired. This intelligence, along with Pomeroy's personal prompting, caused Carney, who had been hesitating, to go ahead with his previously formed intention of seeking election to the Senate in 1864.[10]

The legislature which convened at Topeka on January 12 was predominantly and intensely anti-Lane. The Carney forces, led by the veteran ex-Lane politicos, Sam Wood and Jim Legate, controlled its organization and by means of skillful maneuvering, persuasive blandishments, and perhaps bribery succeeded in forming an overwhelming coalition in favor of Carney's election to the Senate.[11] By the third of February, Representative D. Rog-

[10] Miller-Burlingame-Speer Article.
[11] Charles Robinson to Mrs. Robinson, January 19, 1864, Robinson

ers of Neosho County, a Lane adherent, was writing a friend that "Thomas Carney will be elected U.S. Senator by a large majority in spite of everything the friends of Lane can do. I do not think Lane will get over twenty votes in the House and not more than five in the Senate . . . I wish you were here to see the feeling against Lane." [12] Six days later Rogers' prediction was substantially borne out. Meeting in joint session, sixty-eight legislators voted to elect Carney United States Senator for the term beginning March 4, 1865. Since Carney was the only candidate and they believed that the election was illegal, Lane's followers abstained from the balloting, with the exception of Representative H. Cavender of Anderson County, who went on record as being "against a fraud." [13] Three nights later Carney held a $2,000 "victory banquet," featuring champagne and oysters, at the Topeka House. His happy guests got so drunk that the local Presbyterian preacher felt called upon to condemn the celebration in a special sermon.[14]

Lane was fully and acutely aware of the opposition against him back home. Even before the election of Carney he began taking measures to regain his popularity and retain his control of the Republican Party and politics of Kansas. It was at this point that his relationship with Lincoln became supremely important. Despite his association with the anti-Schofield, radical movement he continued to enjoy the friendship and confidence of the President. In addition, Lincoln regarded him as the political and popular leader of Kansas and desired his assistance in securing renomination. But perhaps of greatest moment, Lincoln apparently was convinced, largely as a result of Lane's representations,

---

Papers, KSHS; Leavenworth *Daily Conservative*, January 17, 19, February 21, 23, 1864; *Council Grove Press*, February 8, 1864; *White Cloud Kansas Chief*, February 4, 11, 1864.

[12] D. Rogers to J. C. Redfield, February 3, 1864, D. Rogers Papers, KSHS.

[13] *Senate Journal, 1864*, pp. 3–4, 200–201; *House Journal, 1864*, pp. 294–295.

[14] Diary of Isaac T. Goodnow, February 12, 1864; *Kansas State Record* (Topeka), March 8, 1864.

that Carney, McDowell, Wood, and the other members of the Kansas anti-Lane faction were leagued with Pomeroy in support of Chase.[15] Lincoln therefore accorded Lane a free hand in dispensing Federal appointments in Kansas. Lane used this patronage power to prod wavering adherents back into line or to replace those who had failed to sustain him with men upon whom he could rely. By obtaining extended furloughs for his friends in the army, they were enabled "to do duty for Lane in Kansas, in browbeating and intimidating his opponents." He also had Sidney Clarke, provost marshal of the state, appoint deputies in every county, and, as if local talent were insufficient, he imported outsiders to aid him in his campaign. One of these was a "Dr. King," described as a brilliant speaker and singer, but with no moral character, who while in Kansas "defiled all the women and swindled all the men that were susceptible to his charms." [16]

Another of Lane's outsiders was Hawkins Taylor of Iowa,

[15] Troy *Kansas Chief*, February 7, 1889; *White Cloud Kansas Chief*, October 13, 1864. See also W. W. H. Lawrence to Lane, February 15, 1864, Robert Todd Lincoln Collection, Library of Congress, stating that Carney, Pomeroy, McDowell, Legate, and several Indian agents were using their influence and positions to defeat Lincoln. Lane turned this letter over to Lincoln. Despite Carney's contact with Pomeroy and Chase it is not clear from available evidence whether he and McDowell were in fact anti-Lincoln. Their newspaper, the Leavenworth *Daily Times*, came out in favor of Lincoln for President on February 9, 1864, and continued to support him. Pomeroy, of course, was avowedly opposed to Lincoln and even advocated disbanding the Republican Party (*Council Grove Press*, April 30, 1864). The Atchison *Champion*, which reflected Pomeroy's views, continued to criticize Lincoln through the spring of 1864. Wood as early as the spring of 1863 came out against Lincoln, denouncing him as "altogether too truckling and timeserving for the position he occupies" (*Council Grove Press*, April 13, 1863). Wood favored Fremont or Chase (*ibid.*, May 7, 14, 28, 1864). See also on this subject Delahay to Lincoln, August 8, 1864, Ewing to W. P. Dole, August 26, 1864, Carney to W. P. Dole, September 22, 1864, Ed. Russell to Lincoln, September 22, 1864, and Conway to Lincoln, October 20, 1864, all in Robert Todd Lincoln Collection.

[16] Troy *Kansas Chief*, February 7, 1889; *White Cloud Kansas Chief*, March 3, July 7, 14, October 13, 1864; *Freedom's Champion* (Atchison), February 25, 1864.

who came to Kansas in the capacity of Federal Mail Agent. Taylor arrived in Topeka—"literally a mud town"—on the day after Carney's senatorial election. After getting a rapid fill-in on the political situation from Richard Hinton, correspondent of the *Conservative*, he held a "caucus" with John Speer and Sidney Clarke in which they mapped out a campaign to destroy the popularity of the legislature and Carney. Then, during the succeeding weeks, he, Speer, Clarke, and other Lane workers toured the state arranging and conducting anti-Carney meetings and engaging in numberless private conversations with editors and other influentials. In the course of his travels he discovered that every Kansas politician, in the opinion of all the other politicians, was a "shyster" and that as a consequence this appellation had no real significance. He found, too, that "half the men of Kansas were in the army, or at the front in some capacity, and that an overwhelming proportion of the home men were in office, either in the civil or military service of the United States or state government." Practically all who did not have an office were "hoping for or expecting an appointment in some of the services named, and it was of much interest to them all to have a United States senator as friend who controlled the appointing power at Washington." The essence of Kansas politics, he soon perceived, derived from the fact that the Government had

surrounded the state on the east and south with a line of forts, and each fort being a sort of mint in a small way to contractors, caused the Lane and anti-Lane fight to embrace the military commanders in the field, and at each of these military forts, making the contest a mixture of principle and dollars and cents, and a good deal more of the latter.

Taylor and his co-workers labeled the election of Carney a "fraud" and claimed that his principal legislative backers, Wood and Legate, were both, "by common consent, at the head of all the political Kansas shysters." Such pro-Lane papers as the *Conservative*, the Lawrence *Tribune*, the Wyandotte *Gazette*, the

Junction City *Union*, the Topeka *Record*, and the Emporia *News*, all of whose editors had government offices and printing for which they were beholden to Lane, filled their pages with resolutions, editorials, and letters denouncing Carney and the "Fraud." This agitation continued week after week and gradually produced a public feeling which, if not exactly pro-Lane, was anti-Carney and "anti-fraud." Thus men who earlier in the winter had extolled Carney now criticized him severely on account of the election, which they denounced as being unconstitutional and undemocratic.[17]

Carney and his supporters tried desperately to defend themselves against the powerful Lane counterattack. They argued that since the Federal Constitution gave the states the right to fix the time and mode of electing U.S. Senators and since the laws of Kansas prescribed only the mode and not the time the election was completely legal. They declared, too, that in holding the election they had merely done what Lane himself had intended to do until he discovered that the legislature was hostile to him. But the Lane forces ignored this assertion and pointed out with considerable justice that choosing a Senator a year ahead of time not only was contrary to accepted practice, but also had deprived the voters of a chance to express their preferences through the election of legislators committed to various senatorial aspirants.[18]

By April, Carney decided that the election had been a bad blunder. He came to this conclusion, however, less because of the storm raised by the Lane faction than because he had discovered that Pomeroy had misled him as to the attitude of the

[17] Taylor, "Year in Kansas," Topeka *Commonwealth*, December 4, 1886; Leavenworth *Daily Conservative*, February 24, 1864; *White Cloud Kansas Chief*, March 3, 1864; *Olathe Mirror*, January 23, 30, February 20, 1864; *Nemaha Courier* (Seneca), February 13, 20, March 12, 1864; *Weekly Osage Chronicle* (Burlingame), February 6, 13, 1864.

[18] Leavenworth *Daily Conservative*, February 11, 1864; *Council Grove Press*, February 8, 15, 1864; *White Cloud Kansas Chief*, February 25, 1864; *House Journal, 1864*, pp. 504-508.

Senate Republican leaders. Soon after the election he received a letter from Pomeroy congratulating him on its outcome, but also containing these chilling words: "The next Legislature will, no doubt, ratify the action of the present, thus giving you the seat beyond question." Greatly alarmed, Carney hastened to Washington as soon as the legislature adjourned to ascertain the true state of affairs there. Much to his dismay and disgust he learned that no such caucus as described by Pomeroy had ever occurred and that Wade, Chandler, and Sherman had not promised to defend his right to a seat in the Senate. On the contrary, all these men said that such a course on their part would establish a dangerous precedent which might well result in the premature loss of their own Senate seats. Pomeroy, in short, had used Carney as a mere pawn in his own campaign against Lane and then had discarded him.[19]

Carney postponed abandoning his claim to the senatorship in the hope of gaining control of the Republican State Convention, which was scheduled to meet in Topeka on April 21 in order to select delegates to the party's national convention at Baltimore. But the Lane forces retained their grasp on the party machinery, and when the convention assembled, they completely dominated it. Jennison, on whom Carney relied to control the southern Kansas delegates, could not even obtain a seat for himself. There was nothing left for Carney to do except to resign "all claims to the Office of United States Senator into the hands of the people." He remained steadfastly determined, however, to end Lane's political domination and succeed him as Senator. Feeling against Lane was still strong and widespread. By effecting an agreement with the Democrats, Carney and the other anti-Lane Republicans felt that they stood an excellent chance of carrying the November elections and of securing a majority in the legislature. Meanwhile, they drew encouragement from the Leavenworth election of April 4, in which McDowell badly defeated Anthony for mayor in a contest marked by street

[19] Miller-Burlingame-Speer Article.

riots and attempts by Anthony to seize the ballot boxes and use military force.[20]

The next clash between Lane and Carney occurred in May. Once again military patronage was the issue. Early in the month Curtis requested Carney to furnish more troops for the defense of the border. Carney eagerly acquiesced. By May 12 he was in Washington, offering the services of two regiments of 100-days men. Lane and Wilder protested to the President, claiming that Carney wanted only to obtain patronage. Lincoln did not give a definite reply to Carney, but informed him of Lane and Wilder's opposition and said that since they composed a majority of the Kansas congressional delegation he must respect their wishes.[21] Angered, Carney on May 13 wrote the following letter to Lincoln:

I have to ask that you will either accept or reject the proposition I made in my communication on the 12th inst. I hope however that you will not allow the lives and homes of the citizens of Kansas to be jeopardized, by the objections you suggested in our conversation, that "Senator Lane would probably oppose the raising of the troops, or if raised would oppose the appropriation for their pay, in consequence of the patronage thus conferred on the Governor of Kansas."

Lincoln, now irritated also, returned Carney's letter with this endorsement:

The within letter is to my mind so obviously intended as a page for a political record as to be difficult to answer in a straight forward business-like way. It is not my recollection that I said to you, "Senator Lane would probably oppose raising troops in Kansas, because it would confer patronage on you." What I did say was that he prob-

---

[20] "Harny" to J. F. Legate, April 18, 1864, and "McBride" to Carney, April 18, 1864, Stevens Papers; *Council Grove Press*, April 30, 1864; Leavenworth *Daily Conservative*, March 20, 30, April 5, 6, 22, 23, 24, 1864; Leavenworth *Daily Times*, April 5, 1864; *White Cloud Kansas Chief*, April 7, 1864; *OR*, ser. I, XXXIV, pt. 3, 53–56, 84.
[21] James F. Legate to Wood, May 19, 1864, Wood Papers.

ably would oppose it because you and he were in a mood of opposing whatever the other should propose! I did argue, generally, too, that in my opinion there is not a more foolish or demoralizing way of conducting a political rivalry, than these fierce and bitter struggles for patronage.[22]

Lincoln, in fact, was heartily tired of the whole Kansas imbroglio. When Pomeroy kept soliciting him to appoint one Ellsworth Cheeseborough assessor of the District of Kansas, in preference to the candidate recommended by Lane, Thomas Sternbergh, Lincoln gave vent to his annoyance by writing: "I wish you and Lane would make a sincere effort to get out of the mood you are in. It does neither of you any good—it gives you the means of tormenting my life out of me, and nothing else." [23] Yet Lane's nominee, it should be noted, received the post. As one of Pomeroy's friends wrote to John Ingalls from Washington early in May, "Lane is very powerful with the President. My own impression is that Pomeroy has a good deal of influence *with Chase and the Radicals*, but *none* with *Lincoln*." [24]

At the Baltimore convention in June, Lane played a prominent part in helping to secure Lincoln's renomination.[25] Following the convention he returned to Kansas, where during July and August he toured about mending his political fences and making speeches in favor of Lincoln. In these speeches he always took care to identify himself with the President and the regular Republican or Union Party and to accuse Carney and his other opponents of "dividing" the party and aiding the Copperheads. As usual with him, however, he devoted a large portion of these

[22] Correspondence published in Leavenworth *Daily Conservative*, July 31, 1864.

[23] Lincoln to Pomeroy, May 12, 1864, Basler, ed., *Complete Works of Lincoln*, VII, 338.

[24] Albert H. Horton to John Ingalls, May 1, 1864, John J. Ingalls Papers, KSHS. Horton was coeditor with Ingalls of the Atchison *Champion*.

[25] W. O. Stoddard, "The Story of a Nomination," *North American Review*, no. 328 (March, 1884), pp. 263–273.

harangues to self-praise and justification. The following excerpts from his speech at Troy are representative:

> Before I was elected my enemies said I would have no influence, but now they complain Jim Lane has too much influence.

> When I reached home, after an absence of many months, I found a baby, a little boy four months old, that I had never seen before.

> I love my wife.

> Jim Lane loves the women.

> Jim Lane is a friend of the negro.

> I once rode thirty miles to kick a man, to make him an open enemy.

> They tell you they are opposed to Jim Lane, but do not tell you who they are in favor of. They oppose me, but do not favor anybody else.

> They have called your humble servant all the hard names they could think of, but a fool—they have never yet called Jim Lane a fool.[26]

The Lane faction dominated the Republican State Convention which met at Topeka on September 8 to select the state ticket and to choose the congressional candidate. After six ballots the delegates nominated Colonel Samuel J. Crawford of Garnett for Governor. They required only one ballot to nominate Sidney Clarke to replace A. C. Wilder in the House of Representatives. The convention adjourned the same day it convened.[27]

The gubernatorial candidate, Samuel Crawford, was colonel of the Second Kansas Colored Regiment and had a creditable war record. He was little known, however, and the Republican press hastened to build him up. He owed his nomination largely to the delegates from the Kansas regiments at Fort Smith. These

---

[26] *White Cloud Kansas Chief*, August 4, 1864.
[27] Leavenworth *Daily Conservative*, September 9, 10, 1864.

regiments were for the most part officered by Lane supporters, and the rank and file did not participate in choosing the delegates. Crawford's candidacy was designed by Lane to appeal to the soldier vote and to the patriotic fervor of the noncombatant citizen.[28]

Sidney Clarke, the congressional candidate, was provost marshal of the state and had a reputation tarnished by involvement in a government claims scandal. Lane had neither intended nor desired his nomination. But Clarke, by making a number of trades and alliances with various elements in the convention, had confounded the prophets who had felt certain that Carter Wilder would be renominated. When Lane met Clarke shortly after the convention, he angrily predicted that Clarke would drag the entire Republican ticket down to defeat, himself with it.[29]

Indeed, Clarke's candidacy was a bitter pill which many Republicans, especially in Leavenworth, refused to swallow. Chief among these was "Web" Wilder, who believed that Lane had cheated his brother out of the nomination. Wilder was no longer connected with the *Conservative*, having sold it to Marcus H. Weightman in order to assume the post of Surveyor General of Kansas and Nebraska. He now publicly broke with Lane and strove to discredit him by charging that his advocacy of Lincoln was insincere. Weightman also was offended by Clarke's nomination and in reporting the convention declared: "The ticket is a poor one, will not be elected, and will have our undivided opposition." Ten days later, however, he abandoned this blanket

[28] *White Cloud Kansas Chief*, October 6, 1864; Leavenworth *Daily Times*, September 24, 1864; "George A. Crawford," *KHC*, VI (1897–1900), 245. See also two undated and unlabeled newspaper clippings in S. J. Crawford Scrapbooks, vol. II, KSHS (hereafter cited as Clippings, Crawford Scrapbooks, vol. II). One of the clippings contains the testimony of Jacob Stotler, president of the convention, who stated that Lane announced his desire for Crawford's nomination at a meeting in St. Louis prior to the convention.

[29] Stotler, in Clippings, Crawford Scrapbooks, vol. II; "Session of 1865," Emporia *Weekly Globe*, January 20, 1887, Kansas Legislature Clippings, Scrapbook, vols. I–II, KSHS.

condemnation and supported all but Clarke. In order to counteract the anti-Clarke feeling in Leavenworth, Anthony and Clarke purchased the *Evening Bulletin* of that town.[30]

The anti-Lane Republicans held their convention in Topeka on September 13. They entitled themselves the "Regular Republican Union Party" and chose for their gubernatorial candidate Solon O. Thacher of Lawrence and for their congressional nominee Brigadier General Albert L. Lee of Doniphan County. Thacher was judge of the Fourth Judicial District and had long figured in Free State and Republican politics as a member of the conservative faction. He had close financial ties to the Carney group as president of the Leavenworth, Lawrence, and Fort Gibson Railroad Company, of which James McDowell was treasurer. Lee was the chief of cavalry of the Union army in Louisiana. His nomination was obviously intended to counteract Crawford's military glamor. The convention went on record as favoring the re-election of Lincoln and called on "all good men, irrespective of party, to unite in putting down the 'one man power' in Kansas." Its nominees were supported by such leaders as Carney, Pomeroy, Robinson, Cyrus K. Holliday, and George Crawford, who had been Colonel Crawford's chief rival at the Lane Republican convention. The Leavenworth *Times*, the Lawrence *Journal*, the Oskaloosa *Independent*, the *White Cloud Kansas Chief*, and the Atchison *Champion*, whose editor, Ingalls, was the candidate for Lieutenant Governor, placed its ticket at their mastheads. The *Conservative* advocated Lee until October 7, when it returned completely to the Lane fold under the new ownership of John W. Wight. Local conventions of "Union Republicans" throughout the state chose candidates for the legislature, most of whom were committed, either overtly or implicitly, to vote for Carney as the next Senator.[31]

[30] Leavenworth *Daily Conservative*, September 7, 1864; Leavenworth *Daily Times*, September 20, October 8, 1864.

[31] Leavenworth *Daily Times*, June 9, September 16, 1864; Leavenworth *Daily Conservative*, September 16, October 7, 1864.

On the same day that the anti-Lane Republicans met, the Democrats also convened in Topeka. As in 1862 they did not name a state ticket, declaring it "inexpedient" to do so, but instead tacitly endorsed the candidates of the "Union Republicans." In fact, they were almost moribund, being without an effective organization or a single important newspaper. At their June 1 convention to select delegates to the Democrat National Convention in Chicago, they had announced themselves in favor of "making Kansas a free white State"—a platform at least five years out of date. Yet there were an estimated 8,000 to 9,500 Democratic voters in the state, and the anti-Lane Republicans counted heavily on their assistance for victory. Wrote Thacher to McDowell: "The Lane ticket is terribly weak. If the Democrats will only act fair we can rid the State of the hold of these fellows [the Lane faction]." Lane partisans accused Thacher and his followers of being "copperheads" and secret supporters of McClellan, the Democratic presidential candidate.[32]

Some of the anti-Lane Republicans refused to go along with the Union Republican convention in favoring Lincoln's reelection. Under the name "Radical Democrats" they held yet another convention in Topeka on September 13 and issued a statement denouncing Lincoln as a "King George" and urging that he withdraw from the Republican nomination so that loyal men could support that party.[33] The leader of the anti-Lincoln movement was Robinson. He had been embittered toward the President as a result of his experiences while Governor. He regarded Lincoln as being "corrupt, weak & spiteful" and as having "no principle whatever on any subject."[34] During the summer of 1864 his journalistic organ, the Lawrence *Journal*, beat the drums for Chase and Fremont and printed the anti-Lincoln speeches

[32] Leavenworth *Daily Conservative*, July 3, 1863, September 15, 16, 1864; Thacher to McDowell, September 9, 1864, McDowell Papers; Wilder, *Annals*, pp. 390–393.

[33] *Kansas State Journal* (Lawrence), September 15, 1864.

[34] Robinson to Mrs. Robinson, February 28, 1864, Robinson Papers, KSHS.

of Wendell Phillips. He presided over the Radical Democrat convention and along with Pomeroy was named by it as a delegate to a convention of anti-Lincoln ultraradicals at Cincinnati.[35]

Although the Radical Democrats attracted little attention and exercised even less influence, there were a fairly large number of Kansans in 1864 who were not at all friendly toward Lincoln, mainly because of his backing of Lane and particularly because of his appointment of Delahay to a United States judgeship. These people, most of whom were anti-Lane politicos and disappointed office seekers, tended to agree with the Lawrence *Journal* when it declared that "Lincoln is Lane" and with the Atchison *Champion* when it asserted that the Delahay appointment was "an act of unjustifiable insolence."[36] The overwhelming vote that Kansas gave Lincoln in 1864—the largest proportionately of any Northern state—was not entirely the result of admiration for him, but in part because, as a goodly number of Kansans saw it, there was no alternative if the war was to be concluded victoriously and the South and slavery crushed.

In many respects the nominations made by the conventions were mere formalities. The real issue was Lane versus Carney, the actual stakes the United States Senate and political control of the state. Attaining white heat in the winter, the struggle raged through the spring and summer with ever-increasing in-

[35] *Kansas State Journal* (Lawrence), June 30, July 7, September 15, 1864.

[36] *Kansas State Journal* (Lawrence), August 4, September 8, September 22, 1864; *Freedom's Champion* (Atchison), March 10, 1864; *Council Grove Press*, April 16, May 7, 14, 28, July 9, 1864; *White Cloud Kansas Chief*, September 8, 22, 1864—all gave vent to criticism of Lincoln, ranging from mild to extremely bitter. The 1864 Kansas legislature passed a resolution against the Delahay appointment, but Lincoln pushed it through the Senate (*Freedom's Champion* [Atchison], March 10, 1864). Delahay subsequently was forced to resign from his judgeship for flagrant misconduct (Paul M. Angle, ed., *New Letters and Papers of Lincoln* [Boston and New York, 1930], p. 243). Carman and Luthin call the Delahay appointment "undoubtedly . . . the most disastrous of Lincoln's personal appointments" (Carman and Luthin, *Lincoln and the Patronage*, p. 118).

tensity. Both sides fought desperately and without scruple. Lane cracked the patronage whip ruthlessly, employed a huge "corruption fund," and made deals and promises with reckless abandon.[37] His journalistic adjuncts denounced all who opposed him as "copperheads" and "soreheads" and smeared Carney with charges of peculation in office, fraudulent business operations, bribery, perjury, consorting with Washington prostitutes, attempted rape, and drunkenness.[38] The pro-Carney papers countered with the somewhat more credible accusation that Lane was a large-scale thief and a wholesale seducer. The Lawrence *Journal* probably went too far, however, when it claimed that he conducted women to his office in the Capitol at Washington and then attempted "liberties" with them. The anti-Lane press made much, too, of an incident in which the Senator was beaten up by a Washington milliner to whom he had made "an insulting proposition." [39]

Toward the middle of October, Lane's prospects of success appeared dim, and Robinson was gleefully writing his wife, "I think the old devil has gone up." Much of the discontent that resulted in the Carney senatorial election persisted, and Lane had received heavy blows in the disaffection of D. W. Wilder and Leavenworth over the Clarke nomination. On October 10, the Republicans of Leavenworth County held a meeting which was controlled by Wilder and other anti-Lane men. They adopted a resolution calling for the election of a Senator from Leavenworth, that is, Carney, and when Anthony attempted to break up the gathering, some of those present knocked him unconscious. Lane was deeply disturbed by the feeling against him in Leavenworth

[37] M. H. Insley to Lane, December 3, 1864, James H. Lane Collection, University of Kansas; *White Cloud Kansas Chief*, July 7, 14, September 8, 1864.

[38] For the attack on Carney, see Leavenworth *Daily Conservative*, August 9, 1864. The *Conservative* at this time was still under the management of "Web" Wilder.

[39] *Kansas State Journal* (Lawrence), August 4, 1864; *White Cloud Kansas Chief*, May 19, September 1, 8, October 13, November 3, 1864.

and was reported as being "very quiet and very blue." John Speer found him alone in a Leavenworth hotel room, lying in bed although it was daytime and suffering from "appalling melancholy," even "aberration of mind." [40] But before the election took place, the political situation was radically altered by a series of military events over which neither Lane nor his enemies had any control, but which were to be very helpful to the former and extremely harmful to the latter.

[40] Robinson to Mrs. Robinson, October 16, 1864, Robinson Papers, KSHS; Leavenworth *Daily Conservative*, October 11, 1864; Speer, *Life of Lane*, pp. 333-334.

# XI

# *The Great Raid*

MILITARILY, the situation in Kansas during the spring and summer of 1864, following Curtis' assumption of command, was relatively quiet. Steele's Arkansas campaign kept the Confederates fully occupied in that quarter, and in the Indian Territory Stand Watie's rebel Indians posed no appreciable threat. The bushwhackers, on the other hand, centered their activities along the north side of the Missouri River and east of Kansas City. As in previous years Union grand strategy called for a strictly defensive policy in the Trans-Missisippi. "West of the Missisippi," wrote Grant to Halleck in June, "I would not attempt anything until the rebellion east of it is entirely subdued." In the meantime all available troops would be concentrated in Virginia and Georgia.[1]

Then, with the coming of autumn, full-scale warfare again erupted in Missouri. On September 19 a Confederate army of 12,000 cavalry moved northward from Arkansas. In command was Sterling Price, and with him were the hard-riding Missourians of Shelby and Marmaduke and the Arkansas troops of General James Fagan. Price was determined to make one final effort for the Confederate cause in Missouri. His plan was to

[1] *OR*, ser. I, XXXIV, pt. 4, 515.

strike at St. Louis and Jefferson City, march up the Missouri River to Kansas City, and retreat southward by way of Kansas and the Indian Territory. Recruits, plunder, and the destruction of Union military installations were his main objectives.[2]

Schofield's successor, Rosecrans, had been aware for some time that Missouri was threatened with invasion, but he had relied on Steele to keep the Confederates south of the Arkansas River. Steele, however, had remained behind the fortifications of Little Rock and had done nothing to halt Price. This failure left Rosecrans in an extremely perilous situation. His army numbered only 17,000, most of it was scattered throughout Missouri fighting guerrillas, and a large portion of it consisted of militia and recruits. As soon as he learned that Price had evaded Steele, he began hurriedly concentrating all available troops and at the same time obtained permission to use Major General A. J. Smith's infantry corps, then at Cairo, Illinois, en route to join Sherman. Definite information as to Price's movements was lacking, and Rosecrans at first though that his destination was western Missouri. Therefore, when he received word on September 24 that Shelby was south of Pilot Knob, he ordered Ewing to go there and ascertain whether Price was moving in that direction. If so, Ewing was to delay him as long as possible in order to gain additional time for strengthening the defenses of St. Louis.[3]

Ewing arrived at Pilot Knob on September 26 and on the following day was attacked by Price. Although the Confederates heavily outnumbered his garrison, Ewing beat off the assault and retained possession of the fort. He lost nearly one-fourth of his command, however, and realized that another Confederate attempt would be successful. Hence, under cover of night, he evacuated the fort and slipped away to the northwest. By his gallant stand at Pilot Knob, called by one writer "the Thermopylae of the West," Ewing accomplished his mission of discovering

[2] *Ibid.*, XLI, pt. 1, 626–627; *ibid.*, pt. 2, pp. 1023–1024, 1040–1041.

[3] *Ibid.*, pt. 1, pp. 307–309, 447; *ibid.*, pt. 2, pp. 717, 967; *ibid.*, pt. 3, pp. 82–83, 113, 124–129.

Price's plans and delaying his advance. Moreover, he inflicted heavy casualties on Price's army, blunting its fighting edge for the remainder of the campaign.[4]

Price merely demonstrated against St. Louis and Jefferson City, as both towns were now too heavily garrisoned to be attacked successfully. On October 10 he reached Boonville, where he remained nearly four days. During this period 1,200 to 1,500 Missourians, including the bushwhackers, led by Bill Anderson, joined his army. He instructed Anderson to cross the Missouri River and operate against the North Missouri Railroad. He also sent orders to Quantrill to strike the Hannibal and St. Joseph, but Quantrill did not receive the orders and took no part in the campaign. Anderson accomplished little and on October 27 was killed by Missouri militia. On October 13, after a skirmish with the advance elements of Major General Alfred Pleasonton's cavalry division, which had been sent by Rosecrans in pursuit of the Confederates, Price left Boonville and headed west toward Kansas.[5]

Word that Price had crossed the Arkansas and would possibly invade Kansas first reached Curtis on September 13 at a camp on the Solomon River, where he had gone to supervise operations against the Indians. Curtis had less than 4,000 regular troops under his command, and he realized that if Price did attempt to enter the state he would have to rely largely on the militia to stop him. Therefore he hurried back to Fort Leavenworth and on September 20 requested Carney to notify the militia to be ready to co-operate with his army against the Confederates. Carney replied that he would do so, but indicated an unwillingness to have the militia serve in the field. Curtis thereupon assured him that if at all possible the militia would be employed solely in garrison duty.[6]

Curtis for a while was under a misconception as to Price's

---

[4] *Ibid.*, pt. 1, pp. 446–450, 628–630, 679–680, 709.
[5] *Ibid.*, pp. 341, 345, 387–388, 424, 630–632.
[6] *Ibid.*, pp. 523; *ibid.*, pt. 3, pp. 279, 290, 523, 528.

movements. Initially he thought that Price was in the vicinity of Fort Gibson. Then a dispatch from Jennison at Fort Scott caused him to believe that Price was at Cane Hill, Arkansas, advancing from there on southern Kansas. Not until September 29 did he receive positive information in the form of a telegram from Rosecrans telling of the battle of Pilot Knob and stating that "the question of Price's being in Missouri is settled." Even then he was unsure whether Price would march toward Kansas, but when a report arrived on October 5 that the Confederates were fifteen miles below Jefferson City he concluded that the danger of his doing so was real and therefore asked Carney to call out the entire state militia.[7]

At this juncture Curtis encountered serious opposition from the Governor. Carney, like many other Kansans, believed it unlikely that Price would invade the state. Consequently he suspected that Curtis' intention to mobilize the militia was simply a political trick cooked up by Lane, with the purpose of taking and keeping the voters away from their homes and the polls until after election day, thus either preventing an election or making it possible for the Lane faction to win it. On the very day that Carney received the request from Curtis to order out the militia, his newspaper organ, the Leavenworth *Times,* openly voiced this suspicion, and on the following day Sol Miller proclaimed in the *Chief:*

People of Kansas, do you know that Gen. Curtis has entered into a conspiracy with Lane, to call out the entire Kansas Militia, to compel their absence at election time? It is the only hope Lane has of succeeding. They admit that the danger is remote, but are determined to make Price's movements a pretext for taking the voters away into Missouri, or from their homes.

Therefore, instead of complying with Curtis' request, Carney asked that the call be deferred pending the receipt of additional information regarding Price's movements. He also suggested

[7] *Ibid.,* pt. 1, p. 523; *ibid.,* pt. 3, pp. 234–235, 351, 650.

that the western counties share more of the burden of supplying the militia, since those on the border had been called upon many times before, those in the interior hardly at all.[8] As Carney's political strength lay in the eastern, Lane's in the western, counties, the motive behind this proposal is clear.

Carney's reluctance to order out the militia was intensified when on October 8 Blunt arrived in Leavenworth to take command of the District of Southern Kansas. He correctly believed that Sykes's removal was made by Curtis at the prompting of Lane, who wanted Blunt to be in position to control the Kansas troops and militia. But on October 9 word came from Rosecrans that Price had left Jefferson City and was moving westward in the direction of Leavenworth. This left Carney little choice except to issue a proclamation calling the militia into "the tented field until the rebel foe shall be baffled and beaten back." At the same time Curtis placed the state under martial law and directed "all men, white or black, between the ages of eighteen and sixty," to join some military organization.[9]

Intense excitement now gripped the state. Rumors circulated that Price was already above Kansas City. In Lawrence an accidental discharge of firearms created a near panic. At Leavenworth the sound of bells ringing and cannon firing to summon a citizens' defense rally caused "wild anxiety" as the townspeople thought that the rebels were upon them. All business halted throughout the state, and every man capable of bearing arms marched or rode in wagons to the threatened border. Those who remained behind, the very young and the extremely old, organized home guard units.[10]

---

[8] *Ibid.*, pt. 3, p. 650.

[9] *Ibid.*, pp. 467–470, 762–765; Charles Robinson to Mrs. Robinson, October 9, 1864, Robinson Papers, KSHS; Blunt, "Civil War Experiences," p. 252; Speer, *Life of Lane*, p. 286.

[10] Britton, *War on the Border*, II, 437; Richard Cordley, *Pioneer Days in Kansas* (Boston, 1903), p. 242; Eldridge, *Early Days in Kansas*, pp. 199–200; Richard J. Hinton, *Rebel Invasion of Missouri and Kansas and the Campaign of the Army of the Border against General Sterling Price, in*

Carney placed General George Deitzler in command of the militia. Deitzler's "staff" was a veritable roster of the anti-Lane faction—Charles Robinson, "Web" Wilder, Solon Thacher, John Ingalls, and Mark Parrott.[11] At first the militia concentrated at Olathe, but when the water supply proved inadequate, they moved on to Shawneetown. By October 16 about 10,000 militiamen were assembled near the border, with another 2,600 stationed at interior points. Nearly all the militia were poorly equipped and armed and badly deficient in training and discipline. Their only uniform consisted of a red badge pinned to their hats.

Curtis divided his forces, which he entitled "the Army of the Border," into two divisions. The first of these he assigned to Blunt, who organized it into three brigades under Jennison, Moonlight, and Blair. Blunt advanced his division to Hickman Mills, Missouri, on October 14, where it formed the right wing of Curtis' army. The other division, composed entirely of militia, was commanded by Deitzler and constituted the left wing. In all, Curtis had approximately 14,000 men in the field. His plan was to make a first stand along the Big Blue, then in front of Kansas City, and finally, if overpowered, at Wyandotte. Accordingly he had field works constructed at all these places by colored troops and civilian volunteers.[12]

Day after day passed, however, without any sign of Price's army or authentic news as to its location and movements. Many Kansans decided that Price was not coming or had retreated to the south and that there was no actual peril of invasion.[13] In

---

*October and November, 1864* (Chicago and Leavenworth, 1865), pp. 38, 54. Hinton, a correspondent of the Leavenworth *Daily Conservative*, served on Blunt's staff during the operations against Price.

[11] Charles Robinson to Mrs. Robinson, October 16, 1864, Robinson Papers, KSHS.

[12] *OR*, ser. I, XLI, pt. 1, 473; *ibid.*, pt. 3, p. 897; Blunt, "Civil War Experiences," p. 253; Hinton, *Rebel Invasion*, p. 60.

[13] O. E. Learnard to Mrs. Learnard, October 15, 1864, Learnard Collection, vol. IV (Learnard was on the staff of Deitzler); Cordley, *Pioneer Days*, pp. 245–246.

particular the suspicions of the anti-Lane men became rearoused. By October 15 they were almost convinced that the mobilization of the militia was a political trick of the wily Senator after all. The pro-Carney Oskaloosa *Independent* of that date expressed this view, and on the following day Charles Robinson wrote his wife from Shawneetown:

It is beginning to be thought that our being called out is all a sham & trick of Lane & Curtis's to make political capital. We cannot hear anything of importance as to the movements of Price. We think that we are being kept in ignorance of the true condition of affairs in order to keep the people out as long as possible. Steps are being taken to ascertain the facts. I have no doubt Price has gone South & that there are only a few guerrillas prowling about. Nobody thinks we shall have anything to do but go home in a few days & attend to our business.[14]

At Hickman Mills on October 16 a serious disturbance occurred among the militia in Blunt's division. Lieutenant Colonel James D. Snoddy, a pro-Carney newspaper editor from Mound City, asked Blunt to permit his regiment to return to Linn County. Blunt refused, whereupon Snoddy started to march home anyway. Backed by another regiment, Blunt personally blocked the attempted desertion and placed Snoddy and Brigadier General William H. Fishback, who was also involved in the mutiny, under arrest. Blunt's action, however, did not prevent numerous desertions by the militia several days later when his division moved to the Big Blue.[15]

The Leavenworth *Times*, the Lawrence *Journal*, and other anti-Lane papers soon began declaring that Price was no longer in Missouri and that the campaign against him was "an egregious

[14] Robinson to Mrs. Robinson, October 16, 1864, Robinson Papers, KSHS. A week previously Robinson had been sure that Price was coming toward Kansas (see Robinson to Mrs. Robinson, October 9, 1864, Robinson Papers, KSHS.

[15] *OR*, ser. I, XLI, pt. 1, 572, 619–620; *ibid*., pt. 4, pp. 18, 22–23, 57–58, 94, 97; Hinton, *Rebel Invasion*, pp. 65–66.

humbug." [16] Carney adherents circulated copies of these pub-
lications among the militia, who increasingly manifested a desire
"to go home and attend to their fall plowing." Many of the
militia regiments refused to cross the state line into Missouri or,
if they did so, to go any distance. Deitzler, who believed that
Price was south of the Arkansas River and had so told his troops,
supported them in their refusal. The Leavenworth militia in particular were recalcitrant. On October 19 they burned Lane in
effigy and paraded a jackass with Blunt's name on it through the
camp at Shawneetown. And when, on the following day, they
were ordered to march into Missouri, over one-half of them went
back to Leavenworth. Political speeches at the Shawneetown
camp by Lane and Blunt did not improve matters. [17]

By October 20 Carney had about decided that the danger of
an invasion had ceased to exist, if in fact it ever had existed. He
therefore asked Curtis to revoke martial law and, according to
a subsequent charge by his opponents, prepared a proclamation
disbanding the militia. [18] The *Times* of that date, in an editorial
captioned "How Much Longer, Oh Lord, How Much Longer,"
also demanded that martial law be lifted and declared that the
militia should be permitted to go home. But at this juncture,
before a real crisis involving the militia could develop, definite
news as to Price's whereabouts at last arrived. An advance detachment of Blunt's division had encountered Shelby at Lexington on the nineteenth. Heavy skirmishing had followed, with

[16] Leavenworth *Daily Times*, October 17, 18, 19, 1864; *White Cloud
Kansas Chief*, October 13, 20, 1864; Oskaloosa *Independent*, October 15,
1864. The Kansas City *Western Journal of Commerce*, October 22, 1864,
stated that the general opinion was that Price had gone south.

[17] *OR*, ser. I, XLI, pt. 4, 96, 118, 144; *Kansas Weekly Tribune* (Lawrence), October 27, 1864; Oskaloosa *Independent*, October 29, 1864; Hinton, *Rebel Invasion*, pp. 80–81; Crawford, *Kansas in the Sixties*, pp. 143–
144; Blunt, "Civil War Experiences," p. 253; Cordley, *Pioneer Days*, pp.
245–246.

[18] *OR*, ser. I, XLI, pt. 4, 142–143; Leavenworth *Daily Conservative*,
October 26, 27, 1864; *Kansas Weekly Tribune* (Lawrence), November
3, 1864; Blunt, "Civil War Experiences," p. 256.

Blunt slowly falling back toward Independence. Blunt immediately reported the action. There was no longer any doubt, even among the most skeptical Carney supporters, that Price was coming.[19]

Blunt continued to retreat before the advancing squadrons of Shelby until he arrived, on the morning of October 20, at the Little Blue, nine miles east of Independence. He decided that this stream would be the best place to make a stand against the enemy and hence called on Curtis to send him reinforcements. Curtis, however, refused to abandon his plan of fighting the main battle at the Big Blue. Carney and the militia generals were unalterably opposed to having the state troops serve more than a few miles beyond the Kansas border, and he believed that in choosing a battle line it was necessary "to have united councils as well as a strong position." Therefore he ordered Blunt to conduct only a delaying action at the Little Blue with Moonlight's brigade.

At noon on the twenty-first Marmaduke's division appeared and endeavored to force its way across the bridge that spanned the Little Blue. Moonlight's troops were strongly posted behind stone walls overlooking the river and were armed with rapidfire rifles and a battery of howitzers. They held off the Confederates for several hours, and finally Price had to bring up Shelby's division to assist Marmaduke. This added pressure was too much, and Moonlight was obliged to give way. He retreated in good order through Independence and on to the Big Blue. The Confederates followed only as far as Independence, where they went into camp for the night.[20]

Curtis now had his entire army, including the militia, in position behind trenches and barricades along the Big Blue. He hoped to hold Price at this line until Pleasonton could close up from the rear and destroy him. But when Price attacked at mid-

---

[19] *OR*, ser. I, XLI, pt. I, 574, 633; Leavenworth *Daily Conservative*, October 21, 1864; Hinton, *Rebel Invasion*, p. 52.

[20] *OR*, ser. I, XLI, pt. I, 476, 683; *ibid.*, pt. 4, p. 145; Blunt, "Civil War Experiences," pp. 254-255; Britton, *War on the Border*, II, 448-449.

day on October 22, he broke through the Union defenses with ease. Shelby crossed the river above and below Byram's Ford, which was supposed to have been guarded by Jennison's brigade, and turned the right flank of the Army of the Border, forcing it to fall back northward to Westport. Several regiments of raw militia tried to stem Shelby's advance on the prairies south of Westport, only to be ridden down and captured "en masse." According to Confederate sources Shelby could have kept on going, but withdrew on his own accord with the approach of darkness. Federal accounts, on the other hand, state that Curtis' troops rallied and drove Shelby back, after which they voluntarily retired again to Westport.[21]

Meanwhile, to the east, Pleasonton's cavalry division was over a day's march behind the Confederates, not having reached Lexington until the morning of October 21. Pleasonton was ignorant of Curtis' plans and movements and feared that the Kansas troops were not yet ready or able to co-operate effectively with his force. But on the night of October 21, Daniel Boutwell, a volunteer scout from Curtis' army, contacted Pleasonton after a daring ride through guerrilla-infested country and told him that Curtis was preparing to withstand Price on the Big Blue. Upon receiving this information Pleasonton quickened his pursuit. At 4 P.M., October 22, he reached Independence, where he engaged Price's rearguard under Marmaduke. By nightfall he had driven Marmaduke to the Big Blue and inflicted heavy losses on his

[21] For Confederate accounts of the Battle of the Big Blue, see *OR*, ser. I, XLI, pt. I, 634-635, 658; John N. Edwards, *Shelby and His Men; or, The War in the West* (Cincinnati, 1867), p. 425; Joseph O. Shelby, "Price's Raid," letter by Shelby published in the *Kansas City Journal*, November 24, 1881, Kansas in the Civil War Clippings, Scrapbook, vol. I, KSHS. For the Union versions, see *OR*, ser. I, XLI, pt. I, 478-485, 526, 575, 584-585, 593; Thomas Moonlight, letter of December 5, 1881, unlabeled newspaper clipping in Kansas in the Civil War Clippings, vol. I; Hinton, *Rebel Invasion*, pp. 128-132; Crawford, *Kansas in the Sixties*, pp. 146-148. See also the Diary of Samuel J. Reader, October 21, 22, 1864. Reader was an officer in a militia regiment from the Topeka region, was captured at the Big Blue, and later escaped.

division. Among those killed during the day while fighting Pleasonton's troops was George Todd.[22]

Messengers from Pleasonton saying that he had closed up with Price reached Curtis and Blunt at sundown—the first intelligence they had received in three days of his movements. Yet, notwithstanding this heartening news, Curtis ordered Blunt's division to fall back to Kansas City. Blunt countermanded the order, however, and, backed by Lane, Samuel Crawford, and other members of Curtis' staff, persuaded Curtis to retain the army in front of Westport.[23] During the night Curtis and Blunt withdrew Deitzler's militia from the northern portion of the Big Blue and placed them in the trenches south of Kansas City as a reserve. Large numbers of the militia discovered a "peculiar attraction" in the north side of the Kansas River, and the staff officers had to threaten, then plead, to keep them in line.

The morning of Sunday, October 23, dawned clear and cold. On the prairie in front of Westport both Blunt and Shelby advanced to attack. At first the battle went in favor of Shelby, as his men forced Blunt almost into the streets of Westport. Shelby, however, was fighting only to cover the retreat of the rest of Price's army. Up to this point, he later declared, the campaign had been a "walkover," but now the Confederates were in danger of being surrounded. Hence Price's only desire now was to escape to the south with his immense train of plunder.

At this juncture disaster struck the rear of the Confederate army. Price had assigned Marmaduke's division to protect the

[22] *OR,* ser. I, XLI, pt. 1, 340, 683; *ibid.,* pt. 4, pp. 163, 183–184; Hinton, *Rebel Invasion,* pp. 117–119.

[23] Blunt, "Civil War Experiences," pp. 258–259; Moonlight, Letter on the Price Raid, Kansas in the Civil War Clippings, vol. I; Crawford, *Kansas in the Sixties,* pp. 148–150. Crawford asserts that Curtis wanted to retreat all the way back to Leavenworth and that he abandoned this intention only when the staff officers threatened to dispose of him and put Blunt in command. This is undoubtedly greatly exaggerated. Blunt, who had little love for Curtis and plenty for himself, does not mention any such threat in his "all is revealed" account and states that Curtis wished to fall back only as far as Kansas City, which is far more likely than Leavenworth, being in accordance with Curtis' original plan.

train, which he had sent off to the southwest along the Fort Scott road. Marmaduke endeavored to prevent Pleasonton from crossing the Big Blue at Byram's Ford, but a savage onslaught by Pleasonton drove him back. Price, fearful for the safety of his train, ordered Shelby to come to Marmaduke's assistance. But as Shelby started to do so the Union forces at Westport, heavily reinforced with militia, counterattacked. Soon Shelby not only was withdrawing to aid Marmaduke, but was being driven back by Curtis and Blunt. Pleasonton's troopers intercepted him, and his men had to fight their way through the Union lines. They then retreated till they caught up with the remainder of Price's army, which was now in full flight to the south.[24]

Blunt and Curtis pushed on till they met Pleasonton at a farmhouse ten miles south of Westport. The generals held a conference and determined to pursue Price in order both to destroy him and to protect southern Kansas. Pleasonton, however, wanted to return to Missouri. He maintained that Curtis had enough men to take care of Price, whereas his horses and soldiers were exhausted from thirty days of constant marching. Carney and Deitzler, who were also present, objected. They argued that the Kansas militia should be allowed to go home first. Curtis and Blunt supported this view, and Pleasonton finally acquiesced. Curtis then rescinded martial law in northern Kansas and ordered the militia from that area mustered out. He retained the militia from southern Kansas since that section was still threatened. These matters settled, the conference ended, and the combined forces of Curtis and Pleasonton continued to Little Sante Fe, where they encamped for the night.[25]

[24] Blunt, "Civil War Experiences," p. 258; Hinton, *Rebel Invasion*, pp. 144–145. The above account of the Battle of Westport is based on the following sources: *OR*, ser. I, XLI, pt. 1, 486, 576, 635, 658–659; *ibid.*, pt. 4, p. 209; Hinton, *Rebel Invasion*, pp. 166–181; Shelby, "Price's Raid," *Kansas City Journal*, November 29, 1881; Crawford, *Kansas in the Sixties*, p. 157; Blunt, "Civil War Experiences," pp. 259–260. Again there are differing Confederate and Federal versions, and the versions even contradict themselves. It would require a special monograph to collate them.

[25] *OR*, ser. I, XLI, pt. 1, 341, 491–492; Hinton, *Rebel Invasion*, pp. 175–177.

At sunrise on October 24 the Union forces were on the march. Curtis was in command, with Blunt's division in advance and Pleasonton's following. A separate column under Moonlight moved parallel to Price's right flank in order to prevent him from raiding Mound City and Fort Scott. Price had retreated all night, but was less than five miles ahead. The country along the line of march was entirely desolate. Here and there were the stark chimneys of burned houses—called by Missourians "Jennison's monuments." The road was littered with broken wagons, caissons, rifles, blankets, bits of harness, and other debris. The Union troops captured many Confederates who had fallen along the way, sick, wounded, or exhausted.

The day's march ended near Trading Post, Kansas. The advance guard found the body of an elderly preacher lying in a field, shot by some of Price's men. His family was "frantic and crazed with terror and grief," his cabin plundered and afire. A dead horse had been dumped into the well. The Confederates had robbed and murdered three other settlers in the neighborhood and shot at several more.[26] These and other atrocities were probably committed by Shelby's Missourians, in whose ranks were numerous bushwhackers. Shelby's chief of staff, Major John N. Edwards, wrote a few years later:

Shelby was soothing the wounds of Missouri by stabbing the breast of Kansas. . . . He was fighting the devil with fire and smoking him to death. Haystacks, houses, barns, produce, crops, and farming implements were consumed before the march of his squadrons, and what the flames spared the bullet finished. . . . If the crows could not fly over the valleys of the Shenandoah without carrying rations, the buzzards of the prairies had no need of haversacks.[27]

During the day the Union forces had gained ground on Price and were within striking distance. Blunt, "with great pertinacity," urged Curtis to move around Price's western flank so as to block

[26] *OR*, ser. I, XLI, pt. 1, 492; Hinton, *Rebel Invasion*, pp. 183–190.
[27] Edwards, *Shelby*, pp. 447–448.

his retreat, thereby compelling him to fight or surrender. Curtis, however, thought that this plan was impracticable and rejected it. He then proceeded to waste several hours shifting Pleasonton's division to the front. At daybreak Sanborn's brigade of Pleasonton's division attacked the Confederates in their camp south of Trading Post. They offered little resistance but simply resumed their retreat, departing in great haste and leaving behind cattle, captured Negroes, and partially cooked provisions. They attempted a stand at the ford of the Marais des Cygnes, only to abandon the position quickly when Sanborn again charged their line.

Price continued to retreat until he reached Mine Creek. Here he was forced to halt, for his train had become bogged down in the ford and blocked the crossing. In order to save the train he turned back with Fagan's and Marmaduke's divisions and prepared to give battle. But before he could complete his dispositions, Pleasonton's troopers were upon him. They thundered across the plain at a gallop and struck Price's lines with a terrific impact. Panic broke out among the Confederates. Men and regiments threw away their guns and fled across Mine Creek like a "herd of buffalo." Pleasonton's troops captured over 500 Confederates, including General Marmaduke. Only the timely intervention of Shelby's division, frantically summoned to the front by Price, saved the Confederate army from complete rout and destruction.

Price made another stand two miles north of the Marmiton River. The fighting that followed was neither vigorous nor important. Only one of Pleasonton's brigades, McNeil's, attacked, and a Confederate countermove nearly flanked it. The rest of Pleasonton's division was strung out over the countryside, badly disorganized, both men and horses exhausted. Blunt's division had failed to catch up with the battle and could not be expected to come up before nightfall. Consequently Pleasonton turned his division westward to Fort Scott to secure food and rest. Blunt, by some mix-up, did not receive orders sent him by Curtis to keep after Price, but also marched to Fort Scott. As a result Price continued his retreat unpursued.[28]

Soon after arriving at Fort Scott, Curtis abolished martial law in southern Kansas and relieved the militia of that section from further duty. He felt that the danger to the state was over and that the regular troops would now be sufficient to dispose of Price. At noon on October 26 his army resumed the pursuit, stopping for the night at Shanghai, Missouri. The next day, however, Pleasonton notified Curtis that he was withdrawing himself, one of his brigades, and his artillery from the army. He gave personal illness and the great fatigue of his troops and horses as the reason. Curtis protested, but since the army was now in Missouri, Pleasonton was subject only to the orders of Rosecrans, who telegraphed him permission to do as he desired. Pleasonton left the brigades of Sanborn and McNeil with Curtis. Probably the real reason he departed was because he had quarreled with Curtis over the credit and spoils of the victories at Westport and Mine Creek.

Curtis took up the march again and on the morning of October 28 reached Carthage, Missouri. Blunt pushed ahead with his division and came upon the Confederates at Newtonia. Although he had only 1,000 men and was far in advance of the rest of the army, he attacked in a desperate personal gamble to win the glory of an independent victory. But a Confederate counterattack led by Shelby soon placed Blunt in a perilous situation. His troops, however, held on until Sanborn's brigade arrived. The combined forces of Sanborn and Blunt then forced Price to retreat once more, and that evening the Army of the Border occupied Newtonia.[29]

[28] *OR*, ser. I, XLI, pt. 1, 335, 341, 493–496, 502–503, 559, 637, 659–660, 684, 70; Edwards, *Shelby*, pp. 450–455; Hinton, *Rebel Invasion*, pp. 179–235.

[29] *OR*, ser. I, XLI, pt. 1, 314, 342, 504–507, 547–549, 577, 638; Blunt, "Civil War Experiences," pp. 262–263; Edwards, *Shelby*, pp. 455–456; Hinton, *Rebel Invasion*, pp. 266–275.

Before Curtis could follow Price any farther, Rosecrans ordered Sanborn and McNeil back to their districts in Missouri. This left Curtis with only Blunt's depleted command and therefore with no alternative except to break off the pursuit. Much disappointed, he was in the course of returning to Kansas when he received instructions from Grant to keep after Price until he was driven south of the Arkansas River. Backed by this higher authority, he countermanded Rosecrans' orders and regained control of 1,800 of Pleasonton's troops. He then turned about and resumed the pursuit.[30] On November 6, after a march in a snowstorm through the rugged country of northwestern Arkansas, he reached Cane Hill, which had been evacuated by the Confederates two day previously. Two days later his advance guard rode up to the banks of the Arkansas River at Pheasant Ford, only to find that Price's army had already passed over. One of his batteries fired a parting salvo across the river, and the campaign came to an end.[31]

The same day that Curtis terminated his pursuit of Price, the voters of Kansas went to the polls. For a while the Leavenworth *Times*, whistling in the political dark, claimed a victory for the anti-Lane Republicans, but it was soon apparent that the regular Republican ticket had won a complete and decisive triumph. Crawford received 13,387 votes and carried twenty-eight of the state's thirty-five counties. Thacher got only 8,448 votes and lost even in his home county of Douglas. Lee came much closer to defeating Clarke, losing by only a little over 1,000 votes and probably justifying Sol Miller's assertion that he would have won had he been able to campaign personally. Most importantly,

---

[30] *OR*, ser. I, XLI, pt. 1, 511–514. Rosecrans' action in withdrawing the troops from Curtis was in direct violation of the orders he had received from Halleck and Major General E. R. S. Canby, commander of the Military Division of the Mississippi. See Canby to Halleck, October 15, 1864, *ibid.*, pt. 3, p. 879; Halleck to Rosecrans, October 27, 1864, *ibid.*, pt. 4, p. 274.

[31] *Ibid.*, pt. 1, pp. 516–517; Hinton, *Rebel Invasion*, pp. 292–293.

insofar as Lane was concerned, most of the men elected to the legislature were committed to his re-election as Senator.[32]

Having expected to win, the anti-Lane forces were badly downcast by defeat.[33] Yet in large measure only their own political ineptitude was to blame. Carney's premature attempt to secure election to the Senate had been a disastrous blunder. Prior to the election his popularity had been growing and Lane's waning. Had he waited until 1865 it is very likely that he would have been elected in the regular manner. As it was, the "Fraud" gave Lane "the opportunity of a lifetime," since "a better thing for the furtherance of his political ambition could not have happened." [34] Many people turned against Carney because they resented his trickery and despised his clumsiness. In the words of a contemporary observer, they decided not to

> tie up to the rotten hulk of a man, of half the brains of Gen. Lane, who was trying to steal into office by the same arts Gen. Lane had so often used. If the people are to be humbugged, they prefer that it should be done by a master hand, and not by a botch at the trade. If they cannot have an honest man in the Senate they prefer that the *rascal* who represents them, should be a man of brains.[35]

Even more damaging to the anti-Lane faction were the mistakes it committed during the Price raid. Carney's unwillingness to call out the militia, the foolish statements of the *Times*, the Lawrence *Journal*, Deitzler, and other Carney adherents that

[32] All election statistics are taken from the figures published in Wilder, *Annals*, pp. 398–404.

[33] *White Cloud Kansas Chief*, November 17, 1864.

[34] "Session of 1865," Emporia *Weekly Globe*, January 20, 1887, Crawford Scrapbooks, vol. II.

[35] Leavenworth *Daily Conservative*, November 24, 1864, quoting the Troy *Investigator*. See also *Freedom's Champion* (Atchison), January 19, 1865. Marshall M. Murdock, editor of the *Weekly Osage Chronicle* (Burlingame), said in the January 30, 1864, issue of his paper that he preferred Lane to Carney as Senator, despite his trickery, because of his superior intelligence.

Price was not in Missouri, the mutinies and desertions in the militia traceable to the statements, and Carney's intention to disband the militia with Price only a few miles from the state, all combined to make the Governor and his faction appear not only unpatriotic but fatuous. The Lane newspapers did not fail to make the most of these errors by "Carney and his bolting copperhead crew" and to contrast them unfavorably with the supposedly heroic exploits of Lane and Crawford in repelling Price and saving Kansas. Lane, it will be recalled, was very despondent over his chances before the raid. "Web" Wilder and John Speer, an opponent and a friend, both held that the raid "made Lane successful." [36]

Another extremely important reason for the failure of Lane's enemies was his monopoly of Federal patronage, resulting from his personal and political friendship with Lincoln.[37] By skillful and ruthless employment of this powerful weapon he retained control of the regular Republican organization, and this in itself possibly assured his triumph. An analysis of the 1864 state election returns indicates that the Lane candidates must have derived much of their support from straight-ticket voting. All these candidates received slightly over 10,000 civilian votes, with the exception of Clarke and the nominees for Attorney General and Associate Justice, who received respectively 9,156, 9,229, and 9,833 civilian votes. In contrast, the anti-Lane ticket probably received the support of only about 4,000 Republicans. This number is obtained by subtracting the civilian vote for Crawford, about 10,200, from the civilian vote for Lincoln, about 14,200. The difference, when added to the civilian vote for McClellan, 3,794, gives a figure very close to the 7,840 civilian votes re-

[36] *Freedom's Champion* (Atchison), January 19, 1865; Leavenworth *Daily Conservative*, October 26, 27, November 2, 3, 4, 6, 1864; *Kansas Weekly Tribune* (Lawrence), November 3, 1864; Wilder, *Annals*, p. 406; Speer, *Life of Lane*, p. 334.

[37] See *White Cloud Kansas Chief*, November 24, 1864; *Freedom's Champion* (Atchison), January 19, 1865.

ceived by Thacher. Thus almost half the votes obtained by the anti-Lane candidates came from Democrats.[38]

The 1865 legislature convened on January 10. Lane's followers, confident and jubilant, leased the Topeka House and made whisky and women available to all who desired them. The anti-Lane members engaged in frantic last-minute efforts to agree on a senatorial candidate to oppose Lane. Ewing, as always ambitious, presented himself, then quickly withdrew when he saw that his cause was hopeless. A former member of the Carney administration offered $1,000 bribes to lukewarm Lane men, but had few if any takers. On January 12 the legislature went into joint session and on the first ballot, by a vote of 82 to 16, re-elected Lane to the United States Senate for six more years. Someone waved a handkerchief from a window in the capitol, and the military band waiting outside struck up "Hail to the Chief." The legislature then adjourned, and Topeka was given over to the revelry of the politicians. A newspaper reporter described Lane as being "affable, sociable, and entertaining." The election was "the most complete victory of his political career," and these "the happiest days of his life in Kansas." [39]

[38] The above calculations are based upon the 1864 state election returns as published in Wilder, *Annals*, pp. 398–404, and Andreas, *History of Kansas*, p. 235. Of course there were many nominal Democrats who voted for Lincoln and the Lane candidates, but these would be canceled out by those who voted for Lincoln and the anti-Lane candidates. Sol Miller, *White Cloud Kansas Chief*, July 14, November 17, 1864, claimed that Lane received sizable Democratic support.

[39] *White Cloud Kansas Chief*, March 9, 1865; Leavenworth *Daily Conservative*, January 17, 1865; *Freedom's Champion* (Atchison), January 19, 1865; *Senate Journal, 1865*, p. 34; Edwin C. Manning, "The Kansas State Senate of 1865 and 1866," KHC, IX (1905–1906), 364; "Session of 1865," Emporia *Weekly Globe*, January 20, 1887, Crawford Scrapbooks, vol. II.

# XII

## *Wartime Kansas*

THE history of Kansas during the Civil War was not solely one of bushwhackers and politicians, of border raids and factional brawls. Other aspects were equally important and certainly no less interesting. Some of these—economic conditions, refugees, the Negro, Copperheads, jayhawking, Indian affairs, and railroads—are the subjects of the present chapter.

Kansas prospered economically during the Civil War. The severe drought that ruined the 1860 crop came to an end in April, 1861, as heavy rains fell throughout the state. By early summer the editor of the Elwood *Free Press* was able to say that "a year of plenty is to succeed a year of famine." In fact, so large a crop was harvested that the problem for a while was one of surplus, not scarcity.[1] But heavy government military buying soon provided a ready and profitable market for this surplus and eventually absorbed nearly all the agricultural output of the state. Money became plentiful and circulated freely, and business was proportionately lively. Late in 1862 another editor frankly asserted: "Financially, the existence of the present war has proved a godsend to Kansas."[2]

[1] *Fort Scott Democrat*, April 6, 1861; Elwood *Free Press*, June 29, 1861; Leavenworth *Daily Conservative*, July 2, 4, 1861.
[2] *Neosho Valley Register*, quoted in the Leavenworth *Daily Conserva-*

Crop conditions during the succeeding war years were generally good. Southern Kansas suffered from a minor drought in the spring and late summer of 1862, but the state as a whole was not affected, and it produced 262,953 bushels of wheat and 6,407,000 bushels of corn.[3] The season of 1863 was probably the best of all, with adequate rains and no difficulties from grasshoppers, which had caused trouble in both the previous years.[4] No figures are available on grain production in 1863, but Charles Robinson informed Amos Lawrence that "crops are *excellent*."[5] The 1864 harvest was also good, although prospects at first were unfavorable owing to a lack of sufficient rainfall until July.[6] There was another drought in 1865, and wheat output declined to slightly less than the 1860 figure.[7] By then, however, the war was over.

Many settlers, "the smarter ones," abandoned agriculture nearly altogether and turned to stock raising. Kansas, especially the southern part, was well suited to this industry. Moreover, there was a great and increasing demand for cattle, mules, and horses from the army, the East, and above all the overland trade. This trade used up hundreds of oxen and mules annually and provided a steady and remunerative source of income for stockmen and farmers.[8] It was by far the major business in wartime Kansas.

---

*tive*, November 12, 1862. See also Oskaloosa *Independent*, November 16, 1861, affirming the same.

[3] Fort Scott *Bulletin*, June 14, 1862; E. B. Whitman to G. L. Stearns, Lawrence, September 7, 1862, Stearns Papers; Andreas, *History of Kansas*, p. 254.

[4] Leavenworth *Daily Conservative*, May 21, 30, July 3, 1863; Andreas, *History of Kansas*, p. 325.

[5] Robinson to Lawrence, June 27, 1863, Lawrence Papers; *Council Grove Press*, August 24, 1863.

[6] Leavenworth *Daily Conservative*, July 6, 10, 24, 1864; *Senate Journal*, *1865*, p. 16.

[7] Leavenworth *Daily Conservative*, July 10, 1865.

[8] C. M. Chase to the Sycamore, Ill., *True Republican and Sentinel*, August 16, 1863, Chase Letters; Stark, ed., *Kansas Register of 1864*, pp. 73–75.

All the vast territory west to Santa Fe and Salt Lake and south to the Arkansas River was dotted with forts, Indian agencies, and trading posts which drew their supplies from the state, and there was also a great traffic with the gold mines of Colorado and California. Thousands of wagons, teamsters, freight agents, oxen, mules, and horses were engaged in this "commerce of the plains," and during the grazing season the freight caravans moved in seemingly endless procession across the prairies.[9]

Leavenworth was the center of the overland trade. During the single year of 1864, boasted the *Conservative* early in 1865, its wholesalers sold to dealers in the interior of the state goods worth some $18,740,000, and its freighters shipped to New Mexico, Utah, Colorado, and other western points 40,000,000 pounds of freight. Under the stimulus of this business the city experienced a tremendous "boom." Its population swelled from 5,000 to at least 15,000 and perhaps to as many as 23,000.[10] Many new stores and other commercial establishments came into being, and the old ones expanded. Thomas Carney, his partner Thomas C. Stevens, and other "merchant princes" built opulent homes atop the bluffs overlooking the Missouri River. The Planter's House, the Mansion House, and other hotels were crowded with civil and military officials, and the streets resounded to the tramp of marching regiments on their way south. Thousands of travelers and immigrants passed through the town, going both east and west. There were over 200 saloons, a dozen brothels, and several theaters. Touring companies presented plays such as *Peg Woffington, Love's Sacrifice, Uncle Tom's Cabin*, and *Deborah, the Forsaken*. In December of 1863 John Wilkes Booth appeared in *Richard III, Hamlet*, and *Othello* and also in *Richelieu, Satan in Paris*, and *The Marble Heart; or, The Sculptor's Dream*. Large

[9] Leavenworth *Daily Conservative*, May 4, 1865; Eldridge, *Early Days in Kansas*, p. 197.

[10] Leavenworth *Daily Conservative*, May 30, 1863, May 4, 1865; *Freedom's Champion* (Atchison), March 31, 1865, quoting a New York correspondent. Richardson, *Beyond the Mississippi*, p. 550, estimated Leavenworth's population as 22,000 in 1866.

audiences attended his performances, and "Web" Wilder acclaimed his acting. Those who did not care for Shakespeare and melodrama went to the lectures of "J. M. Searl, Grand Master of the Occult Sciences and Interpreter of Ancient Necromancy" or saw Miss Sallie Thayer in "a new side-splitting act entitled 'Sallie and her hoops.' "

Second to Leavenworth in economic activity and prosperity was Atchison, with a population that reached 8,000 by the end of the war. Atchison's position on the westernmost bend of the Missouri River made it the principal transshipment point for goods going from the East to the West. In 1865 its ox and mule trains hauled 21,541,830 pounds of freight westward, most of it to Denver and the Colorado gold-mining regions. An estimated 4,917 wagons, 6,164 mules, 27,685 oxen, and 1,256 men participated in this business. While traveling "across the continent" in the spring of 1865 Samuel Bowles, editor of the Springfield, Illinois, *Republican,* reported that a single firm in Atchison, occupying a "modest building," was "selling one million dollars yearly to small traders, or to fill up forgotten places in large trains." Bowles also commented on the fact that although long trains of heavily laden wagons left daily the immense warehouses and yards of Atchison remained constantly packed with mining machinery, provisions, and agricultural implements.[11]

Another town that boomed with the outbreak of the war was Fort Scott, which became the center of military affairs in the southwest. In the summer of 1863 it had a population of between one and two thousand permanent residents and as many more transients. Large numbers of troops were also stationed there at various times, especially prior to the Arkansas campaign of 1862, and the merchants benefited accordingly. It was a "fast town," where it was easy to promote horse races, fights, and drunken

---

[11] *Freedom's Champion* (Atchison), March 31, 1865; Root and Connelley, *Overland Stage,* p. 419; Samuel Bowles, *Across the Continent* (Springfield, Ill., 1865), p. 5.

sprees. It contained many "well-stocked" stores, a first-class hotel (the Wilder House), numerous "beer saloons," a dozen or so billiard parlors and bowling alleys, and a theater in a barn with two or three changes of scenery and "one or two tolerable performers for stars, and a half a dozen very scurvy stock performers." Some Kansas troops encamped near the town found a play presented by a touring company "too wanton for even the morals of soldiers" and so proceeded to cut the guy ropes of the tent in which the show was being held.[12]

The progress and prosperity of Lawrence naturally received a tremendous setback from the Quantrill raid. For several weeks following the massacre the people were in a stupor, and many of them asserted that the town had received a deathblow and would never recover, or if it did, the Missourians would only come and destroy it again.[13] But the majority of the inhabitants decided to remain and rebuild, and by autumn a number of new buildings were completed, a still larger number were well under way, and "Lawrence began to look like a town again." Money and supplies sent by other Kansas towns and from the East materially aided the work of reconstruction. Most of the "Boston Relief Fund," raised principally by Amos Lawrence, went to businessmen, "the wants of the poor having been met by other friends." Much of the fund, however, got into the hands of men whose need for it was questionable.[14]

This is the statistical summary of Kansas' progress during the Civil War: land in farms, 1,778,400 acres in 1860, 3,500,000 acres in 1865; value of farms, $12,258,239 in 1860, $24,796,535 in 1865; value of all property, $31,327,890 in 1860, $72,252,180 in

[12] C. M. Chase to the Sycamore, Ill., *True Republican and Sentinel*, August 19, 1863, Chase Letters; Albert Greene, "The Army of the Frontier," *KHC*, XIV (1915–1918), 287–288.

[13] O. E. Learnard to Mrs. Learnard, September 13, 1863, Learnard Collection, vol. IV.

[14] Richard Cordley to Amos Lawrence, April 18, 1866, and John S. Brown to Amos Lawrence, May 24, 1864, Lawrence Papers.

1865.[15] Although most of the growth indicated by these figures probably dates from the spring of 1864, it is clear that economically the Civil War was on the whole beneficial to Kansas. This wartime prosperity contrasted sharply with the drought and depression that immediately preceded it when the Democrats were in power and no doubt provided an additional reason why Kansans became infatuated, as it were, with the Republican Party.

Of course not all Kansans benefited from the war. Hundreds were killed or driven from their homes by the bushwhackers and the Indians. Casualties among Kansas troops were extremely heavy, and the number of those who lost husbands, fathers, brothers, sons, and friends at the front must have been proportionately great. The poor were hard-hit by inflation, and Leavenworth had a sizable population of destitute and jobless, many of them the wives and children of soldiers. By the fall of 1863 Sarah Everett of Osawatomie was doubtlessly not the only person in the state asking the question, "Will the war ever end?" [16]

One of the most notable and dramatic features of wartime Kansas was the great influx of refugees, both Negro and white, from Missouri, Arkansas, and even Louisiana and Texas. Most of the Negroes came on their own volition or were "liberated" by Lane, Jennison, and the other jayhawkers. They began coming as soon as warfare broke out in Missouri. Often they brought with them the mules, horses, wagons, furniture, provisions, and other property of their erstwhile masters. By 1863 there were 8,000 of them who had "crossed over into Canaan," and by the end of the war the state's colored population had swollen from

[15] Figures taken from the Kansas State Census of 1865, the original returns of which are in the Kansas State Archives, Kansas State Historical Society. This census was taken in May, 1865, and therefore measures precisely the condition of Kansas at the end of the Civil War.

[16] *OR*, ser. III, V, 667; Gates, *Fifty Million Acres*, pp. 99–100; *House Journal, 1865*, pp. 287–288; Leavenworth *Daily Conservative*, August 11, 1864; Sarah Everett to "Jennie," November 4, 1863, *KHQ*, VIII (November, 1939), 377.

a mere 816 in 1860 to almost 13,000. The majority of the former slaves congregated at Leavenworth, Lawrence, Wyandotte and in Linn County, in that order. Leavenworth in the summer of 1862 had 1,500 colored residents, two Negro churches, and a Negro school with 128 students. Lawrence attracted a great many fugitives owing to its reputation as an "abolition center." Wyandotte by 1865 had 1,504 Negro inhabitants—one-half of its total population.[17]

White Kansans welcomed the Negroes as laborers. Such a severe shortage of manpower existed in the state by the middle of the war that Governor Carney felt it necessary to caution recruiting officers to go slow in their efforts. "A great many farms are not cultivated in this section," wrote Sam Reader of Indianola to a relative back East, "for want of working men." "It would be a great blessing," he added, "if more darkies would understand their rights and come to our aid." Kansas farmers eagerly sought the Negroes brought out of Missouri by the Lane Brigade in the autumn of 1861, and the Lawrence *Journal* accused Lane of asking and accepting money for providing them. The large crop of 1863, affirmed the *Conservative*, was made possible only by Negro hands. "Almost every farm is supplied with labor in the shape of one or two large, healthy negroes." [18]

Many of the former slaves, however, were reluctant to work. To them slavery and work were synonymous, and initially, at least, they adopted the attitude that when one ended so should the other. Mrs. Orpen remembered seeing young children in the fields hoeing corn while the "negroes who abounded in the neighborhood . . . would not work, no matter what pay was

---

[17] Statement of Pomeroy in *Congressional Globe*, 37th Cong., 3d Sess., p. 597; Kansas State Census of 1865, Kansas State Archives; Leavenworth *Daily Conservative*, July 8, 1862.

[18] Carney to Colonel W. R. Judson, February 23, 1863, "Kansas Regiments," *Report of the Adjutant General*, p. 84; "The Letters of Samuel James Reader, 1861–1863," *KHQ*, IX (May, 1940), 151; *Kansas State Journal* (Lawrence), March 13, 1862; Leavenworth *Daily Conservative*, May 27, August 6, 1863.

offered." A newspaper correspondent from Illinois described a colony of "contrabands" near Fort Scott, its members sprawled out on the ground in "squads," completely unconcerned about the future, and declining to accept any of the jobs offered them. They preferred, stated the correspondent, to exist on the hospitality of their fellows who had erected "little shanties and were earning a living." Only a few professional abolitionists were prepared to accord the Negro refugees equal rights and treatment. Most Kansans considered the Negro to be "greatly inferior to the white man" and regarded him with a mixture of contemptuous amusement and distrustful fear. At Indianola, in the fall of 1864, an attempt by some Negro children to attend the same school as the white resulted in the parents of the latter withdrawing their children from the school and in the white students throwing stones at the colored.[19]

The prevailing wartime attitude in Kansas toward slavery was summed up by the editor of the Oskaloosa *Independent* in September, 1861:

When the present rebellion first broke out, there was but one sentiment among loyal citizens—that of maintaining the government against the rebels, and of avoiding the Slavery issue, as such, in the contest. . . . But of late . . . there is an evident change in public feeling on the subject of Slavery. . . .

While no one, or at least none but a mere handful [*sic*] of rabid abolitionists, wishes the war to assume the Slavery issue as the leading feature or the main end to attain, yet there is a growing desire to have the institution, which is either the real cause of the rebellion, or the instrumentality used by ambitious demagogues to carry out their treason, put out of the way.

Sol Miller agreed with this analysis and added that even recent proslavery men were advocating that the slaves of "traitors" be

---

[19] Orpen, *Emigrant Days,* pp. 60–61; C. M. Chase to the Sycamore, Ill., *True Republican and Sentinel,* August 19, 1863, Chase Letters; *Olathe Mirror,* June 20, 1861; Diary of Samuel Reader, September 12, 25, October 16, 1864.

liberated. Kansans generally favored emancipation both as a war measure and as "an act of justice," but placed main emphasis on the first reason. They believed that "the preservation of the Union and the preservation of slavery, both, are utterly impossible" and that "one or the other must go down." Therefore they decided that they "could but accept the issue, and war on slavery." [20]

The white refugees did not come to Kansas voluntarily as did most of the Negroes. They had been driven from their homes by secessionists and guerrillas or wished to evade service in the Confederate army. Sol Miller estimated their number as six or seven thousand by the fall of 1864.[21] They were very bitter toward their former neighbors who had forced them to flee and were intensely anxious to obtain vengeance. In turn, they were especially hated by the bushwhackers, who mercilessly killed all whom they recognized during raids into Kansas. These refugees were a factor in state politics, siding for the most part with the Lane faction: Lane's advocacy of marching into Missouri and making up the losses of Union men appealed to them. Hundreds of them enlisted in Kansas regiments, some of which contained as many, if not more, Missourians than Kansans. The presence of these vengeance-minded Missourians in the Kansas regiments was an important cause of the marauding perpetrated by these regiments in their expeditions into Missouri. Even some former Confederate soldiers were to be found in the ranks of the Kansas troops. In all, probably one-third of the 20,000 men

[20] *White Cloud Kansas Chief*, November 28, 1861. See also *Lawrence Republican*, September 12, November 28, 1861; *Kansas State Record* (Topeka), September 7, 1861; *Kansas State Journal* (Lawrence), September 26, December 5, 13, 1861; Oskaloosa *Independent*, September 28, October 5, 1861; *Freedom's Champion* (Atchison), November 9, December 14, 1861; *House Journal, 1865*, p. 395; *Council Grove Press*, December 14, 1863; *Olathe Mirror*, June 20, 1861. See as well *Weekly Osage Chronicle* (Burlingame), February 6, 1864; *House Journal, 1865*, p. 413; Diary of Samuel J. Reader, September 12, 25, October 10, 1864.
[21] *White Cloud Kansas Chief*, November 17, 1864.

raised by Kansas during the course of the war came from out of the state.[22]

The overwhelming majority of Kansans were intensely, even intolerantly, pro-Union. A New York *Tribune* correspondent, following a trip through the state, declared that he would not for his life "go into any part of Kansas and advocate the rebel cause. No one dare do it. The mere suspicion that one is disloyal may result in his being shot."[23] On the other hand, there seems to have been very little active disloyalty in the state, as distinguished from political dissent or simple pro-Southern leanings. Contemporary reports concerning the presence of the pro-Confederate secret societies known as "Blue Lodges" and "Knights of the Golden Circle" are vague and inconclusive. Most of the really serious and determined Confederate sympathizers probably either went South or, like Quantrill and Anderson, became bushwhackers.

The outstanding instances of persecution of so-called "copperheads" occurred in Leavenworth. There, in June, 1861, the rabidly radical Anthony shot R. C. Saterlee, editor of the Leavenworth *Herald*, for printing supposedly unpatriotic remarks. For a while following Saterlee's death Leavenworth was without a Democratic journal, but in February, 1862, the Democratic *Daily Inquirer* came into being with Burrell E. Taylor as editor. A mob, angered by its criticism of the Administration, gathered for the purpose of wrecking it, but was dissuaded by, of all people, "Web" Wilder.[24] On June 15, however, Blunt, who had been sharply criticized by the *Inquirer*, ordered it suppressed and arrested Taylor and the publisher for "giving aid and comfort to the Confederacy." This action was highhanded and unwar-

[22] *Senate Journal, 1866*, pp. 22–24.

[23] Quoted in *Freedom's Champion* (Atchison), March 31, 1865. The *Olathe Mirror*, June 31, 1861, stated that "no Secesh dares openly declare himself so in Kansas."

[24] Leavenworth *Daily Conservative*, March 1, 1862. The *Inquirer* was printed on the presses of the *Conservative*. This may have had something to do with Wilder's uncharacteristic action.

ranted. A writ of habeas corpus speedily released both men, and the paper resumed publication.[25] But on February 9 a mob, led by Jennison and Anthony, after breaking up a Democratic "peace" meeting, sacked the offices of the *Inquirer* and drove Taylor from the town. The city authorities attempted to halt the mob; street-fighting ensued; and on February 10 Blunt imposed martial law.[26] In May, Anthony, now mayor, arrested David H. Bailey, editor of the *Times*, for "disturbing the peace" by publishing an article criticizing the generalship of General Hooker in Virginia and fined him twenty dollars. Bailey refused to pay the fine and spent three hours in jail before obtaining a release on a writ of habeas corpus. He then sued Anthony, who was fined fifty dollars and costs.[27]

Throughout the war Kansas Republicans, already waving the bloody shirt, labeled their Democratic rivals as "seceders" and "copperheads," notwithstanding the fact that many of them, notably John A. Halderman of Leavenworth, served with conspicuous gallantry in the Union army. In 1862 the Democrats claimed, probably with much justification, that "terrorism" in various localities prevented them from voting.[28] Much of the odium that descended on the Democrats nationally as the result of their peace and anti-emancipationist policies fell also upon the Democrats of Kansas. Numerous Democrats, George Crawford being perhaps the most prominent, joined the "Union Party," as the Republicans styled themselves, and even those old "pro-slavery villains" of territorial days, Sheriff Sam Jones and Judge Samuel D. Lecompte, became Republicans.[29] Although certain individual Democrats such as Cyrus K. Holliday of Topeka and George W. Glick of Atchison exercised considerable personal influence, the

[25] Leavenworth *Daily Conservative*, June 17, 1862.

[26] *Ibid.*, February 8, 11, 14, 1863.

[27] *Council Grove Press*, May 25, 1863; Leavenworth *Daily Times*, September 21, 23, 1863.

[28] *Topeka Tribune*, October 4, 1862.

[29] Samuel N. Wood, "The Pioneers of Kansas," *KHC*, III (1883–1885), 430.

Democrats as a party emerged from the war an extremely weak minority, the victims of history and their own mistakes.

The jayhawkers and Red Legs by no means restricted their marauding to Missouri. They also committed countless acts of robbery and terror in Kansas itself. In Kansas as in Missouri they covered and excused their deeds by claiming that they were merely putting down the "secesh." For a while they received widespread praise and support from Kansans who imagined that their motives were identical with their professions and that they were performing a worth-while service in repressing pro-Southern elements and guarding the border. Their leading eulogist was Wilder in the Leavenworth *Conservative*. Declaring that "the essence of Jayhawking is Democracy," he defied their critics by stating:

Jayhawking was got up in Kansas. It's one of our things. It works well; we believe in it, we are going to have it. It don't make any difference whether the authorities, civil or military, believe in it or not. Kansas don't care much for authorities; never did, never will.[30]

But when it became obvious that the jayhawkers plundered and killed indiscriminately, and not only in Missouri, commendation turned to condemnation. Only Wilder continued to extol them, and even he had to admit that one of his heroes, Marshall Cleveland, was a "desperado" after he robbed two banks in Kansas City.[31]

The state and military authorities made repeated but sporadic efforts to suppress jayhawking. In August, 1861, Governor Robinson sent a posse into Johnson County after receiving a letter stating that at Olathe the people were more afraid of the jayhawkers than of an invasion from Missouri and that "a secret organization had been formed for the purpose of plundering the

[30] Leavenworth *Daily Conservative*, September 20, 1861.
[31] *Ibid.*, November 17, 1861. The above discussion of Kansas attitudes toward jayhawking is based on a reading of the Kansas press of the summer and fall of 1861.

people: ostensibly to operate against those who are reputed as lukewarm on the Union question, but really to rob every man of property." Several months later he had troops stationed at various points in northern Kansas at the urging of Judge Samuel A. Kingman, who also declared that the populace feared the jayhawkers as much as they did the Missourians. Robinson's efforts, however, failed to check jayhawking, and in his message to the 1862 legislature he announced that the state was "overrun with thieves and highway robbers," for which he blamed the war and (by implication) Lane. On February 8, 1862, General Hunter, at Robinson's request, placed all of Kansas under martial law.[32]

Blunt, when he assumed command, retained martial law and issued new orders designed to eradicate jayhawking. But the practice continued unabated, and by the spring of 1863 the Red Legs had come into being. In April, Blunt sent the Ninth Kansas into West Missouri to operate against this organization and the bushwhackers, with instructions to shoot "on the spot" persons "caught in the act of thievery or other lawlessness, or in the possession of stolen property."[33] Some, though, expressed doubts concerning Blunt's sincerity in combating the Red Legs, since Captain Tough, one of their reputed leaders, was his chief of scouts.[34] Ewing's sensational Olathe speech denouncing those who were "stealing themselves rich in the name of liberty" and his attempt to suppress the Red Legs at Leavenworth have been described. Stirred to action by this speech, law-abiding settlers in many counties formed vigilante bands which hunted down the

[32] E. S. Lowman to Robinson, August 13, 1861, Robinson Papers, KSHS; Kingman to Robinson, November 25, 1861, and Major Charles Halpine to Robinson, January 24, 1862, Governors' Correspondence (Charles Robinson), Military Affairs, 1861–1862, Kansas State Archives; *Kansas State Journal* (Lawrence), August 29, 1861, January 23, 1862; *OR*, ser. I, VIII, 547–548.

[33] *OR*, ser. I, XIII, 572; *ibid.*, XXII, pt. 2, 139, 222–223; Leavenworth *Daily Conservative*, June 5, 1862; Blunt, "Civil War Experiences," p. 259.

[34] Oskaloosa *Independent*, April 25, 1863; *Olathe Mirror*, February 13, 20, 1864.

Red Legs and other jayhawkers and either killed or drove them away.[35] But to the end of the war and for a long time afterward banditry was a serious problem in the state.

Throughout much of the war Kansans feared that the Confederate Indians in the Indian Territory would invade their state. This apprehension, however, was largely groundless. The Confederates in that region lacked both the means and the organization for offensive operations, and Blunt's campaigns of 1862 and 1863 forced them back nearly to the borders of Texas. Kansans also were uneasy concerning the Osages, who inhabited a long belt of territory in the southern part of the state. But they gave no serious trouble and in the summer of 1863 wiped out a party of Confederates who were on their way west to negotiate with the Plains Indians.[36]

Fortunately for Kansas the western Plains Indians did not go on the warpath in 1861, when they could have caused tremendous difficulty owing to the lack of troops, the drought, and the menace of Confederate invasion. During 1862 and 1863 they committed only minor depredations in the Republican and Solomon River regions. But in July of 1864 a full-scale Indian war broke out. The Kiowas, Arapahoes, and Comanches roamed up and down the Santa Fe Trail from the Cimarron to Council Grove robbing stations and ranches, stealing horses, and killing or wounding about eighteen people. In August the Cheyennes and Arapahoes struck the fringe of settlements along the valley of the Little Blue in "one of the most thoroughly planned, skilfully executed, and disastrous raids in the history of the Western states." The settlers fled in terror, some going to Marysville, others to the number of 200 collecting in a fortified camp near the present site of Clay Center. Most of them returned to their claims after scouts reported the departure of the Indians, but a sizable number retreated to less exposed areas. Throughout the

[35] Leavenworth *Daily Conservative*, May 16, June 9, 1863; *Kansas State Journal* (Lawrence), August 6, 1863.
[36] P. P. Elder to Blunt, May 17, 1863, *OR*, ser. I, XXIII, pt. 2, 286.

remainder of 1864 and into 1865 the Indians continued their forays in northern Kansas, directing them mainly against the horse stations, ranches, wagons, and stagecoaches of the over-land lines, which as a result were badly crippled in their opera-tions.[37]

In consequence of the Indian outbreak, Curtis in July took the field in person at the head of 100 regulars and 300 militia. He proceeded as far west as Fort Larned but was unable to engage the marauders. Late in September, Blunt, in command of the District of the Upper Arkansas, went on an "Indian Hunt" with 400 troops. According to his own account he routed 1,500 In-dians in a battle northwest of Fort Larned, pursued them for two days, and failed to destroy them completely only because his horses gave out. Actually, however, the battle was a mere skir-mish in which a small detachment under Major Scott J. Anthony did all the fighting, and Blunt's attack only exasperated the In-dians, who were conducting peace negotiations at Denver, and caused them to retaliate on the Smoky Hill settlements.[38]

Many Kansans firmly believed that the Confederates incited the Plains Indians to attack the state. Although there is some evidence that Southern agents attempted to contact the Co-manches, Kiowas, and Cheyennes, there is none to indicate that they influenced the action of these or other tribes. The Plains Indians were indifferent as to whether the whites called them-selves Confederates or Federals, and they raided the western settlements of Texas as frequently as they did those of Kansas, Nebraska, and Minnesota. The real causes of the Indian uprisings were the usual ones: the encroachment of white settlers on the Indian hunting grounds, the massacre and spoilation of the buffalo

[37] *Ibid.*, XIII, 381–384; *ibid.*, XXII, pt. 1, 813–814; *ibid.*, pt. 2, p. 144; *ibid.*, XLI, pt. 2, 446, 484; Andreas, *History of Kansas*, pp. 916, 1015, 1056, 1274, 1313; Bowles, *Across the Continent*, p. 5.

[38] *OR*, ser. I, XLI, pt. 2, 484; Leavenworth *Daily Conservative*, August 5, 6, 1864; Leavenworth *Daily Times*, October 28, 1864; Blunt, "Civil War Experiences," pp. 251–252; George Bird Grinnell, *The Fighting Cheyennes* (Norman, Okla., 1956), pp. 161–164.

herds by professional hunters, personal outrages committed by settlers and soldiers, the selling of whisky to the Indians by unscrupulous traders, and the savage desire of the Indians for plunder and
excitement.[39]

Kansas land held by Indians living on reservations totaled
9,986,442 acres—nearly one-fifth of the entire area of the state
and including some of its most fertile soil. With complete and
passionate unanimity the settlers of Kansas desired that either
the Indians be removed from this land or that the land be removed from the Indians. They did not conceive of the Indians
as possessing any rights to this land, but as merely presenting an
irritating obstacle to its acquisition. Whether they were petty
speculators, prospective homesteaders, or railroad promoters they
demanded that the holdings of the Indians be thrown open to
exploitation. Many of them contemptuously disregarded legal
formalities and simply "squatted" on the Indian tracts, where
they ignored the protests of the Indians and defied the sporadic
efforts of the Government to drive them off. An able scholar had
in mind the attitudes and policies of the pioneers of Kansas toward
the Indians when she wrote that "never in all history . . . has
the insatiable land-hunger of the white man been better illus-
trated than in the case of the beginnings of the sunflower state." [40]

Beginning early in 1863 Kansas officials, both state and Federal, launched a determined drive to acquire the reservations.
First Carney proposed to the legislature that it request Washington to extinguish all Indian land titles in the state, a recommendation which it quickly adopted. Next Lane, seconded by
Pomeroy, had the Senate pass a bill authorizing the President
to negotiate treaties with the Kansas Indians which would provide for their removal to the Indian Territory. Finally, that

[39] See *OR*, ser. I, XXXIV, pt. 4, 150, 404; *ibid.*, XLI, pt. 2, 209; *ibid.*,
XXII, pt. 2, 316.
[40] *Senate Journal*, 1864, p. 24; Anna Heloise Abel, "Indian Reservations
in Kansas and the Extinguishment of Their Titles," *KHC*, VIII (1903–
1904), 72–109; Abel, *Slaveholding Indians*, III, 23–24.

summer, Indian Commissioner Dole went to Kansas and drew up treaties with the Creek, Sac and Fox, Osage, Shawnee, and New York Indians calling for their transfer to the Indian Territory. None of these agreements, however, went into effect. Bad enough to begin with, the Senate, at the behest of Lane and Pomeroy, attached amendments to the treaties which made them absolutely intolerable to the Indians, who refused to ratify them. As a result a general removal of the Indians did not take place until after the war.[41]

The prime influence behind the movement to deprive the Indians of their lands was that of the Kansas railroad interests. These interests centered in Leavenworth, Atchison, and Lawrence. Of the three, the first was the most important and the only one to achieve tangible results during the war period. But before relating its history, it would be well to state that the desire of Kansans in the 1860's for railroads was matched only by their need for them. To them the coming of the railroads meant the coming of prosperity, new opportunities, and wonderful conveniences of commerce and travel. In later years they were to regret the favors they showered upon the railroad companies, but for the time being they were willing to do or promise almost anything to assist the railroad promoters and to secure lines to their communities or through their farming regions.

In 1861 the leaders of the Leavenworth railroad group were Thomas Ewing, Jr., James C. Stone, A. J. Isaacs, and James H. McDowell. They constituted the "Executive Committee" of the Leavenworth, Pawnee & Western Railroad Company. Although the company completed surveys of the portion of the line between Leavenworth and Fort Riley in 1857, its further progress was stymied during the ensuing three years by lack of capital.[42] As with other railroad enterprises of the time, it pro-

[41] *Kansas State Journal* (Lawrence), January 22, 1863; *Congressional Globe*, 37th Cong., 3d Sess., pp. 505, 527; Abel, "Indian Reservations in Kansas," *KHC*, VIII (1903–1904), 72–109.

[42] U.S. Congress, Senate, *Report of the United States Pacific Railway*

posed to supply this lack by acquiring land which could be sold to settlers or mortgaged in return for loans. Therefore in May, 1860, it concluded a treaty with the Delaware Indians, who occupied a large reservation north of Lawrence. This treaty authorized the Delawares to sell 223,966 acres of the reserve to the LP&W at their appraised value but at not less than $1.25 per acre.[43] But when the time came to pay for this land, the Leavenworth associates did not have sufficient money to do so. They therefore resorted to a very ingenious but rather dubious device. Principally through the efforts of Ewing they induced President Lincoln to issue an executive order postponing the date of payment. Then, with the assistance of the Office of Indian Affairs, they negotiated a supplementary treaty. Under its terms the LP&W was to buy the Delaware lands by paying for them with bonds which were to be secured by a mortgage on 100,000 acres of these lands. In other words, the company would use part of the lands to acquire all of the lands, which was tantamount to a confession on its part that the price it proposed to pay for them was far less than their actual market value. The Indians signed the new treaty on July 2, 1861, and the Senate ratified it on August 6, 1861. During the course of these transactions the LP&W bribed Lane, Pomeroy, Conway, Delahay, and Robert G. Corwin.[44]

Ewing and his partners next gained possession of the valuable

_____

*Commission*, Sen. Ex. Doc., 50th Cong., 1st Sess., vol. III, no. 51, pt. 4, pp. 1595–1596 (hereinafter cited as *Report of the Pacific Railway Commission*); Andreas, *History of Kansas*, p. 245; John D. Cruise, "Early Days on the Union Pacific," *KHC*, XI (1909–1910), 534–535.

[43] *A Compilation of All the Treaties between the United States and the Indian Tribes Now in Force as Laws* (Washington, 1873), pp. 350–352.

[44] *Report of the Pacific Railway Commission*, pp. 1674–1675; Basler, ed., *Complete Works of Lincoln*, IV, 400–402; *Treaties between the United States and Indian Tribes*, pp. 350–362; document entitled "Proposition for Sale," and Ewing to James C. Stone, December 31, 1861, in Ewing Papers, KSHS; Leavenworth *Daily Conservative*, March 4, 1862; *White Cloud Kansas Chief*, June 23, 1864; Robinson, *Kansas Conflict*, p. 418.

Pottawatomie Reserve northwest of Topeka by a treaty signed on November 5, 1861, and approved by the Senate on April 15, 1862. In order to secure passage of the treaty the LP&W once more had to "provide for" Lane and Pomeroy, as well as distribute stock and lands to D. W. Wilder, Secretary of the Interior Caleb Smith, and others both in Washington and in Kansas.[45] Yet, even with the Pottawatomie lands added to the Delaware, they found it impossible to attract the necessary Eastern capital to begin actual construction. Therefore they had their projected road included in the Pacific Railroad Act of July 1, 1862. This act granted the LP&W "every alternate section of public land, designated by odd numbers, to the amount of five alternate sections per mile" on each side of its line. This line was to run from the south side of the mouth of the Kansas River to the one-hundredth meridian between the Platte and Republican rivers, where it was to connect with the main track of the Union Pacific from Omaha. Ewing, Stone, and Isaacs endeavored to have Leavenworth made the terminus, but the Missouri railroad interests successfully opposed them. As before, they were obliged to distribute "favors" to Lane and Pomeroy and also to such Kansas "worthies" as Fielding Johnson, Josiah Miller, Chester Howard, Robert Stevens, Frederick Stanton, Mark Delahay, S. N. Simpson, William Ross, Cyrus Holliday, and Attorney General Samuel N. Stinson.[46]

On September 19, 1862, the LP&W let a contract to Ross, Steele & Company, a Canadian firm, to construct its line. This company began work in November, 1862. By June of the following year it had expended $50,000 but had only one mile graded, and the funds of the LP&W were exhausted. At this point a new group headed by John C. Fremont and Samuel Hallett of New

[45] Ewing to Dole, December 27, 1861, to John P. Usher, November 19, 1861, to R. McBratney, December 27, 1861, Ewing Papers, KSHS; *Report of the Pacific Railway Commission*, pp. 1598–1600, 1616–1619.

[46] *Report of the Pacific Railway Commission*, pp. 1595–1598, 1622, 1676; *Congressional Globe*, 37th Cong., 2d Sess., pt. 4, Appendix, p. 383.

York, backed by Eastern capital, purchased the controlling interest in the LP&W and renamed it the Union Pacific Railway, Eastern Division. Hallett canceled the contract with Ross, Steele & Company and ordered it to stop work. When it refused, he obtained the services of a squadron of United States cavalry and in a "pitch in" on August 5 drove its laborers from the construction area.[47]

With Hallett in personal charge, grading operations on the main line of the Union Pacific, Eastern Division, began near Wyandotte on September 7, 1863. The road started at the state line on the south bank of the Kansas River, went west one mile, then crossed over to the north side and proceeded up the Kaw Valley. By November it was graded as far as Lawrence and surveyed as far as Topeka. It did not, however, pass through either of these towns, but about three miles north of them. The citizens of Lawrence and Topeka, greatly alarmed, asked Hallett why he was by-passing their communities. Hallett replied that they both were so distant from the direct line that Congress would not appropriate the subsidies provided by the charter of the company if he directed the track to either of them. He further declared that only if they each voted him $100,000 would he change the route. He likewise demanded $100,000 from Wyandotte to connect that town directly.

Lane was personally interested in having the road pass close to Lawrence. He owned land along the north bank of the river opposite Lawrence which he had received for his support of the Delaware Treaty. Moreover, the road as it was presently graded passed through a farm belonging to Charles Robinson. Therefore Lane proceeded to deprive Hallett of his excuse for running the line north of Lawrence by having thirty-four Senators and President Lincoln sign a memorial requesting Hallett to construct his railroad along the upper bank of the Kansas River. Hallett at first agreed to do so, but later reneged and at-

[47] *Kansas Weekly Tribune* (Lawrence), June 4, 1863; Cruise, "Early Days on the Union Pacific," *KHC*, XI (1909–1910), 535–536.

tempted to extort $300,000 and $200,000 in bonds from Lawrence and Topeka respectively. Lane then induced the Senate to amend the Pacific Railroad Bill so as to require the Union Pacific, Eastern Division, to enter the two towns. This pressure had the desired effect. On June 13 Hallett notified Lane that he would relocate the road as demanded. In return Lane promised that Lawrence would pay the additional costs of grading, $30,000. Lawrence had previously voted to provide the railroad with depot grounds and remunerate it "for all accommodations." [48]

Construction crews began laying tracks in April, 1864. By November 26 they reached Lawrence, and on December 19 the first regular train ran between that town and Wyandotte. On January 18, 1865, the legislature accepted an invitation from the Union Pacific, Eastern Division, to take "a free ride from Topeka to Wyandotte and back again." Since the tracks extended only as far as Lawrence, the legislators, as well as the state officials, Supreme Court judges, and "miscellaneous citizens" who joined them, traveled some twenty miles of the way on horseback, in carriages, or even on foot. They boarded the waiting cars at Lawrence, "and soon, for the first and only time in Kansas history, the whole state administration—legislative, executive, judicial, and military, with an enthusiastic social accompaniment —was being hurtled towards the Missouri border." After arriving at Wyandotte they attended a grand ball at a warehouse on the levee, during which "the doors were taken off their hinges." On the following morning, Saturday, the Government of Kansas

[48] Leavenworth *Daily Times*, September 27, 1863; *Kansas Weekly Tribune* (Lawrence), December 31, 1863, February 4, June 28, August 1, 1864; *Congressional Globe*, 38th Cong., 1st Sess., pp. 2417–2418; *House Journal, 1864*, pp. 508–510; Speer, *Life of Lane*, pp. 272–277. Lane's efforts in this embroglio probably regained him much support and helped him win the 1864 elections. Hallett was murdered on July 27, 1864, by O. A. Talcott, chief engineer of the UP, ED, whom Hallett had beaten up and dismissed for reporting to Lincoln that Hallett's construction work was below the required quality and that Hallett was dishonest and heavily in debt.

reboarded the train and headed back to Lawrence and Topeka, having celebrated in fitting fashion the "forging of the first link in the chain which was to bind the mouth of the Kaw to Golden Gate." [49]

[49] *Kansas Weekly Tribune* (Lawrence), December 1, 22, 1864; *Senate Journal, 1865*, pp. 76, 94; *House Journal, 1865*, pp. 98–100, 120, 123; Manning, "The Kansas Senate of 1865 and 1866," *KHC*, IX (1905–1906), 365.

# XIII

# *The End of the War*

"RICHMOND TAKEN!" "LEE SURRENDERS!" "OUR NATION SAVED!" Thus in large black capital letters Kansas newspapers proclaimed the long-awaited, greatly welcomed news. In Leavenworth the people celebrated with processions, prayers, and pyrotechnics. At Oskaloosa the citizens "got up quite a bonfire and had considerable of a jollification" around a liberty pole. The *Olathe Mirror* announced that "Humanity, Truth and Right have succeeded, Treason, Anarchy and Ruin have been thwarted." Atchison was bright with illuminations all through the night. The typesetters of the local *Champion* were so excited that they misprinted the date of the issue telling of Appomattox as "April 11, 165." And in Lawrence, which had more reason than any other town to rejoice, the people hauled out the historic cannon "Old Sacramento" and fired salvo after salvo, while Lane and Robinson appeared on the same platform to address the happy throng.

A week later, black-bordered newspaper columns related the horrifying story of the President's assassination. "Yesterday," wrote Colonel Martin in the April 16 *Champion*, "was a bright, balmy and beautiful day, but oh! how sad and mournful to the nation." All business houses closed, and the buildings were draped in black. People gathered in little groups on the streets and discussed the calamity in subdued voices. Others "seemed struck dumb" and could only weep. Governor Crawford appointed April 23 as a day of fasting and prayer, and during all the latter part of the month the towns of Kansas held public services and funeral processions in commemoration of the man who had led the nation to victory. The war had ended, but in tragedy and gloom.

Remnants and aftereffects of the war, however, lingered on for many months. The Confederate Trans-Mississippi armies did not lay down their arms until June, and it was July before promises of amnesty and protection induced most of the bushwhackers to surrender. Within Kansas the crime and violence engendered by the jayhawkers long remained rampant. One editor sarcastically commented that "horse stealing and robbery seems to be the most respectable mode of making a living just at the present time." [1] The *Conservative* was shocked by the "cheapness of blood" and reported that "not a paper from any locality came to hand without an account of bloodshed, either in some broil, or more frequently in the commission of some crime." "There are hundreds of men in the State," it added, "who would shoot a human being as soon as they would a dog." [2]

Despite these disturbed postwar conditions, which were aggravated by drought and grasshopper troubles, so many immigrants poured into Kansas that in the spring of 1866 Governor Crawford optimistically predicted that by the end of the year the population of the state would reach "three hundred thousand persons." [3] The new settlers came in parties, usually jogging along in covered wagons. Almost all the men were ex-soldiers who carried one or two revolvers and wore some part of their

[1] *Council Grove Press*, September 22, 1865.

[2] Leavenworth *Daily Conservative*, May 21, 1865.

[3] Crawford to Blunt, March 1, 1866, Governors' Correspondence (Samuel J. Crawford), 1865–1867, Kansas State Archives. The population of Kansas increased to 364,000 by 1870.

old uniform.[4] Between 1865 and 1870 an estimated 75,000 of them entered the state, where during the ensuing four decades they built the schools, churches, and courthouses, operated the businesses and tilled the farms, and completely dominated politics and government. "In every school district the school board were old soldiers; in every county the commissioners, and most of the other officers, were old soldiers." Session after session of the legislature was filled with men who had served in the Union army, and for years practically all the governors were members of the G.A.R.[5] Nearly one-half of Kansas' 107 counties today bear the names of Civil War soldiers or statesmen, and upon the spacious lawns about the county seats are still to be seen the statues and cannons put there by the veterans so that future generations would remember and honor them.

Most of the men who have figured in the pages of this work were still relatively young in 1865 and hence lived for many years thereafter, although not always happily. Blunt, who recovered much of his prestige in the Price Raid, resigned his commission in June and resumed the practice of medicine in Leavenworth. In 1869 he moved to Washington, where he became a professional claim solicitor. The Justice Department in 1873 indicted him and several others for conspiring to defraud the Government, but the courts dismissed the case two years later. Early in 1879 he became a patient at St. Elizabeth's hospital for the insane in the District of Columbia, and there he died on July 25, 1881. Martin Conway, the most radical of all the radicals, died in the same institution a few months later.[6]

Ewing left the army in February, 1865, with the brevet rank of major general for his services at Pilot Knob. Having abandoned all hope of political preferment in Kansas, he did not re-

[4] Eugene F. Ware, "The Neutral Lands," *KHC*, VI (1897–1900), 152.
[5] William A. Calderhead, "The Service of the Army in Civil Life after the War," *KHC*, XII (1911–1912), 16–17.
[6] Blunt, "Civil War Experiences," p. 211; Andreas, *History of Kansas*, pp. 302–304.

turn there, but became a Washington lawyer and lobbyist. He also quit the Republican Party and was an aspirant for the Democratic vice-presidential nomination in 1868. Previously he had declined an offer from President Johnson of the office of Secretary of War. In 1870 he took up residence in his native state of Ohio and twice won election to the House of Representatives. In 1879 he waged an unsuccessful campaign for Governor, a campaign in which Bingham's painting, "Order No. 11," was used against him. He spent his last years in New York, where he died in 1896 as the result of a streetcar accident.[7] His abilities were greater than his fortune, and although he had a distinguished career, it did not fulfill his ambition.

D. R. Anthony attempted to become mayor of Leavenworth again in April, 1865, only to be defeated by Thomas Carney. Several weeks after the election he engaged in a shooting affray with Jennison, whose gang had assaulted him a few days before, but neither man suffered injury. He remained violently active in Leavenworth journalism and politics until the end of the century, a persistent and sometimes successful seeker of the mayorship. Prior to his death in 1904, he expressed regret that he had not been more "radical."[8]

Jennison emerged from the Price campaign with his reputation more tainted than before. During the fighting between Lexington and Westport the men of his regiment, the Fifteenth Kansas, gave no quarter to prisoners and even executed some Kansas militiamen whom they claimed to have mistaken for bushwhackers. While participating in the pursuit of Price they lynched several Confederate prisoners, and at Carthage, Missouri, in Jennison's own words, they shot and hanged a number of "skulking, whining rebels," although "it wasn't a very good

---

[7] Harrison Hannahs, "General Thomas Ewing, Jr., *KHC*, XII (1911-1912), 280-282; Albert H. Horton, "The Judiciary of Kansas," *ibid.*, III (1883-1885), 394-395; *Dictionary of American Biography* (New York, 1928-1937), VI, 238-239.

[8] Leavenworth *Daily Conservative*, March 29, 30, April 20, May 18, 1865; *The Annals of Kansas, 1886-1925* (Topeka, 1954), I, 410.

time for hanging either." On the return march from the Arkansas River they continued these atrocities and were also guilty of "indiscriminate pilfering and robbing of private citizens, and especially of defenseless women and children."[9] Upon arriving back in Kansas, Jennison quarreled bitterly with Blunt, who arrested him and had him court-martialed. He escaped with a mere reprimand but later another court martial resulted in his being dishonorably dismissed from the army.[10] The war now being over, he went to Leavenworth where in subsequent years he operated a saloon and bred horses. Death came to him fairly early, in 1884, at the age of fifty.[11]

"Web" Wilder continued to edit newspapers and mix in politics until his death in 1911. He helped found the Kansas State Historical Society and in 1875 brought out the first edition of his *Annals of Kansas*, a useful book, but not always accurate and often ludicrous both for what it includes and for what it excludes. He took part in the "Old Settlers" quarrel over who "saved Kansas" in the fifties and, as might be expected, was a passionate advocate of John Brown.[12]

Quantrill, who in the spring of 1864 had been supplanted by Todd and Anderson as the leader of the bushwhackers, stayed in hiding in Missouri throughout the summer and fall of 1864. In January, 1865, with several dozen of his old followers, he crossed the Mississippi River into Kentucky. Some speculate that he intended to go to Washington and assassinate Lincoln. However, he passed the winter and spring committing petty robberies in central Kentucky. On May 10, 1865, a party of "Federal guerrillas" surprised his band near Louisville. They shot Quan-

---

[9] "Kansas Regiments," *Report of the Adjutant General*, pp. 239-242; Hinton, *Rebel Invasion*, p. 185; Leavenworth *Daily Times*, November 29, 1864; *OR*, ser. I, XLI, pt. 4, 591.

[10] *OR*, ser. I, XLI, pt. 4, pp. 842-843, 846.

[11] Leavenworth *Daily Times*, March 19, 1865; Leavenworth *Daily Conservative*, April 27, 1865; C. M. Chase Letters, letter of November 24, 1873.

[12] *KHC*, XII (1911-1912), 416.

trill through the spine, captured him, and took him to Louisville, where he died on June 6 in a hospital. He was buried "in a grave deep enough to keep him till the judgment day."[13]

Pomeroy, blandly distributing bribes, secured re-election to the Senate in 1867. He aligned himself with the congressional radicals during the Reconstruction era and achieved considerable influence and power in Washington. He was well on his way to re-election for a third term in 1873 when, in one of the most dramatic incidents in Kansas history, State Senator A. M. York stood up before the legislature, produced a packet containing $7,000, and announced that he had received the money from Pomeroy in return for pledging his vote to him. Pomeroy was ruined by York's disclosure, and the legislature elected John James Ingalls as his successor. He retired to Massachusetts, lived comfortably on the fortune he had accumulated in Kansas and Washington, ran as the Prohibitionist Party candidate for President in 1884, and died almost unnoticed in 1891.[14] Mark Twain, in his novel *The Gilded Age*, gave him lasting fame as "Senator Dilworthy" of "The Happy Land of Canaan."

Thomas Carney attempted to secure the Republican nomination for Congress in 1866. His principal backer was, surprisingly enough, Jim Lane. Failing, he retired from active participation in politics and devoted himself to business affairs. To this he was much better suited. Before his death in 1888 he became "the most successful businessman in Kansas."[15]

Charles Robinson resided on a large farm near Lawrence until his death in 1894. Although he declared that he was through with politics after his retirement from the governorship, he remained active in the public arena to the end. From 1874 to 1878 he served as State Senator. In 1886 he left the Republican Party and ran against its candidate for Congresss. Four years later he was

[13] Connelley, *Quantrill*, pp. 459–480.

[14] Albert R. Kitzhaber, "*Götterdämmerung* in Topeka: The Downfall of Senator Pomeroy," *KHQ*, XVIII (August, 1950), 243–278.

[15] Lane to McDowell, June 24, 1866, McDowell Papers; William E. Connelley, ed., *History of Kansas* (Chicago and New York, 1928), II, 656–659.

the gubernatorial nominee of the Populists, Democrats, and Greenbacks. Defeated in this election, in 1892 he helped organize the fusion of Democrats and Republicans which resulted in the Populist victory of that year. Although engaged in the politics of the present, he did not forget those of the past. In various speeches and writings, and especially in his autobiography, *The Kansas Conflict*, he continued his old quarrel with Jim Lane, John Brown, and other enemies of the early days. Their champions angrily attacked him, and a bitter controversy ensued which in some degree persists to this day.[16]

Lane, after his victory in the 1864 election, was besieged with pleas for office. Some of these requests were frank, others were veiled, but all amounted in substance to the following communication from E. C. K. Garvey of Tecumseh: "In the distribution of your patronage remember your promises to your friends." In Washington the Senator was literally pursued on the streets by dozens of Kansas office seekers, who on one occasion had to be subdued by the police when they tried to storm his boarding-house. Meanwhile he himself pulled wires to become Secretary of the Interior, a post which would have enormously facilitated his railroad schemes and provided him with a fortune in graft. During this period also he began laying plans to unseat Pomeroy in 1866.[17]

Upon Andrew Johnson's succession to the presidency, Lane endeavored to establish with him the same relationship he had so profitably possessed with Lincoln. In return for a continued monopoly of Federal patronage in Kansas he supported Johnson's Reconstruction policy. The majority of Kansans, however, backed Congress and the Radical program, and the tide of public sentiment in the state turned strongly against him. At the same time the Chicago *Tribune* and the Boston *Commonwealth*

[16] Blackmar, *Charles Robinson*, pp. 292, 300–301, 308.

[17] Garvey to Lane, November 18, 1864, Delahay to Lane, November 23, 1864, J. S. Emery to Lane, November 23, 1864, Lane Collection, University of Kansas; *White Cloud Kansas Chief*, March 23, 30, 1865; Lane to L. C. Reaves of Beardstown, Ill., December 8, 1864, quoted in Carman and Luthin, *Lincoln and the Patronage*, p. 309.

published articles linking him to the corrupt activities of a contractors' ring in the Indian Territory. He fought desperately to preserve his power, and, as so often in the past, he seemed headed for ultimate victory when, late in June, while in St. Louis, he collapsed both physically and mentally. Friends took him to a farm near Leavenworth to recuperate, but on July 1 he placed the barrel of a pistol in his mouth and shot himself. He lingered for ten days and then "the scheming brain worked and suffered no more." Soon afterwards a friend of Robinson's wrote: "His suicide was his own verdict on his life & actions." [18]

Lane's macabre death fittingly marks the end of the Civil War era in Kansas history. This era began in 1854 with the fateful Kansas-Nebraska Bill and was distinguished by the predominance of the slavery issue and by the existence of the border conflict with Missouri. It was, from the standpoint of primary interest, essentially political in character. Henceforth the major concern of Kansans—and the main theme of their history—was economic. Young Preston Plumb of Emporia well expressed the spirit of his fellow Kansans as they moved into the new era. Upon returning home from the army in the summer of 1865, he wrote to a friend:

There is going to be a chance to make some money in the next five or ten years which neither of us may ever have again. I have determined to avail myself of it. I shall devote all my energy and powers to securing my share of it. We have had a good time as boys . . . now we are men.[19]

Kansas had entered the Gilded Age.

[18] S. C. Smith to Robinson, August 5, 1866, Robinson Papers, KSHS. The above account of Lane's last days and suicide is based on the following sources: an article by Sol Miller in the Troy *Kansas Chief*, February 7, 1889, in Robinson Scrapbooks, vol. III; Speer, *Life of Lane*, pp. 313–316; Stringfellow, "Jim Lane," *Lippincott's Magazine*, V (March, 1870), 277–278; Robinson, *Kansas Conflict*, pp. 457–460; Fisher, *Gun and Gospel*, p. 229; Stephenson, *Political Career of Lane*, pp. 154–159.

[19] Quoted in William E. Connelley, *The Life of Preston B. Plumb* (Chicago, 1913), pp. 209–210.

# Bibliography

THE main sources employed in preparing this book were the manuscripts and newspapers listed below and *The War of the Rebellion: A Compilation of the Official Records of the Union and Confederate Armies.* The most useful newspapers were the Leavenworth *Daily Conservative,* Leavenworth *Daily Times, Freedom's Champion* (Atchison), *Kansas State Journal* (Lawrence), and *White Cloud Kansas Chief.* These and most of the other newspapers listed are in the extensive files of the Kansas State Historical Society, Topeka, Kansas. The most valuable manuscript collections, all in the possession of the Kansas State Historical Society, were the Charles and Sara T. Robinson Papers, consisting of the personal correspondence of Governor Robinson and his wife; the James L. McDowell Papers, containing letters by and to that leading businessman and politician; the George Luther Stearns Papers, chiefly useful for his correspondence with various Kansas radical leaders; the Samuel Newitt Wood Papers, the correspondence of a prominent politician and newspaper editor; and the C. M. Chase Letters, written by Chase while traveling through Kansas in the summer of 1863. The Thomas Ewing, Jr., Papers, which are divided between the Kansas State Historical Society and the Library of Congress, contain this important figure's family, business, military, and political correspondence, and the John M. Schofield Papers at the Library of Congress contain little which is not more readily available in the general's memoirs. Since the writing of this book, the papers of Daniel R. Anthony have become available at the Kansas State Historical Society. I have consulted them, however, and find that they serve only to confirm the conclusions previously arrived at concerning this colorful individual, especially as to his responsibility for Kansas depredations in Missouri in 1861.

Unfortunately only a few of the letters of this book's central figure, James Henry Lane, have survived or been collected. His papers on file at the Kansas State Historical Society and the University of Kansas Library, Lawrence, Kansas, are extremely limited and miscellaneous in nature, as are those of his rival Senator, Samuel Clarke Pomeroy, at the Kansas State Historical Society.

The *Kansas Historical Collections* contain a multitude of significant and informative articles and reminiscences by men and women who lived in Kansas during the Civil War period. Other important materials were found in the *Kansas Historical Quarterly*, especially the memoirs of General James G. Blunt. Some of the papers in the *Kansas Historical Collections*, however, must be used with utmost caution, as either the authors' memories had failed or they were deliberately romanticizing. The various scrapbooks listed, especially the Charles Robinson Scrapbooks and the Samuel J. Crawford Scrapbooks, contained some extremely valuable and otherwise unavailable items.

## MANUSCRIPTS

A. Kansas State Historical Society
    Sherman Bodwell Diary, 1861–1865
    August Bondi Papers
    Edward Bumgardner Papers
    C. M. Chase Letters

Mark W. Delahay Papers
James Stanley Emery Papers
Thomas Ewing, Jr., Papers
Hugh Dunn Fisher Papers
Simon M. Fox Papers
Isaac T. Goodnow Diary
Alfred Gray Papers
John A. Halderman Papers
James and John Hanway Papers
Richard Josiah Hinton Papers
Thaddeus and Theodore Hyatt Papers
John J. Ingalls Papers
James Henry Lane Papers
Amos A. Lawrence Papers
James L. McDowell Papers
James Montgomery Papers
Thomas Moonlight Papers
H. Miles Moore Papers
Fletcher Pomeroy Diary (typewritten copy)
Samuel Clarke Pomeroy Papers
Samuel J. Reader Diary
Charles and Sara T. Robinson Papers
D. Rogers Papers
George Luther Stearns Papers
Thomas C. Stevens Papers
Samuel Newitt Wood Papers
B. University of Kansas Library
George W. Collamore Collection
James Henry Lane Collection
Oscar Eugene Learnard Collection
Charles and Sara T. Robinson Collection
"Personal Recollections of Mrs. Sara T. D. Robinson of the Quantrill Raid of August 21, 1863"
C. Kansas City, Kansas, Public Library
William E. Connelley Collection
Charles Robinson Papers
D. Library of Congress

Thomas Ewing, Jr., Papers
Robert Todd Lincoln Collection
John M. Schofield Papers

## ARCHIVES

Kansas State Archives, Kansas State Historical Society
   Governors' Correspondence (Charles Robinson), 1861–1863
   Governors' Correspondence (Thomas Carney), 1863–1865
   Governors' Correspondence (Samuel J. Crawford), 1865–1868
   Kansas Adjutant General's Correspondence, 1861–1866
   Kansas State Census, 1865

## NEWSPAPERS

*The Council Grove Press*, 1863–1865
Elwood *Free Press*, 1861
Emporia *News*, 1861–1862
Fort Scott *Bulletin*, 1862
*The Fort Scott Democrat*, 1861–1862
*Freedom's Champion* (Atchison), 1861–1865
*Kansas State Journal* (Lawrence), 1861–1865
*Kansas State Record* (Topeka), 1861–1863
*Kansas Weekly Tribune* (Lawrence), 1863–1865
*Lawrence Republican*, 1861–1862
Leavenworth *Daily Conservative*, 1861–1865
Leavenworth *Daily Times*, 1861–1865
Leavenworth *Herald*, 1861
*The Nemaha Courier* (Seneca, Kansas), 1863–1865
*Olathe Mirror*, 1861–1865
Oskaloosa *Independent*, 1861–1864
*The Topeka Tribune*, 1861–1862
*The Weekly Osage Chronicle* (Burlingame, Kansas), 1863–1864
*Western Journal of Commerce* (Kansas City, Mo.), 1861, 1863–1865
*White Cloud Kansas Chief*, 1860–1866

## SCRAPBOOKS

A. Kansas State Historical Society
    Samuel J. Crawford Scrapbooks (3 vols.)
    Governors of Kansas, Clippings
    Kansas Biographical Scrapbook
    Kansas History, Clippings (4 vols.)
    Kansas in the Civil War, Clippings (3 vols.)
    Kansas Legislature, Biography
    Kansas Legislature, Clippings (2 vols.)
    Kansas Reminiscences by Kansas Authors
    Joel Moody Scrapbooks (4 vols.)
B. University of Kansas Library
    Charles Robinson Scrapbooks (4 vols.)

## PUBLIC DOCUMENTS

A. State

    *Kansas Constitutional Convention: A Reprint of the Proceedings and Debates of the Convention Which Framed the Constitution of Kansas at Wyandotte in July, 1859.* Topeka, Kansas, 1920.

    *Kansas Public Documents.* 1861–1866.

    *The Laws of the State of Kansas.* 1861–1866.

    *Proceedings in the Cases of the Impeachment of Charles Robinson, Governor, John W. Robinson, Secretary of State, George S. Hillyer, Auditor of State, of Kansas.* Lawrence, Kansas, 1862.

    *Report of the Adjutant General of the State of Kansas, 1861–'65.* Topeka, Kansas, 1896.

    *Senate and House Journals of the Legislative Assembly of the State of Kansas.* 1861–1866.

B. Federal

    *A Compilation of All the Treaties between the United States and the Indian Tribes Now in Force as Laws.* Washington, 1873.

*The Congressional Globe.*

U.S. Bureau of the Census. *Eighth Census of the United States, 1860: Mortality and Miscellaneous Statistics.* Washington, 1866.

——. *Eighth Census of the United States, 1860: Population.* Washington, 1864.

U.S. Congress, Senate. *Report of the United States Pacific Railway Commission.* Sen. Ex. Doc., 50th Cong., 1st Sess., vol. III, no. 51, pt 4. Washington, 1885.

*The War of the Rebellion: A Compilation of the Official Records of the Union and Confederate Armies.* 128 vols. plus atlas. Washington, 1881–1901.


## BOOKS, PAMPHLETS, AND ARTICLES

Abel, Anna Heloise. "Indian Reservations in Kansas and the Extinguishment of Their Titles," *Kansas Historical Collections*, VIII (1903–1904), 72–109.

——. *The Slaveholding Indians.* 3 vols. Cleveland, Ohio, 1915–1919.

Adams, Franklin G. "The Capitals of Kansas," *Kansas Historical Collections*, VII (1903–1904), 331–351.

"Address of Ex-Governor James W. Denver," *Kansas Historical Collections*, III (1883–1885), 359–366.

"Address of Gov. John A. Martin," *Kansas Historical Collections*, III (1883–1885), 372–384.

Andreas, Alfred Theodore. *History of the State of Kansas.* Chicago, 1883.

Angle, Paul M., ed. *New Letters and Papers of Lincoln.* Boston and New York, 1930.

*The Annals of Kansas, 1886–1925*, vol. I. Topeka, Kansas, 1954.

Baker, Floyd P. "The Kansas Legislature in 1862," *Kansas Historical Collections*, III (1883–1885), 101–109.

Ballard, David E. "The First State Legislature," *Kansas Historical Collections*, X (1907–1908), 232–237.

Bartles, William L. "Massacre of Confederates by Osage Indians in 1863," *Kansas Historical Collections*, VIII (1903–1904), 62–66.

Basler, Roy P., ed. *The Collected Works of Abraham Lincoln*. 8 vols. New Brunswick, N.J., 1953.

Birdsall, A. *The History of Jackson County, Missouri*. Kansas City, Mo., 1881.

Blackmar, Frank W. "The History of the Desert," *Kansas Historical Collections*, IX (1905–1906), 101–114.

———. *The Life of Charles Robinson: The First State Governor of Kansas*. Topeka, Kansas, 1902.

Blunt, James G. "General Blunt's Account of His Civil War Experiences," *Kansas Historical Quarterly*, I (May, 1932), 211–265.

Botkin, Theodosius. "Among the Sovereign Squats," *Kansas Historical Collections*, VII (1901–1902), 418–441.

Bowles, Samuel. *Across the Continent*. Springfield, Ill., 1865.

Bradley, Glenn D. *The Story of the Santa Fe*. Boston, 1920.

Brewerton, G. Douglas. *The War in Kansas*. New York, 1856.

Britton, Wiley. *The Civil War on the Border*. 2 vols. New York, 1899.

———. *Memoirs of the Rebellion on the Border—1863*. Chicago, 1882.

Brown, George W. *Reminiscences of Gov. R. J. Walker*. Rockford, Ill., 1902.

Bumgardner, Edward. *The Life of Edmund G. Ross*. Kansas City, Mo., 1949.

Calderhead, William A. "The Service of the Army in Civil Life after the War," *Kansas Historical Collections*, XII (1911–1912), 14–24.

Carman, Henry J., and Luthin, Reinhard H. *Lincoln and the Patronage*. New York, 1943.

Carr, Lucien. *Missouri: A Bone of Contention*. Boston and New York, 1888.

Case, Theodore S., ed. *History of Kansas City, Missouri*. Syracuse, N.Y., 1888.

Clarke, Henry S. "W. C. Quantrill in 1858," *Kansas Historical Collections*, VII (1901–1902), 218–223.

Coffin, William H. "Settlement of the Friends in Kansas," *Kansas Historical Collections*, VII (1901–1902), 324–361.

Cole, Fannie E. "Pioneer Life in Kansas," *Kansas Historical Collections*, XII (1911–1912), 353–358.

Connelley, William E. *An Appeal to the Record*. Topeka, Kansas, 1903.

———. *The Life of Preston B. Plumb*. Chicago, 1913.

———. *Quantrill and the Border Wars*. Cedar Rapids, Iowa, 1910.

———, ed. *A Collection of the Writings of John James Ingalls*. Kansas City, Mo., 1902.

———, ed. *History of Kansas*. 5 vols. Chicago and New York, 1928.

———, ed. "Some Ingalls Letters," *Kansas Historical Collections*, XIV (1915–1918), 94–122.

Cordley, Richard. *A History of Lawrence, Kansas, from the First Settlement to the Close of the Rebellion*. Lawrence, Kansas, 1895.

———. *Pioneer Days in Kansas*. Boston, 1903.

Cornish, Dudley T. "Kansas Negro Regiments in the Civil War," *Kansas Historical Quarterly*, XX (May, 1953), 417–429.

Crawford, Samuel J. *Kansas in the Sixties*. Chicago, 1911.

Cruise, John D. "Early Days on the Union Pacific," *Kansas Historical Collections*, XI (1909–1910), 529–549.

Dalton, Kit. *Under the Black Flag*. Memphis, Tenn., c. 1914.

Deatharage, Charles P. *Early History of Greater Kansas City*. Kansas City, Mo., 1927.

Delahay, Mary E. "Judge Mark W. Delahay," *Kansas Historical Collections*, X (1907–1908), 638–641.

Drought, W. S. "James Montgomery," *Kansas Historical Collections*, VI (1897–1900), 242–243.

Edwards, John N. *Noted Guerrillas; or, The Warfare of the Border*. St. Louis, 1877.

———. *Shelby and His Men; or, The War in the West*. Cincinnati, 1867.

Eldridge, Shalor Winchell. *Recollections of Early Days in Kansas*. Topeka, Kansas, 1920.

Ewing, Cortez A. M. "Early Kansas Impeachments," *Kansas Historical Quarterly*, I (August, 1932), 307–325.

Fisher, H. D. *The Gun and the Gospel*. 4th ed. Kansas City, Mo., 1902.

Fox, Simon M. "The Story of the Seventh Kansas," *Kansas Historical Collections*, VIII (1903–1904), 13–49.

"The Frontier Guard at the White House, Washington, 1861," *Kansas Historical Collections*, X (1907–1908), 419–421.

Gates, Paul Wallace. *Fifty Million Acres: Conflicts over Kansas Land Policy, 1854–1890*. Ithaca, N.Y., 1954.

Geary, Daniel. "War Incidents at Kansas City," *Kansas Historical Collections*, XI (1909–1910), 282–291.

"George A. Crawford," *Kansas Historical Collections*, VI (1897–1900), 237–248.

Gleed, Charles S. "The First Kansas Railway," *Kansas Historical Collections*, VI (1897–1900), 357–359.

Glick, George W. "The Drought of 1860," *Kansas Historical Collections*, IX (1905–1906), 480–485.

——. "The Railroad Convention of 1860," *Kansas Historical Collections*, IX (1905–1906), 467–480.

Gowing, Clara. "Life among the Delaware Indians," *Kansas Historical Collections*, XII (1911–1912), 183–193.

Greene, Albert Robinson. "Campaigning in the Army of the Frontier," *Kansas Historical Collections*, XIV (1915–1918), 283–310.

——. "The Kansas River—Its Navigation," *Kansas Historical Collections*, IX (1905–1906), 317–358.

Grinnell, George Bird. *The Fighting Cheyennes*. Norman, Okla., 1956.

Hannahs, Harrison. "General Thomas Ewing, Jr.," *Kansas Historical Collections*, XII (1911–1912), 276–282.

Haskell, John G. "The Passing of Slavery in Western Missouri," *Kansas Historical Collections*, VII (1901–1902), 28–39.

——. "Speculative Activities of the Emigrant Aid Company," *Kansas Historical Quarterly*, IV (August, 1935), 235–267.

Hickman, W. Z. *History of Jackson County, Missouri*. Topeka, Kansas, and Cleveland, Ohio, 1920.

Hinsey, F. W. "The Lawrence Massacre," *Kansas City Star*, July 19, 1903.

Hinton, Richard J. "Pens That Made Kansas Free," *Kansas Historical Collections*, VI (1897–1900), 371–382.

——. *Rebel Invasion of Missouri and Kansas and the Campaign of the Army of the Border against General Sterling Price, in October and November, 1864.* Chicago, Ill., and Leavenworth, Kansas, 1865.

Holcombe, R. I., comp. *History of Vernon County, Missouri.* St. Louis, 1887.

Horton, Albert H. "The Judiciary of Kansas," *Kansas Historical Collections,* III (1883–1885), 389–396.

Horton, James C. "Business Then and Now," *Kansas Historical Collections,* VIII (1903–1904), 143–148.

———. "Peter D. Ridenour and Harlow W. Baker: Two Pioneer Kansas Merchants," *Kansas Historical Collections,* X (1907–1908), 589–619.

———. "Reminiscences of Hon. James C. Horton," *Kansas Historical Collections,* VIII (1903–1904), 199–205.

Hougland, D. P. "Voting for Lincoln in Missouri in 1860," *Kansas Historical Collections,* IX (1905–1906), 509–520.

Hull, O. C. "Railroads in Kansas," *Kansas Historical Collections,* XII (1911–1912), 37–46.

Kitzhaber, Albert R. "*Götterdämmerung* in Topeka: The Downfall of Senator Pomeroy," *Kansas Historical Quarterly,* XVIII (August, 1950), 243–278.

Langsdorf, Edgar. "Jim Lane and the Frontier Guard," *Kansas Historical Quarterly,* IX (February, 1940), 13–25.

———. "S. C. Pomeroy and the New England Emigrant Aid Company, 1854–1858," *Kansas Historical Quarterly,* VII (August, November, 1938), 227–245, 379–398.

Learnard, O. E. "Organization of the Republican Party," *Kansas Historical Collections,* VI (1897–1900), 312–316.

Leech, Margaret. *Reveille in Washington, 1860–1865.* Garden City, N.Y., 1941.

"Letters of John and Sarah Everett, 1854–1864," *Kansas Historical Quarterly,* VIII (February, May, August, November, 1939), 3–34, 143–174, 279–310, 350–383.

"Letters of Julia Louisa Lovejoy," *Kansas Historical Quarterly,* XVI (May, 1948), 175–211.

"The Letters of Samuel James Reader, 1861–1863," *Kansas Historical Quarterly,* IX (February, May, 1940), 26–57, 141–174.

Lowman, H. E. *Narrative of the Lawrence Massacre.* Lawrence, Kansas, 1864.

Lyman, William A. "Origin of the Name 'Jayhawker' and How It Came to Be Applied to the People of Kansas," *Kansas Historical Collections,* XIV (1915–1918), 203–207.

McAllaster, O. W. "My Experience in the Lawrence Raid," *Kansas Historical Collections,* XII (1911–1912), 401–404.

McClure, James R. "Taking the Census and Other Incidents in 1855," *Kansas Historical Collections,* VIII (1903–1904), 227–250.

Malin, James C. "Dust Storms: Part One, 1850–1860," *Kansas Historical Quarterly,* XIV (May, 1946), 129–144.

——. "Dust Storms: Part Two, 1861–1880," *ibid.,* XIV (August, 1946), 265–296.

——. *John Brown and the Legend of Fifty-Six.* Philadelphia, 1942.

——. *Background of the Nebraska Question.* Lawrence, Kansas, 1954.

——. "Notes on the Writing of General Histories of Kansas," *Kansas Historical Quarterly,* XXI (Autumn, 1954), 184–223.

Manning, Edwin C. "The Kansas State Senate of 1865 and 1866," *Kansas Historical Collections,* IX (1905–1906), 359–375.

Martin, George W. "A Chapter from the Archives," *Kansas Historical Collections,* XII (1911–1912), 359–375.

——. "The Territorial and Military Combine at Fort Riley," *Kansas Historical Collections,* VII (1901–1902), 361–390.

Miller, George. *Missouri's Memorable Decade, 1860–1870.* Columbia, Mo., 1898.

Miller, Wallace E. *The Peopling of Kansas.* Columbus, Ohio, 1906.

Moore, H. Miles. *Early History of Leavenworth City and County.* Leavenworth, Kansas, 1906.

Morrill, Edmund N. "The Early Settlers of Kansas: Their Trials, Privations, Hardships, and Sufferings," *Kansas Historical Collections,* V (1891–1896), 148–154.

Nicolay, John G., and Hay, John. *Abraham Lincoln.* 12 vols. New York, 1914.

"Origins of County Names," *Kansas Historical Collections,* VII (1901–1902), 472–474.

Orpen, Adela Elizabeth. *Memories of the Old Emigrant Days in Kansas, 1862–1865.* Edinburgh and London, 1926.

Palmer, Henry E. "The Black-Flag Character of War on the Border," *Kansas Historical Collections,* IX (1905–1906), 455–466.

——. "The Lawrence Raid," *Kansas Historical Collections*, VI (1897–1900), 317–325.

Prentis, Noble L. *Kansas Miscellanies*. Topeka, Kansas, 1889.

"Report of the Kansas Relief Committee to and including March 15, 1861." Kansas Relief Pamphlets, Kansas State Historical Society.

Richardson, Albert D. *Beyond the Mississippi*. Hartford, Conn., 1867.

Riegel, Robert Edgar. *The Story of the Western Railroads*. New York, 1926.

Robinson, Charles. *The Kansas Conflict*. Lawrence, Kansas, 1898.

Rollins, C. B., ed. "Letters of George Caleb Bingham to James S. Rollins," *Missouri Historical Review*, XXXIII (October, 1938), 45–78.

Root, Frank A., and Connelley, William E. *The Overland Stage to California*. Topeka, Kansas, 1901.

Schofield, John M. *Forty-six Years in the Army*. New York, 1897.

Shannon, Fred Albert. *The Organization and Administration of the Union Army, 1861–1865*. 2 vols. Cleveland, 1928.

Simpson, Benjamin F. "The Wyandotte Constitutional Convention," *Kansas Historical Collections*, II (1879–1880), 236–247.

Speer, John. "The Burning of Osceola, Mo., by Lane and the Quantrill Massacre Contrasted," *Kansas Historical Collections*, VI (1897–1900), 305–312.

——. *Life of Gen. James H. Lane*. Garden City, Kansas, 1896.

Spencer, Joab. "The Methodist Episcopal Church, South, in Kansas—1854 to 1906," *Kansas Historical Collections*, XII (1911–1912), 135–182.

Spring, Leverett Wilson. "The Career of a Kansas Politician," *American Historical Review*, IV (October, 1898), 80–104.

——. *Kansas: The Prelude to the War for the Union*. Boston, 1890.

Stark, Andrew, ed. *Kansas Annual Register of the Year 1864*. Leavenworth, Kansas, 1864.

"Statement of Capt. J. A. Pike concerning the Quantrill Raid," *Kansas Historical Collections*, XIV (1915–1918), 311–318.

Stearns, Frank Preston. *The Life and Public Services of George Luther Stearns*. Philadelphia and London, 1907.

Stephenson, Wendell H. *The Political Career of General James H. Lane*. Topeka, Kansas, 1930.

Stoddard, W. O. "The Story of a Nomination," *North American Review*, no. 328 (March, 1884), pp. 263–273.

Stringfellow, Jacob (Nicholas Verres Smith). "Jim Lane," *Lippincott's Magazine*, V (March, 1870), 266–278.

Switzler, W. F. *History of Missouri*. St. Louis, 1879.

Taylor, Hawkins. "My Year in Kansas," *Topeka Commonwealth*, December 4, 1886.

Taylor, Richard Baxter. "Kansas Newspaper History," *Kansas Historical Collections*, II (1879–1880), 164–182.

Tomlinson, William P. *Kansas in Eighteen Fifty-Eight*. New York, 1859.

Union League of America. *Proceedings of the National Convention*. Washington, 1863.

Wardell, Morris L. *A Political History of the Cherokee Nation, 1838–1907*. Norman, Okla., 1938.

Ware, Eugene F. "The Neutral Lands," *Kansas Historical Collections*, VI (1897–1900), 147–169.

Webb, William L. *Battles and Biographies of Missourians*. Kansas City, Mo., 1900.

Wilder, Daniel Webster. *The Annals of Kansas*. Topeka, Kansas, 1886.

Williams, T. Harry. *Lincoln and the Radicals*. Madison, Wis., 1941.

Wood, Samuel N. "The Pioneers of Kansas," *Kansas Historical Collections*, III (1883–1885), 426–431.

# Index